# Walter Scott and the Limits of Language

## Alison Lumsden

Edinburgh University Press

Edinburgh University Press Ltd
22 George Square, Edinburgh

www.euppublishing.com

Typeset in Times New Roman and
printed and bound in Great Britain by
CPI Antony Rowe, Chippenham and Eastbourne

A CIP record for this book is available from the British Library

ISBN 978 0 7486 4153 6 (hardback)

Arts & Humanities
Research Council

# Contents

*For Wayne*

# Acknowledgements

First and foremost I must express my gratitude to the Arts and Humanities Research Council (AHRC). Their generous award from the Research Leave Scheme enabled the completion of this project. Warmest thanks are also extended to David Hewitt for his invaluable advice, help and encouragement and for his support as a colleague over many years; his passion for Scott has helped keep alive my own enthusiasm. Gratitude is also due to my fellow General Editors on the Edinburgh Edition of the Waverley Novels, Ian Alexander, Peter Garside, Claire Lamont and G. A. M. Wood; their wisdom and good humour has made it a pleasure to work with them. Thanks are also extended to those who have been of support in the wider Scott community; Jane Millgate, Penny Fielding, Gerard Carruthers, Graham Tulloch and Douglas Gifford have helped me in many ways. I am also grateful for the invigorating discussions I have had with my Scott students and in particular with my postgraduates. Ainsley McIntosh deserves a special thanks not only for her comments on the manuscript and for proof reading the text but for the warmth of her friendship. Beyond the Scott community, many friends and colleagues have provided support, kindness and a passion for scholarship and literature; I would particularly like to thank Shane Alcobia-Murphy, Louise Bowen, Patrick Crotty, Barbara Fennell, Jeannette King, Sofia Sanchez-Grant and Lee Spinks. My sincere thanks are also due to those colleagues at Aberdeen who covered for me while I was on leave; David Duff and Catherine Jones deserve a particular mention. I am also grateful to the anonymous readers of the manuscript for EUP and of the proposal for the AHRC. Their comments were invaluable.

For me this book marks the culmination of many years of work on the Edinburgh Edition of the Waverley Novels and both that project and this study would not have been possible without the support of the National Library of Scotland and the Queen Mother Library at the University of Aberdeen. In particular I would like to thank Dr Iain Brown of the National Library of Scotland and Michelle Gait and June Ellner of Special Collections at the University of Aberdeen. Support staff at the University of Aberdeen have also been of immense help; in particular I would like to thank Maureen Wilkie and her office team and June Middleton. I would also like to thank Jackie Jones and the staff at EUP for their encouragement.

Finally I would like to thank my family for their on-going support, love and kindness, in particular Helen and Isobel Lumsden and the whole Price clan. My deepest gratitude is to Wayne Price who read the manuscript of this book, gave intelligent advice, and brought a story writer's perspective to it. Above all, he has provided his love and companionship throughout this project. All mentioned here and many more have helped with this book in their own ways and I am grateful to them. The errors in it are all my own.

# Abbreviations and
# Shortened Forms of Reference

The texts listed here are referred to several times. Page numbers, or in the case of poems canto and stanza numbers, for quotations from these will be given in brackets after quotation.

Walter Scott, *The Lay of the Last Minstrel: A Poem* (London and Edinburgh: Longman, Hurst, Rees, and Orme and A. Constable and Co., 1805)

——, *Marmion; A Tale of Flodden Field* (Edinburgh and London: Archibald Constable and Company and William Miller and John Murray, 1808)

——, *The Lady of the Lake: A Poem in Six Cantos* (Edinburgh and London: John Ballantyne and Co. and Longman Hurst, Rees, and Orme, and William Miller, 1810)

——, *Waverley* (1814), ed. by P. D. Garside, Edinburgh Edition of the Waverley Novels 1 (Edinburgh: Edinburgh University Press, 2007)

——, *Guy Mannering* (1815), ed. by P. D. Garside, Edinburgh Edition of the Waverley Novels 2 (Edinburgh: Edinburgh University Press, 1999)

——, *The Antiquary* (1816), ed. by David Hewitt, Edinburgh Edition of the Waverley Novels 3 (Edinburgh: Edinburgh University Press, 1995)

——, *The Tale of Old Mortality* (1816), ed. by Douglas Mack, Edinburgh Edition of the Waverley Novels, 4b (Edinburgh: Edinburgh University Press, 1993)

——, *The Heart of Mid-Lothian* (1818), ed. by David Hewitt and Alison Lumsden, Edinburgh Edition of the Waverley Novels 6 (Edinburgh: Edinburgh University Press, 2004)

——, *The Bride of Lammermoor* (1819), ed. by J. H. Alexander, Edinburgh Edition of the Waverley Novels 7a (Edinburgh: Edinburgh University Press, 1995)

——, *Ivanhoe* (1820), ed. by Graham Tulloch, Edinburgh Edition of the Waverley Novels 8 (Edinburgh: Edinburgh University Press, 1998)

——, *The Pirate*, ed. by Mark Weinstein with Alison Lumsden, Edinburgh Edition of the Waverley Novels 12 (Edinburgh: Edinburgh University Press, 2001)

——, *The Fortunes of Nigel* (1822), ed. by Frank Jordan, Edinburgh Edition of the Waverley Novels 13 (Edinburgh: Edinburgh University Press, 2004)

——, *Peveril of the Peak* (1822), ed. by Alison Lumsden, Edinburgh Edition of the Waverley Novels 14 (Edinburgh: Edinburgh University Press, 2007)

——, *Redgauntlet* (1824), ed. by G. A. M. Wood with David Hewitt, Edinburgh Edition of the Waverley Novels 17 (Edinburgh: Edinburgh University Press, 1997)

——, *Chronicles of the Canongate* (1827), ed. by Claire Lamont, Edinburgh Edition of the Waverley Novels 20 (Edinburgh: Edinburgh University Press, 2000)

——, *Count Robert of Paris* (1831), ed. by J. H. Alexander, Edinburgh Edition of the Waverley Novels 23a (Edinburgh: Edinburgh University Press, 2006)

——, *Castle Dangerous* (1831), ed. by J. H. Alexander, Edinburgh Edition of the Waverley Novels 23b (Edinburgh: Edinburgh University Press, 2000)

——, *Reliquiae Trotcosienses Or The Gabions of the Late Jonathan Oldbuck Esq. of Monkbarns*, ed. by Gerard Carruthers and Alison Lumsden (Edinburgh: Edinburgh University Press in association with The Abbotsford Library Project Trust, 2004)

The following texts are referred to several times and they will be referenced in the notes using the following abbreviations.

| | |
|---|---|
| *Prose Works* | *The Prose Works of Sir Walter Scott, Bart.*, 28 vols (Edinburgh: Robert Cadell, 1834–6) |
| *Poetical Works* | *The Poetical Works of Sir Walter Scott, Bart.*, ed. by J. G. Lockhart, 12 vols (Edinburgh: Robert Cadell, 1833–4) |
| *Letters* | *The Letters of Sir Walter Scott*, ed. by H. J. C. Grierson and others, 12 vols (London: Constable, 1932–7) |
| *Life* | J. G. Lockhart, *Memoirs of the Life of Sir Walter Scott, Bart.*, 7 vols (Edinburgh: Robert Cadell, 1837–8) |
| *Journal* | *The Journal of Sir Walter Scott*, ed. by W. E. K. Anderson (Oxford: Clarendon Press, 1972) |

## *Permissions*

All manuscripts referred to in this text are in the National Library of Scotland (NLS) and are quoted with the kind permission of the Keepers. All quotations from the Edinburgh Edition of the Waverley Novels (EEWN) are with the permission of the Editor-in-Chief.

# Introduction:
# The 'Poverty' of Words

In the revised version of the 'General Introduction' to the Edinburgh Edition of the Waverley Novels (EEWN) the editor-in-chief, David Hewitt, contemplates what it has achieved and what it has taught us about Scott. He comments:

> A surprising amount of what was once thought loose or unidiomatic has turned out to be textual corruption. Many words which were changed as the holograph texts were converted into print have been recognised as dialectical, period or technical terms wholly appropriate to their literary context. The mistakes in foreign languages, in Latin, and in Gaelic found in the early printed texts are usually not in the manuscripts, and so clear is this manuscript evidence that one may safely conclude that Friar Tuck's Latin in *Ivanhoe* is deliberately full of errors. The restoration of Scott's own shaping and punctuating of speech has often enhanced the rhetorical effectiveness of dialogue . . . The Historical and Explanatory Notes reveal an intellectual command of enormously diverse materials, and an equally imaginative capacity to synthesise them. Editing the texts has revolutionised the editors' understanding and appreciation of Scott, and will ultimately generate a much wider recognition of his quite extraordinary achievement.[1]

Here Hewitt draws attention to the fact that the research conducted by the Edinburgh Edition team has revealed both a linguistic richness and a linguistic diversity within Scott's fiction that was obfuscated by earlier editions. Much of this has been restored by the Edinburgh Edition and this process has revealed an author who employs a range of vocabulary that has never before been apparent. This complexity is evidenced both by the glossaries which accompany the editions and the emendation lists, which illustrate the ways in which the subtleties of Scott's language were frequently overlooked or misunderstood by those involved in producing earlier versions of his texts.

This information is, of course, documented with considerable detail within individual Edinburgh Edition volumes but it is worth noting some instances here. The glossaries to the volumes, for example, frequently bear testimony to the fact that Scott not only draws on Scots, as one might expect, but also on many European languages. As will be discussed later *The Fortunes of Nigel* has embedded within it passages in dense Scots, French, Spanish, Latin and even Greek. Technical language is often employed too; the language of Scott's own profession of the law features in novels such as *The Heart of Mid-Lothian* and *Redgauntlet*, but perhaps more surprisingly, Scott also demonstrates his understanding of nautical terms in *The Pirate*, and his impressive vocabulary relating to items of medieval military costume in texts such as *Ivanhoe* and *The Betrothed*. The language of rogues, gypsies and pirates is also exploited, with the glossaries indicating how frequently Scott draws on what might be called 'cant'. *Guy Mannering* offers one good example of this and is the first in a series of Scott's novels which incorporate into them the use of such language; there are well over thirty words listed in the notes and glossary derived from thieves' cant alone.

It was precisely this kind of language that frequently disappeared from the first editions of Scott's work, since it was simply unrecognised by printers and compositors and replaced by more commonplace, transparent, terms. An example from *The Pirate* illustrates this point; in the first edition one pirate turns to another towards the end of the novel and says '"But hold your own course—I have done with caring for you"'. While this makes sense of a sort it is bland to say the least and is hardly in the language we might expect a pirate to employ. Upon revisiting the manuscript, however, it is clear that the word is not 'caring', since there are far too many upstrokes in what Scott has written. After careful examination of the manuscript and reference to the *Oxford English Dictionary* it becomes apparent that the word Scott has written is, in fact, 'canning', a nautical term used to describe giving sailing directions to the steersman. This fits well with piratical patois and also adds invigorated meaning to 'hold your own course'. Scott had either gleaned the word from Smollett's *Roderick Random*, where it also occurs, or from his conversations with sailors while on the lighthouse cruise in 1814. It is restored in the Edinburgh Edition (363.42). Graham Tulloch, the editor of *Ivanhoe*, records a similar shift away from archaic terms used by Scott in the manuscript to a modern vocabulary in the first edition; in one instance he records how '"Patch", an old word for a jester . . . becomes the less explicit and less appropriate "wretch" (224.34)' while elsewhere he notes that a description of the Jews as 'dispersed' is altered to the far less appropriate 'despised'.[2] In these examples what is apparent is that Scott's richness of vocabulary has been sacrificed to what was seen as clarity, and as a consequence the complexity of his use and response to language obscured. The premise behind the present study is that this process of 'clarification' also obscured an important critical point; that the creative impulse behind Scott's work was one that privileged the complexities and suggestive potentialities of communication above transparency. As Janet Sorensen has recently noted in an essay that draws attention to the linguistic diversity in the Waverley Novels '[f]ocusing on language in these novels . . . provides a thread that can pull together an array of critical themes'.[3]

While the examples from *The Pirate* and *Ivanhoe* offered above exemplify the ways in which complexity gave way to clarity in the early socialisation of Scott's texts the experience of returning to manuscripts has also illustrated many examples of mis-reading, which have, ultimately, simply ironed out the richness and subtlety of his linguistic approach. Several emendations from *The Heart of Mid-Lothian* prove this point. For example, Scott writes that the Edinburgh district of Portsburgh is inhabited by the 'lower order of artizans and mechanics'.[4] However 'artizans' was misread as the rather fatuous 'citizens' and the social point that Scott is making obscured. Later in the text when Jeanie visits Butler before setting out for London he holds out to her, in the manuscript version, his 'extenuated' hand – one shrunken and wasted by disease – while in the first edition the hand is merely 'extended', prompting an alert reader to ask how else a hand 'held out' may be presented.[5]

Other mis-readings also serve to obfuscate the extent to which Scott's novels operate as matrices of meaning constructed from traces of reference to other texts. One simple example occurs early on in *The Heart of Mid-Lothian*, when Jedidiah Cleishbotham fears that his tales will have lost their 'favour' with the public; in fact the word in the manuscript is 'savour', which is of course a Biblical reference.[6] Here, emendation serves both to correct what Scott has written and to uncover the ways in which his text is comprised of numerous inter-textual moments, and one of the most significant achievements of the Edinburgh Edition is the way in which it has enhanced our understanding of Scott in this respect. In the passage quoted earlier Hewitt notes that '[t]he Historical and Explanatory Notes reveal an intellectual command of enormously diverse materials, and an equally imaginative capacity to synthesise them'. In doing so he draws attention to the ways in which the EEWN has, in fact, uncovered networks of textual reference within the Waverley novel texts. At times these have been obscured by mis-reading, as in the above example from *The Heart of Mid-Lothian*. Elsewhere these references have survived into Scott's texts but it is only with the notes to the Edinburgh Edition that the full range of these source materials, and the extent to which they have been creatively reworked in his fiction is truly revealed. This became evident in the course of editing *The Heart of Mid-Lothian*, for example, when the process of researching the notes for that edition uncovered the full extent of Scott's reworking of source materials within his own text. As he was writing this novel Scott was simultaneously engaged in reviewing Kirkton's *History of the Church of Scotland*, a task which encouraged him to return to the Covenanting histories which he had read in his youth.[7] 'I laid Kirkton aside half finished', he writes to John Murray, 'from a desire to get the original edition of the lives of Cameron, &c., by Patrick Walker, which I had not seen since a boy'.[8] These texts were to have a profound influence on the writing of the novel, for many of Dean's speeches – his diatribe on dancing, for example, or the tale of the man washed down the river – are lifted almost verbatim from Walker. The story of James Russel and the controversy of the names of the days of the week is, similarly, taken from an appendix to Kirkton which gives a life of that character.[9]

This relationship between Scott's sources and his fictional texts illustrates the complex process by which meaning resides in the Waverley Novels and examples of such inter-textual re-workings can be found in nearly every novel edited by the Edinburgh Edition. Similar confluences are also evident in *Peveril of the Peak*. During the course of annotating that novel over sixty pamphlets on the subject of the Popish Plot held in the library at Abbotsford were examined. Just as with *The Heart of Mid-Lothian*, it became evident that Scott had picked up phrases and traces of these source texts which, once discerned, create new nuances of meaning, or echoes, within this fiction, generating levels of meaning and resonance hitherto indiscernible.[10]

Research for the Edinburgh Edition has also uncovered much about Scott's working practices by its return to the manuscript versions of his texts and the close scrutiny of them, and this too contributes to a renewed understanding of his relationship to language. Working as an editor of Scott for the Edinburgh Edition of the Waverley Novels I was in the fortunate position of collating the manuscripts of nearly all of Scott's novels, and many of the existing proof sheets. This offered a unique opportunity to experience at first hand something of the creative process involved in the production of a Waverley Novel. As the Edinburgh Edition has demonstrated the manuscripts of the Waverley Novels are remarkably clean. But, as described in each volume, they also involve thousands of changes generated in the process of writing. Again, examples of these changes are provided for readers in the 'Essay on the Text' sections which accompany the Edinburgh Edition but some reiteration of these will serve to illustrate the creative processes at play in Scott's fiction. In *The Heart of Mid-Lothian*, for example, Jeanie's future husband, Rueben Butler, begins life in the manuscript as the generic schoolmaster 'Tawse' (the Scots word for the leather strap used to punish children, thus making him a counterpart to Thwackbairn). As Scott writes, however, he decides that the character 'Tawse' must occupy a more significant role in the text and it is only in chapter 6 of volume 1 that his name is changed from a comic generic term to the more neutral Butler.[11]

Similar examples of creative evolution can also be found in *The Pirate*. As the editors of that volume suggest, these changes fall into several categories. Often, Scott is seen striving for the right word or expression; 'the original "village" is changed to a "small hamlet" (14.14)', the editors note. 'The original "islands" are more accurately described as "islets" (24.8). Generic "waters" become "lakes and streams" (28.24)'.[12] 'In the same spirit of artistic integrity' they add, 'Scott often replaces a perfectly adequate word or expression with something more vivid' (p. 400), citing as examples the fact that Norna raises herself from a 'stooping' rather than 'reclining' posture, and that the 'deep colouring' of the young men's complexions is changed to 'fresh and ruddy'.[13] Peter Garside summarises the process in relation to *Guy Mannering* commenting that 'commonplace or amorphous words and phrases are replaced by sharper alternatives'.[14] *The Pirate* also offers examples of more extensive manuscript revision. As detailed in the 'Essay on the Text' one significant passage is deleted; in it Scott implies a sexual relationship between Norna and Magnus. If this material had stood Minna and Cleveland would have been half brother and sister and ultimately Scott shies away from this taboo. Echoes of this, however, remain in the tragic nature of their parting and the impossibility of their happiness.[15] More generally the experience of working on Scott's manuscripts suggests that traces of all of his revisions remain, as if echoes of them inhabit the finished texts, haunting the published versions of the novel with other possibilities, other semantic networks which give a sense that what we read is not complete, but somehow partial, an approximation of what can be recounted in any 'final' work of fiction.

To recognise this is, of course, in a sense only to acknowledge that creativity is a process, and we should hardly be surprised to find it at play in the work of one of the most archetypal of Romantic writers. However, such work, and its articulation in scholarly editions, is also a reminder that all creative writing is in a sense never complete, but provisional; that as a writer creates a piece of literature they are inevitably and inescapably aware of alternative linguistic possibilities and the nuances of meaning that are both contained within them and remain elusive.

The cumulative effect of the work of the Edinburgh Edition of the Waverley Novels, then, is to offer us a version of the Author of Waverley which is far more acutely aware of the complexities of language and the modes by which it communicates than earlier versions of his work may suggest. Edinburgh Edition texts draw our attention to the linguistic complexity of Scott's fiction by revealing the richness, diversity and complexity of the language that he employs, by uncovering the ways in which it often is constructed via matrices of meaning echoing earlier inter-textual references, and by revealing that in his working practices Scott's manuscripts are evidence of the provisionality of all linguistic construction.

The present study arises in part out of its author's close involvement with the Edinburgh Edition and builds upon this new awareness of Scott's complex relationship to language and communication. Taking as its starting point an assumption that Scott has a far more acute awareness of the complexities of linguistic communication than has hitherto been recognised, *Walter Scott and the Limits of Language* examines the ways in which a self-reflexivity that has been recognised in Scott's work in recent years in fact arises out of a fundamental scepticism concerning the communicative potentialities of language. It explores the extent to which this is manifested throughout his writing career, the ways in which it generates creativity within his work, and the means by which he explores how the writer can continue to meaningfully create in the face of such fractures and lacunae in communication.

Such an investigation, however, also arises out of the critical context that has surrounded Scott in recent years, for several strands emerge within it that prompt such enquiry. While no study has explored the extent to which Scott's creativity is generated by an anxiety concerning the limits of language much work to date has been suggestive of this. In 1991 at the Fourth International Scott Conference in Edinburgh Jill Rubenstein provided an overview of the current state of Scott criticism and we may take this as a starting point of modern reinterpretation. Her position was one of tempered optimism, recognising an 'encouraging indicator of maturity' in the fact that 'Scott criticism no longer assumes a defensive stance'.[16] New historicist approaches, she suggested, were opening up fresh readings of Scott and his work was increasingly acknowledged as 'reflexive, self-conscious, and more-or-less experimental'.[17] Feminist readings of Scott were only just beginning to emerge. Rubenstein concludes by posing a question, asking '[w]here do we go from here? Are we hapless proponents of an exhausted culture, burdened with just one more "dead white Eurocentric male", as the most radical of the canon revisionists might have it?' Her response is that this is not the case: 'Quite to the contrary' The Author of Waverley is 'a literary figure whose moment has once again arrived'.[18]

Nearly twenty years on it is interesting to revisit Rubenstein's conclusions by considering the directions Scott criticism has taken and what these imply about the questions that still need to be asked about his work. Certainly, it is clear that the major critical reassessment of Scott which Rubenstein anticipated has indeed taken place and it is worth giving an overview of some of this recent criticism here. Perhaps most relevant to the present study is Penny Fielding's *Writing and Orality*. Fielding's book is one of the first to place Scottish fiction in a modern theoretical context, and in it Fielding explores the interplay between writing and orality in the work of Scott, alongside that of James Hogg, Robert Louis Stevenson, and Margaret Oliphant. Central to Fielding's thesis is the concept that the interplay of writing and orality is culturally determined and crucial to both the ways in which the novel developed in the early nineteenth century and its relationship to a burgeoning sense of national consciousness with which, of course, Scott became intimately connected. In *The Grammar of Empire* Janet Sorensen also links questions of language to issues of national identity, discussing this in relation to the process of internal colonisation.[19] Rubenstein recognises that this 'national' strand persisted in Scott criticism in response to his 'problematic . . . attitude to the Union'[20] but devolution has moved this question into new terrain and several recent studies have concerned themselves precisely with Scott's relationship to national identity; in his study *Subversive Scott* Julian Meldon D'Arcy,[21] for example, argues that a renewed understanding of Scott's relationship to national identity is crucial to the critical revision of his work. Discerning in Scott's fiction the construction of a 'dual audience' of Scottish and British readers D'Arcy suggests that Scott is offering a far more overtly nationalist agenda in his fiction than has hitherto been discerned. Arguing that to see the ambiguities that have frequently been recognised in Scott's work as clumsiness or bad writing is to fail to read the text in the correct way, D'Arcy sees these ambiguities and dissonances in the novels as a skilful means of putting forward a covert but persistent national agenda, a 'nationalist subtext which provides considerable evidence to corroborate a claim that, despite his apparently "politically correct" fiction and lifestyle, Walter Scott's Waverley Novels implicitly reveal a Scotsman's passionate concern with the issues of national identity, dignity and independence'.[22]

D'Arcy's study builds on an increasing understanding of Scott's work as dialogic, what he calls the 'prevalent acceptance of the polyphonic nature of Scott's fiction'.[23] Such interpretations of Scott's work were particularly prominent at the Fourth International Conference during which Rubenstein's paper was presented. As the preface to the published volume of its proceedings outlines, 'participants were invited to consider new critical approaches to Scott, and around half of them responded by invoking Mikhail Bakhtin to a greater or lesser extent'.[24] More sustained studies of Scott's work have also been built around a recognition of the competing discourses which inform it. Taking genre as their primary starting point both Ian Duncan's *Modern Romance and Transformations of the Novel* and Fiona Robertson's *Legitimate Histories* offer readings of Scott and his relationship to other fiction that recognise a narrative technique incorporating an interplay of styles and genres,[25] while Ina Ferris's study similarly recognises that such interplay, and its structural implications within Scott's work, inevitably prompted his contemporaries to re-negotiate what could be considered 'literary authority'.[26] Catherine Jones's study *Literary Memory* also recognises an essentially dialogic or polyphonic aspect in Scott's fiction, arguing that creative memory in it is built upon the complex interplay of what she defines as 'associative', 'social', 'legal' and 'fragmentary' memory.[27] More recently, Ian Duncan's *Scott's Shadow* positions the popularity and long reaching influence of Scott's novels as embodying the foundations upon which the novel form was grounded in the nineteenth century.[28]

All of these studies recognise in Scott a more radical or subversive impulse than traditional criticism implies, for as D'Arcy proposes, polyphony and cultural resistance go hand in hand; 'Scott's fiction should therefore be seen as essentially radical', he claims 'its polyphonic nature challenging the status quo'.[29] If we accept this position it is hardly surprising that other critical activity surrounding Scott in recent years has sought to explore it within frameworks which recognise its engagement with aspects of experience beyond the boundaries one would anticipate in his fiction. Both Judith Wilt's *Secret Leaves*[30] and Robert P. Irvine's *Enlightenment and Romance* build on the emerging feminist criticism identified in 1991 and recognise surprisingly feminist agendas within Scott's work.[31] One of the most recent full-length studies to emerge on Scott, Caroline McCracken-Flesher's *Possible Scotlands,* takes Scott's relationship to national identity as its subject and brings the dialogic impulse that has been recognised in Scott to its logical conclusion.[32] McCracken-Flesher suggests that the key to understanding how Scott's work operates in terms of nationhood is to recognise that, far from offering a version of Scotland based on monolithic binary oppositions, 'Scott provided many and contesting visions' of national identity.[33] As a consequence Scott creates a version of Scotland that is not a fixed and determined set of signs but which can be seen as an act of deferral, continually open to new acts of re-negotiation; 'Scott may have seemed to transfer Scotland to the past and dehistoricize the present', she suggests, but 'by the mere entry into narrative he located the nation ever at the point of construction through the lively play of the sign'.[34] Scott's role, consequently, is seen as one of inserting Scotland into the narrative of British identity and therefore enabling the possibility of its cultural renegotiation and reinvigoration at some future point. Scott, McCracken-Flesher argues, provides a template for a modern Scottish national identity by instigating an on-going dialogue on the subject of Scottishness (rather than a closed or fixed version of national identity) which facilitates our understanding of what it is to be Scottish today. Andrew Lincoln's *Walter Scott and Modernity* finds in Scott's work a kind of 'double narrative' which simultaneously evades and confronts what we now recognise as the conditions of 'modernity' so that Scott's 'own contradictory historical romance' can be read as a 'precursor' to our own 'complex response to uncertain times'.[35]

Such a renaissance of critical activity connected to Scott has been crucial in contributing to a renewed understanding of his work and has been significant in shaping the ways in which Scott is interpreted and regarded today. But the nature of this criticism is also revealing, for what it shares is the sense that Scott is in a very significant way relevant, and his work capable of reassessment within surprisingly modern frameworks; feminism, nation-theory, deconstruction, for example. Moreover, work which explores other critical discourses which are appealing and even vital to our own times, such as post-colonialism, is also now taking cognisance of the role that Scott can play in it.[36] What is, perhaps, most notable about this body of work is that in spite of Rubenstein's statement that '[n]ew critical methodologies have been relatively slow to enhance Scott' and that this has saved 'the Great Unknown' from being 'deconstructed into the Great Unknowable'[37] nearly all of the criticism described above is informed, in one way or another, by what we may broadly call 'theory'; Fielding and McCracken-Flesher, for example, are operating largely from the assumptions of post-structuralism, while those studies which place Scott within feminist or post-colonial frameworks are enabled to do so by the discussions of such discourses rendered possible by the broad parameters of postmodernity. Even the Edinburgh Edition of the Waverley Novel's statement that it has produced a 'fresher, less formal and less pedantic' version of the novels than was hitherto available reveals the broader critical contexts in which it has been published; we are operating in an environment where the 'fresh' and less formal is valued and where a 'ragged' version of Scott that reflects a dialogic methodology and one that continually undercuts authority is seen as something to applaud. In short, it is the strand of criticism that recognises Scott as 'reflexive, self-conscious and more-or-less experimental' that has emerged as dominant in the last twenty years. While none of this criticism may have dealt directly with Scott's anxiety concerning the linguistic medium in which his work is operating it is clear that such an anxiety lies somewhere behind the patterns such criticism has identified in his writing.[38] It is that anxiety and the relationship between linguistic scepticism and self-reflexivity in Scott's writing that is the subject of this study.

While it is not possible here to provide an overview of the development of twentieth-century literary theory it is worth pausing to consider the main lines of development in order to reiterate the ways in which they are intimately connected to an anxiety concerning language. Central to all twentieth-century theorising of literature is, of course, Saussure's recognition of the self-enclosed and self-generating systems of language and the challenge this launches to the notion of referentiality. As Dorothy Hale puts it, in Saussure's model 'it is not the "real" world referent that gives rise to language; but rather the human cognitive ability to produce language (language as a signifying system) that dictates the very conditions of the "real world"'.[39] This severance between language and referent, sign and essence is, of course, the release of the genii out of the bottle, and all our thinking about language, and by implication literature, follows on from this moment. As Roland Barthes famously put it, 'the whole of Literature, from Flaubert to the present day, became the problematics of language'.[40] Ludwig Wittgenstein, from whom the present study takes its title, was to develop ideas about the relationship of language to the world in the *Tractatus* suggesting that there is no knowledge of the world outside of language since 'the world is *my* world: this is manifest in the fact that the limits of *language* (of that language which alone I understand) mean the limits of *my* world'.[41] Hale points out that in terms of literary criticism, narratology, the attempt to analyse narrative in a scientific form, was the next step,[42] and from here it is a logical movement to recognise that 'the understanding of narrative, like the understanding of language . . . helps to illuminate the semiotic systems that produce human knowledge'.[43] So too she argues that it is from a fundamental flaw in the narratological project (the attempt to separate discourse from story in a scientific and binary form) that deconstruction arises,[44] in that Barthes' understanding of the text as a 'network of endless semantic possibilities' (and the confluent recognition that none of these possibilities can be final or complete) is in fact 'the logical conclusion of Saussure's 'system without end or centre'. For deconstructionists such as Derrida, of course, these conclusions became the moment when 'language invaded the universal problematic . . . when, in the absence of a center or origin, everything became discourse', what he rather melodramatically calls 'the unthinkable itself'.[45]

For many critics the deconstructionist project, and in particular Derrida's insistence upon an interpretation of discourse as the interplay of endlessly displaced and deferred meanings, seemed to signal a redundancy in literary criticism, a removal from any meaningful engagement with the text which is destined only to repeat its own recognition that texts are self-enclosed systems unable to tell us anything about our own position within the world or our relationships to it. However, as others have recognised, deconstruction potentially has far more to offer than this. Certainly, in terms of literature, it has been useful in reminding us that literary texts are indeed, like all discourse, constructed out of language, and that, by definition, their relationship to what can be known, and perhaps more importantly, what can be communicated, is problematic. It is within this framework, consequently, that literary texts themselves become recognised not as purveyors of universal human truths and knowledge, but rather, as 'language games' (to borrow the term Wittgenstein adopts in his later *Philosophical Investigations*),[46] or systems which themselves (precisely because they are constructed via language) become 'networks of endless semantic possibilities . . . without end or centre'. And while this must be said of all discourse, one could argue, as Bakhtin did, that novels are in some senses privileged sites of discourse where this disjunction is foregrounded, since the text is already proclaiming its own fictionality, the breach it has made between language and referent.[47] The ultimate end point of such thinking is, of course, the turn which the novel took towards self-reflexivity at the end of the twentieth century where proclaiming and critiquing the parameters of its own fictionality became the apparent business of the genre as it foregrounded the question of language within its own narratives.[48]

In her 1991 paper Jill Rubenstein was perhaps rightly suspicious of the worst excesses of deconstruction. Nevertheless it is clear that it is this critical context which has facilitated revisionist readings of Scott and contributed to his on-going rehabilitation. Whether she intended a reference to Wittgenstein or not Rubenstein identified 'the limits of language' as a thread beginning to emerge in Scott criticism[49] and points towards George Levine's tentative claim that Scott deals with the problem of 'how . . . to tell the truth in a form that is by its nature untrue' which gives his work the 'peculiar, almost modern, sort of self-consciousness' that has been so appealing to his recent critics.[50]

Critical theory has, of course, also encouraged a broader re-evaluation of the novel form and this too prompts new questions about Scott, one of its most important exponents. As David Daiches points out in his Foreword to the Edinburgh Edition, 'Scott not only invented the historical novel, but gave it a dimension and a relevance that made it available for a great variety of new kinds of writing, so that Stendhal was to call him "notre pere, Walter Scott"'.[51] Indeed, while there is no room here to elaborate upon all the ways in which Scott was to influence, and continues to influence, those novelists who came after him, it is clear his effect was considerable; a snapshot can be provided if we note, for example, that the *Critical Heritage* volume on Scott includes commentaries by not only Stendhal, but also Thomas Love Peacock, Honoré De Balzac, Henry James, Margaret Oliphant, Robert Louis Stevenson and Mark Twain.[52] Moreover, it is fascinating to note just how often Scott is referred to in Franco Moretti's magisterial work *The Novel*; several of the essays, including Moretti's own, place discussion of Scott at the heart of their examination of the form, and Scott is one of the few writers to whom an individual essay is devoted. It seems, then, that his work is crucial to any discussion of the novel and, by implication, any discussion of Scott should take cognisance of the ways in which our understanding of the form has developed in recent years.

It is fair to say that if critical understanding of Scott has changed dramatically in the past twenty years, so too has our understanding of the novel as a literary artefact and, indeed, our understanding of what criticism of it might involve. Centres for the study of the novel now exist in Aberdeen and Stanford, suggesting a rigorous and contemporary examination of this form in an international context. Moreover, the publication in 2006 of the English version of Franco Moretti's multivolume *The Novel* and of Dorothy J. Hale's volume of the same name suggests a new maturation of theorising about this most diverse of genres;[53] rather than being at the end of its life span, its 'time as a major art form . . . up' as John Barth famously put it,[54] the novel has, rather, apparently come of age.

Hale sums up the history of criticism of the novel in recent years when she writes: 'the field itself has been made and remade over the course of the twentieth century, emerging as a rich problematic rather than a monolithic idea'[55] and this notion of 'problematic' is perhaps what is most characteristic in current theorising of the form. Víktor Shklovsky identified this aspect in Sterne's *Tristram Shandy* as early as 1921: 'Sterne . . . lays bare the technique of combining separate story lines to make up the novel', he writes. 'In general, he accentuates the very structure of the novel. By violating the form, he forces us to attend to it; and, for him, this awareness of the form through its violation constitutes the content of the novel'.[56] To read Hale's volume is to recognise that the history of criticism of the novel in the twentieth century is essentially one of ever-growing understanding of the complexity of it as a genre and of its essentially vexed nature. The development of criticism of the novel involves a growing understanding that its primary features are not those of mimesis and verisimilitude as was once argued, but rather, a self-conscious awareness of its own modes of operation; Sterne's novel, it seems, is increasingly recognised not as an *aberration* in the form but of the *essence* of it. By the late twentieth century, consequently, a critic like Hillis Miller could argue 'Literature depends on the possibility of detaching language from its firm embeddedness in a social or biographical context and allowing it to play freely as fiction'.[57]

Many of the essays in Moretti's volume also reveal a growing awareness of such self-reflexivity as a key feature of the genre. Jack Goody, for example, argues that the novel is, and always was, a vexed form. 'Any form of re-presentation may raise doubts and hence ambivalence about its relationship with the original' he suggests and goes on to point out that this is particularly true when the re-presentation has a linguistic basis:

> Such doubts . . . are inherent in the human situation of language-using animals facing their environment. It is intrinsic to language, and therefore to narrative . . . An account of events is never the events themselves. When it does not even pretend to be such an account but is fictional, the situation is aggravated.[58]

Similarly Luiz Costa Lima suggests that 'not even pretending to be such an account' is intrinsic to the novel form which 'beginning with its medieval manifestations, thematizes the role of language with respect to truth, its *constitutive incompleteness* and, consequently, its fictional status'.[59] An essay by Catherine Gallagher, one of the most significant of current theoreticians of the novel, similarly recognises that the foregrounding of its own fictionality (and by implication its vexed relationship to referentiality) is central to all understanding of the form. 'The novel is not just one kind of fictional narrative among others', she writes, 'it is the kind in which and through which fictionality became manifest, explicit, widely understood, and accepted'.[60] In Moretti's second volume, an essay by John Brenkman seems equally anxious to pull apart the long-accepted connection between the novel and any naïve understanding of realism, arguing against the 'tidy little story' of the novel that sees its narrative as a trajectory from realism to modernism to postmodernism: 'Forget the commonplace that what makes a novel realistic is its intent to mirror a stable reality' he writes. 'That idea has never been more than a caricature of the aesthetic of nineteenth-century realism . . . realism never was a mirror, and reality was hardly more stable in the nineteenth century than today'. Brenkman supports his thesis by suggesting that novels, consequently, do not refer outwards to the idea of a stable external world, but rather, inwards, to other linguistically bound structures or discourses: 'Novels do not reproduce reality; they refer to it, with deep awareness of its elusiveness . . . Novels thus make reference to reality by making reference to other discourses'.[61] Indeed, Ian Duncan has recently suggested that 'Fiction is the discursive category that separates novels from history, from periodicals and other kinds of writing, in its designation of a strategic difference from reality – a distance or obliquity in the relation between narrative and world, a figurative disguise or darkening of the real'.[62]

It is clear, then, that the story of the novel in the twentieth century is one of its increasing theorisation and recognition of its vexed and problematic relationship to the 'real' so that the 'self-reflexive' cast identified in Scott's work is recognised not as an aberration, but increasingly as the dominant feature of the novel form. Moreover, understanding of the novel in recent years has also recognised that its self-reflexivity is intrinsically bound to the ways in which it 'thematizes the role of language with respect to truth' so that a concern with language is seen not just as a twentieth-century phenomenon, but as a dominant within the genre.

It is the aim of this study, therefore, to explore the ways in which Scott's fiction may be illuminated by the recognition that the 'reflexive, self-conscious and . . . experimental' features identified within it in recent years are fundamentally bound up with Scott's anxieties concerning the communicative capacities of the medium in which he is operating. It will argue that while Levine claims that Scott's awareness of a schism between what he describes as 'language and action' does not tend towards the seriousness of modern writers in their 'exposure of the fictionality of language and fictions' and that he does not provide a 'modern' answer to the problem he recognises, Scott's fiction does, in fact, have at its very heart an awareness of the limits (and problematics) of language as a tool for communication, and that it is this which generates creativity throughout his work.[63] As a consequence it will suggest that Scott remains intriguing to all those who are interested in the novel because in his long fictional career he offers us an extraordinarily rich and diverse investigation of the key problems which have emerged in recent years as inherent in the form from its eighteenth-century origins to its modern manifestations.

If a study which seeks to trace Scott's creativity via a concern with language is legitimised by recent criticism of both his own work and the novel more generally, however, it is encouraged by a further strand of recent criticism which, partly generated by new historicist approaches, has sought to read his work in the philosophical and cultural contexts in which it was generated. It has been increasingly acknowledged that Scott was shaped and informed by the writings of the Scottish Enlightenment, and the work of the Edinburgh Edition in uncovering Scott's sources, including the cultural and philosophical contexts in which his work was being produced, has done much to enhance our understanding of this. So too, there have been several studies such as those by Graham McMaster, Catherine Jones and more recently Ian Duncan, as well as a series of major articles by P. D. Garside, which have sought to draw out these connections, demonstrating to great effect that Scott's thinking on subjects such as the nature of society, conjectural history and associative memory reflect the Enlightenment context in which his mind took shape. Andrew Lincoln also draws comparisons between Scott and Hume, recognising that their view of political progress shares a common ground of scepticism.[64]

It is, however, potentially problematic to seek for connections between Scott's Enlightenment roots and his propensities towards a scepticism regarding the nature of language itself since the post-structuralist project, along with the so-called postmodern condition with which it has allegedly gone hand in hand, have in many ways sought to create a schism between their own thinking and that of classic Enlightenment thought, suggesting that their own conclusions, which limit the parameters of the knowable within the closed circuit of language, are in direct opposition to those of the Enlightenment thinkers who sought to expand knowledge through an empirical and rational description of a knowable world. As André Brink reminds us, for many there seems to be an inescapable connection between realism as an artistic mode (and a corresponding faith in a stable, knowable reality) and Enlightenment thought since it appeared to express an 'impressively self-confident faith in reason and in reason's access to the real'.[65] Such an opposition is, however, a gross over-simplification of Enlightenment thought, particularly as it was manifested in Scotland; the literati's critique of what could be known and the mechanisms of how it could be known is far more complex than this.

Ian Duncan argues, indeed, that a direct link between Scott's fictional practice and Enlightenment thought can be traced in David Hume's sceptical philosophy. 'It was Hume who provided the philosophical justification for Scott's combination of history and romance' argues Duncan: 'The Humean trajectory of enlightenment traces a sceptical dismantling of the metaphysical foundations of reality and their replacement with a sentimental investment in "common life," intermittently recognized as an imaginary construction of reality ratified by custom'.[66] Indeed, Duncan goes so far as to argue that Hume's role is crucial not only for Scott, but for authenticating the role of fiction *per se*, 'Hume establishes the philosophical matrix for the ascendancy of fictional realism in modern British literature. Humean empiricism generates a "novelistic" model of the imagination',[67] he claims:

> Hume theorizes a foundational role for fiction and the imagination in the work of representation that constitutes all knowledge. Hume's case, that all representation is a fiction, a *poesis*, since all experience is mediated through the imagination, provides a stronger and more comprehensive theoretical base for fiction than any that had appeared hitherto, delivering it from the sentence of inauthenticity, of categorical opposition to reality. It licenses Scott's own fictional practice, with its deconstruction of the opposition between history and fiction and dialectical reconstitution of their difference in a suspension of empirical realism in the medium of romance . . . Humean skepticism as the persistent condition or inescapable horizon of Reidian common sense—provides the philosophical framework for the fiction of the Scottish post-Enlightenment.[68]

Cairns Craig also recognises a link with Hume, arguing in *Association and the Literary Imagination* that Hume's emphasis on 'association' has long lasting repercussions that extend to postmodernity.[69] More directly relevant for this study, in *Fragments of Union* Susan Manning draws a direct parallel between Hume's philosophy and what we might describe as 'postmodernism' (with all the connotations of self-reflexivity, fragmentation and concern with the limits of language that the moniker implies). While acknowledging that one direction in which Hume can take fiction is 'radical subjectivity and the prison-house of language'[70] she also suggests that 'Hume's "conclusion" in the *Treatise* that matters of personal identity may only resolve themselves as questions of grammar, and that identity itself is a grammatical fiction, offer the possibility . . . that he is the first deconstructionist. To read Hume through the post-modern keyhole is . . . to commit an anachronism: it is however perhaps not only an inevitable one, but a perspective that Hume's writing first made available'.[71]

Both Duncan's and Manning's claim for Hume's role in 'authorising' not only Scott's fiction but fiction in general (or at least a significant strand of it) lies in the emphasis he places upon imagination in the construction of our perceptions. This is, indeed, intrinsic to Hume's sceptical position which leads him to the acknowledgement of the limits of both what is knowable, and perhaps more significantly for the present study, what is *communicable* to another. In his essay 'The Sceptic' for example, he outlines this position, which is essentially his own, describing the extent to which our understanding of all objects, and indeed of all sentiments, is based upon the peculiar and particular formation of the individual mind: 'beauty and worth are merely of a relative nature, and consist in an agreeable sentiment, produced by an object in a particular mind, according to the peculiar structure and constitution of that mind'.[72] 'Objects have absolutely no worth or value in themselves' he continues, 'they derive their worth merely from the passion'.[73] Passion, which is for Hume the motivating factor in all of human experience is, in turn, controlled by the 'fabric of our minds', over which we have little or no control; rather, for Hume, the human mind is governed by association, or mental attraction, motivated primarily by the emotions. In essence, therefore, scepticism acknowledges that the possibilities of human knowledge are limited and even if individual knowledge can be expanded by the working of the mind, communicating it to another remains problematic.

While, Hume suggests, we may have a general sense of the meaning of terms in language, when it comes to particulars there is nearly always a gap (or slippage) between what one person means by a term and what the other understands. This is never more apparent than in matters of taste. 'There are certain terms in every language which import blame' he comments, 'and all men who use the same tongue must agree in their application of them':

> Every voice is united in applauding elegance, propriety, simplicity, spirit in writing; and in blaming fustian, affectation, coldness, and a false brilliancy. But when critics come to particulars, this seeming unanimity vanishes; and it is found, that they had affixed a very different meaning to their expressions.[74]

As a consequence, Hume is forced to conclude that 'Beauty is no quality in things themselves: it exists merely in the mind which contemplates them'[75] and that to 'seek the real beauty, or real deformity, is as fruitless an enquiry as to pretend to ascertain the real sweet or real bitter'.[76] Constructed in the fabric of the individual mind all perceptions are thus unique to the individual and can only be communicated, as Hugh Blair puts it, via the 'play of speech', by a language that remains oblique and potentially as limited as the knowledge it seeks to describe. For Hume, the individual, famously, is 'nothing more than a bundle or collection of different perceptions' and he pushes scepticism beyond the question of what can be known in any particular circumstance, to what is knowable *per se*.

Duncan's reading of Hume suggests that he destabilises any straightforward construction of Enlightenment thought as offering a rational confidence in the 'real'. Rather, as Cairns Craig puts it, Hume's associative conclusions are not only suggestive of the strain which Scottish Romanticism was to take as it explored the idea that there is 'no guarantee of an eternal Idea', only the provisionality of 'temporal associative chains', but they also imply that reality can only be perceived subjectively. Comparing Hume to Coleridge, Craig concludes:

> Humean associationism presents a very different and much more anguished conception of the imagination since, for Hume, the imagination is both the foundation of all our experience and, at the same time, its inevitable dissolution. Only through the workings of the imagination can we discover a stable world . . . but that stable world is, in the end a 'fiction'.[77]

Seen in this way, Hume's philosophy lends itself to a discussion not only of epistemological questions but also ontological ones. As Terrence Penelhum recognises there are in some ways connections between Hume's position and Wittgenstein's later meditations on the role of language since both philosophers question the nature of certainty (or resist Dogmatism) while simultaneously seeking a way to proceed in the world.[78]

While both Manning's recognition of a postmodern tendency in Hume and Duncan's assessment of his role in giving agency to Scott's fictional project are therefore convincing, Hume himself seldom engages directly with the capacities of language, and in spite of Penelhum's recognition of similarities with Wittgenstein Hume does not share the later philosopher's direct engagement with its limits. Indeed Duncan himself does not suggest that the self-reflexive nature of Scott's work owes a great deal to an understanding of the vexed nature of his own medium. Nevertheless, as Manning indicates, 'from a literary point of view the laws of association which underpin [Hume's] "system" are predicated on grammatical and syntactic relationships as much as philosophical principles'[79] and while language itself may not be his key focus his work is indicative of the ways in which a concern with language as an organising structure by which to measure human experience was prevalent throughout Enlightenment thought. The origins, scope, potentialities, and indeed limitations of language are key topics of debate in the Scottish Enlightenment and it is consequently hardly surprising that they should inform Scott's work so fundamentally.

It would be impossible to outline here the many and diverse ways in which Scottish Enlightenment thought engages with the topic of language and its relationship to the nature of knowledge.[80] However it is hardly surprising that such studies adopt the conjectural methodology of other histories of the time, and share a broadly stadial view of the development of language. In his *Of the Origin and Progress of Language* (1773–92), for example, Lord Monboddo seeks to trace the development of language from its common primitive origins to its classical grandeur suggesting that language is intrinsic to civil society and 'the great instrument of social life'.[81] Adam Smith also extends his essentially stadial view of history to the development of language, conjecturing upon its primitive origins. In his 'Considerations Concerning the First Formations of Language' he suggests an essentially Adamic or Nominalist view of the original relationship between words and meaning noting that 'The assignation of particular names, to denote particular objects, that is, the institution of nouns substantive, would probably, be one of the first steps towards the formation of language':

> Two savages, who had never been taught to speak, but had been bred up remote from the societies of men, would naturally begin to form that language by which they would endeavour to make their mutual wants intelligible to each other, by uttering certain sounds, whenever they meant to denote certain objects. Those objects only which were most familiar to them, and which they had most frequent occasion to mention, would have particular names assigned to them.[82]

This directly metonymic model of the relationship between words and meaning is, indeed, recurrent in several Enlightenment thinkers, such as Lord Kames, who suggests that 'language may be considered as the dress of thought',[83] thus apparently assuming no real disjunction between ideas and the ways in which they are conveyed.

However, it is also apparent that for several commentators this straightforward relationship between signifier and signified is problematised as soon as language moves beyond its most basic functions. While Wittgenstein was eventually to conclude that 'Nominalists make the mistake of interpreting all words as *names*, and so of not really describing their use, but only, so to speak, giving a paper draft on such a description'[84] Monboddo himself directly confronts the issue of whether words derive from some connection with the thing they signify or 'whether they are not to be considered as signs of arbitrary institution'.[85] Suggesting that while 'the most perfect language' may be 'that which has proper names for every thing, and uses figurative words only by way of ornament'[86] he also argues that such a language is impossible in civil society because the vastness of knowledge precludes a direct correspondency in language:

> Nor does the most learned man in the world know one hundredth part of those [species] which nature has produced; but if even such as he knows were to be expressed all by separate words, entirely different from one another, so that the one could not suggest the other, it is evident, that the memory would be greatly overburdened, and consequently the language unfit for use; . . . Some other way therefore was to be devised to prevent words from increasing to an unwieldy number.[87]

As a result he observes that 'words are wanted to express many things' and 'this necessity has introduced the use of metaphors and other tropes'[88] concluding that by his own age there is no obvious connection between a word and what it signifies.[89]

In spite of his seeming confidence in a direct confluence between word and thought, Lord Kames also demonstrates a hesitation concerning the ability of words to directly convey meaning. As he points out in his *Elements of Criticism*: 'to ascertain with accuracy even the proper meaning of words, not to talk of their figurative power, would require a large volume'.[90] The figurative nature of language is part of its complexity for Kames, for like Hume he recognises that the imaginative faculty which is thus engendered creates a discrepancy between what is said, and what is potentially communicated. Like Monboddo, he recognises the extent of experience and comments that no one can directly experience all things. Language, consequently, appears to be a valuable tool for communicating what has been perceived by others:

> As the range of an individual is commonly within narrow bounds of space, it rarely happens, that every thing necessary to be known comes under our own perceptions; which therefore are a provision too scanty for the purposes of life. Language is an admirable contrivance for supplying that deficiency; for by language every man may communicate his perceptions to all: and the same may be done by painting and other imitative arts. The facility of communication is in proportion to the liveliness of the ideas; especially in language, which hitherto has not arrived at greater perfection than to express clear and lively ideas.[91]

However, Kames is careful to point out that such vicarious events should not be directly equated with what we have experienced ourselves, since 'poets and orators, who are extremely successful in describing objects of sight, find objects of the other senses too faint and obscure for language'.[92] And therefore 'an idea thus acquired of an object at second hand, ought to be distinguished from an idea of memory'.[93] For Kames experience falls into three categories: things we have experienced first hand, things perceived by the imagination, and those ideas or events we experience second hand via language; the last category must be distinguished from first hand experience precisely because there can be no guarantee that what is said will be communicated to the reader (or listener) in the way that the poet or orator intended: as Goody puts it for our own times 'an account of events is never the events themselves'.

This rupture of any kind of direct relationship between word and meaning is also one identified by Adam Smith as he progresses in his description of the development of language. The stage following an Adamic naming of objects, he suggests, involves a kind of analogy so that, for example, the word used for a particular fountain would become the word used for 'fountain' in general by a process of recognition of similarity. However, Smith recognises that this metaphorical extension of an essentially metonymic link between sign and signified cannot be sustained as soon as language moves beyond the most primitive stages, and that certain classes of word, prepositions, for example, require a degree of abstract thought, and a more oblique relationship between the word and what is being described:

> Now, I say, the original invention of such words would require a yet greater effort of abstraction and generalization, than that of nouns adjective. First of all, a relation is, in itself, a more metaphysical object than a quality. Nobody can be at a loss to explain what is meant by a quality; but few people will find themselves able to express, very distinctly, what is understood by a relation. Qualities are almost always the objects of our external senses; relations never are. No wonder, therefore, that the one set of objects should be so much more comprehensible than the other. Secondly, though prepositions always express the relation which they stand for, in concrete with the co-relative object, they could not have originally been formed without a considerable level of abstraction. A preposition denotes a relation, and nothing but a relation. But before men could institute a word, which signified a relation, and nothing but a relation, they must have been able, in some measure, to consider this relation abstractedly from the related objects; since the idea of those objects does not, in any respect, enter into the signification of the proposition. The invention of such a word, therefore, must have required a considerable degree of abstraction.[94]

This 'considerable degree of abstraction' in the relationship between words and what they mean in fact haunts much of the Scottish Enlightenment's discussion of language, raising far more complex epistemological questions than common perceptions of the period may imply.

Nowhere is the ambiguous and potentially problematic nature of language as a transparent communicative medium more evident, however, than in the frequent discussions of rhetoric which take place during the Enlightenment period. The study of rhetoric had long been a feature of the Scottish education system and in 1759 Hugh Blair was made Edinburgh University's first professor of Rhetoric and Belles Lettres. His lectures offer an important insight into the ways in which language and discourse were perceived by those immersed in the traditions of the Enlightenment.

For Blair, there is no question but that language is essentially mimetic in its impulses, offering a window into a 'true' understanding of the world; the implication throughout his work is that those who can best use language (via the rules of rhetoric) will be best equipped to negotiate their way around the world. Cultivation of rhetoric, consequently, is seen as being in accord with cultivation of reason, the process by which the world may be seen to operate:

> For I must be allowed to say, that when we are employed, after a proper manner, in the study of composition, we are cultivating reason itself. True rhetoric and sound logic are very nearly allied. The study of arranging and expressing our thoughts with propriety, teaches to think, as well as to speak accurately. By putting our sentiments into words, we always conceive them more distinctly.[95]

Blair's justification for the use and study of rhetoric cloaks several problems, however, not least the fact that if language may be used to manipulate it can, by implication, also be used to falsify. As a consequence, Blair's discussion of language contains at its heart a paradox that recurs in much Enlightenment writing on this subject, whereby writers tend to paper over or 'silence' the issue of 'false' rhetoric by suggesting that 'good' rhetoric and virtue are intrinsically combined. To reconcile this paradox Blair proposes that rhetoric in the hands of those who are not virtuous may entertain and amuse but will be recognised as 'artifice, as trick, as the play only of speech; and, viewed in this light, whom can it persuade?'[96] By this argument, Blair concludes, somewhat problematically, that good truth will create good rhetoric, and that sound rhetoric, by implication, can be equated with 'truth'.

Monboddo, however, is far less confident in the implicit relationship between good rhetoric and truth, suggesting that rhetoric may well be used to persuade people of what is false as well as true:

> It follows from what is said, that as rhetoric does not require any scientific knowledge of the subject of which it treats, and speaks to people who have not that knowledge neither, it may persuade what is false as well as what is true; so that truth and falsehood appear to be indifferent to this art, as well as the subject of which it treats. The profession, therefore, of Gorgias the sophist, that he could make the worse reason appear the better, though it was thought a very impudent profession, was nothing more than professing that he understood the rhetorical art, and could make that use of it if he would.[97]

For Monboddo, the problem lies in the fact that words are 'arbitrary systems of institution' and do not necessarily correspond with any essential reality. Where a kind of pure or unornamented language may be hypothetically possible, he implies, a correspondence between rhetoric and truth might be achieved. However, such direct linguistic exchange is impossible in the modern world: 'If the hearers of rhetorical speeches were such as they ought to be, there would be no need of ornaments of speech', he argues. 'They would require no more of the orator, than that he should make himself understood, and not offend their ears; for it would be the matter they would mind, and not the words. But the hearers are such, that they are not to be convinced by reason and argument only, without the blandishment of fine language'.[98] As a consequence he is forced to conclude that the inevitable 'blandishment of language' allows for ambiguity and miscommunication so that rhetoric is 'a most dangerous art' and offers no guarantee that its outcomes will be for good.[99]

Such doubts are present even in those writers who seem most assured about the correspondence of rhetoric and truth. George Campbell, for example, like Monboddo, urges the need for clarity stating that 'in matters of criticism . . . it is of the utmost consequence to ascertain, with precision, the meanings of words, and as nearly as the genius of the language in which one writes will permit, to make them correspond to the boundaries assigned by Nature to the things signified'.[100] However, he too is ultimately far more ambivalent about what kind of 'truth' can be conveyed via language than this would imply, again recognising that listening is an active act, which may generate meanings other than those which are intended. There is, he acknowledges, a discrepancy between what he terms the sense and the expression of every speech: 'in other words, the thought, and the symbol by which it is communicated' or, as he puts it, 'the soul and the body of an oration, or indeed, of whatever is signified to another by language'.[101] 'What is signified to another' he suggests, must rely on the faculty of imagination. Only mathematical demonstration 'disdains all assistance whatever from the fancy'.[102] All other forms of communication rely, it would seem, on the power of imagination to bridge the gap that exists between speaker and 'what is signified to another by language', a recognition that also lies at the heart of Wittgenstein's post-logical positivist reflections.

For many of these commentators then, a Humean conception of the role which the imagination (or individual subjectivity) plays in the act of communication implies that there can be no direct correspondence between words and meaning, no guarantee that what is said is what is communicated. Instead, language becomes an inaccurate medium, 'which is to be regretted', as Kames puts it 'because ambiguity in the signification of words is a great obstruction to accuracy of conception'.[103] While 'accuracy of conception' may have been an ideal for Enlightenment commentators, they are, then, far more sceptical about the possibility that it can be achieved. Hume himself sums up the dilemma in a letter to John Home, where he urges such accuracy of expression arguing that the want of it is the greatest of vices:

> Of all the vices of language, the least excusable is the want of perspicuity; for, as words were instituted by men, merely for conveying their ideas to each other, the employing of words without meaning is a palpable abuse, which departs from the very original purpose and intention of language. It is also to be observed, that any ambiguity in expression is next to the having no meaning at all; and is indeed a species of it; for while the hearer or reader is perplexed between different meanings, he can assign no determinate idea to speaker or writer; . . . For this reason, all eminent rhetoricians and grammarians, both ancient and modern, have insisted on perspicuity of language as an essential quality; without which, all ornaments of diction are vain and fruitless . . .
> . . . Yours, without ambiguity, circumlocution, or mental reservation.
> David Hume[104]

However, if 'perspicuity of language' may be an ideal for Hume, the possibility of achieving this, as his ironic, even self-reflexive, conclusion to the letter implies, is clearly far more difficult.

Scott never directly engages with this language debate in his own prose writings but he was, of course, aware of the work of his Enlightenment predecessors. In *Guy Mannering*, for example, when the Colonel and Dominie Sampson are in Edinburgh, Mr Pleydell calls on them to ask if he can accompany them to worship and Mannering responds '"I should wish to hear some of your Scottish preachers . . . your Blair, your Robertson, or your Henry"' (p. 211). The 'Blair' referred to is Hugh Blair. Mannering also receives cards of introduction for among others, Lord Kames, Adam Smith and, anachronistically, David Hume. More intriguingly, in those excerpts of Mannering's Edinburgh journal restored for the first time by the Edinburgh Edition, Mannering provides (appropriately fragmentary) pen portraits of some of the key Enlightenment figures who Peter Garside identifies as including Lord

Monboddo. 'He questioned me closely about sundry tribes in the East', Mannering records, 'which I endeavoured to answer with great caution, as I have no ambition to be quoted in a new edition of the Origin of \*\*\*' (p. 228). As Garside notes, the asterisks refer to Monboddo's *Of the Origins and Progress of Language* which, while it may have been widely ridiculed by Scott's time, was certainly well known. Scott may not have commented on Enlightenment views of language directly but he was certainly well aware of them.

A final justification for considering Scott's work through the lens of an anxiety about language is also offered by his own commentary on the art of fiction and the relationship it bears to the 'real'. Scott, it is true, never directly engages with the language debate and he is often considered to be the least self-conscious of Romantic writers. As Ioan Williams comments he was a 'practical rather than a theoretical critic'[105] and while other writers of the period (most obviously Wordsworth and Coleridge) provide us with manifestos and treatises concerning the nature of their art Scott offered no such blueprint or commentary, and has, as a result, sometimes been cast as unthinking about his craft. However, Williams's distinction is in some ways a false one for while Scott may not have written directly about the theory of the novel he was a prolific reviewer, and his pieces on Godwin, Maturin, Austen and Mary Shelley's *Frankenstein*, as well as on his own *Tales of My Landlord*, have embedded within them a comprehensive theory of the form. So too, many of his thoughts on the novel can be gleaned from the introductions he wrote for *Ballantyne's Novelist's Library* which include revealing commentaries on authors such as Samuel Richardson, Fielding, Smollett, Sterne and Henry Mackenzie.[106]

While much of this writing, particularly that in the introductions for the *Novelist's Library*, is couched in the politest of nineteenth-century language, one can, nevertheless, piece together Scott's thoughts on the novel from these essays and it is worth taking some time to consider them, for what emerges is Scott's preoccupation both with the concerns which had dominated the eighteenth-century novel and an attempt to move towards a more complex understanding of the relationship between text and the world in which it is located. In his essay on Fielding, for example, he gives an outline of the qualities he sees as necessary in a good novel which seems initially to be articulated in fairly traditional terms: 'Force of character, strength of expression, felicity of contrast and situation, a well-constructed plot, in which the development is at once natural and unexpected, and where the interest is kept uniformly alive, till summed up by the catastrophe—all these', he writes 'are requisites as essential to the labour of the novelist as to that of the dramatist'.[107] As Scott elaborates on what he means by this both in this essay and elsewhere it appears that on the face of it, much of what he writes implies a predilection for what we might broadly term a 'realist', or at least mimetic turn in fiction; certainly, what he seems to praise time and time again is the skill of the writer in painting what is 'true to life', and on several occasions he draws direct analogies between the writer and an artist drawing with a pencil: Richardson's Clarissa, for example, is described as 'a character as nearly approaching to perfection as the pencil of the author could draw'.[108] In his review of Jane Austen's *Emma*, Scott elaborates further, commending that class of literature which has arisen which aligns itself with 'copying from nature':

> a style of novel has arisen, within the last fifteen or twenty years, differing from the former in the points upon which the interest hinges; neither alarming our credulity nor amusing our imagination by wild variety of incident, or by those pictures of romantic affection and sensibility, which were formerly as certain attributes of fictitious characters as they are of rare occurrence among those who actually live and die. The substitute for these excitements, which had lost much of their poignancy by the repeated and injudicious use of them, was the art of copying from nature as she really exists in the common walks of life, and presenting to the reader, instead of the splendid scenes of an imaginary world, a correct and striking representation of that which is daily taking place around him.[109]

For Scott, such literature is seen as being more directly affective, and hence effective, and is valuable in fulfilling what he refers to as the novel's role of instruction, since it demonstrates 'a knowledge of the human heart, with the power and resolution to bring that knowledge to the service of honour and virtue'.[110] Returning to a metaphor of graphic art Scott comments 'The author's knowledge of the world, and the peculiar tact with which she presents characters that the reader cannot fail to recognize, reminds us something of the merits of the Flemish school of painting. The subjects are not often elegant, and certainly never grand; but they are finished up to nature, and with a precision which delights the reader'.[111]

However, while discussions such as these seem to locate Scott very firmly within a tradition which sees art as mimetic and instructive, his exploration of the relationship of the novel to external experience is in fact more complex than this might imply. Much of this review concerns itself with a discussion of the ways in which Austen's novels depart from earlier fiction, which, Scott notes, arose out of the romance tradition. As a consequence 'the author of novels was, in former times, expected to tread pretty much in the limits between the concentric circles of probability and possibility; and as he was not permitted to transgress the latter, his narrative, to make amends, almost always went beyond the bounds of the former'.[112] Such fictions dealt with 'various and violent changes of fortune' and in this 'rests the improbability of the novel'.[113] Austen, on the other hand, 'keep[s] close to common incidents, and to such characters as occupy the ordinary walks of life'.[114] What he is acknowledging in Austen's novels, consequently, is a difference not so much in the *processes* by which the novel relates to life, as in the kind of detail of life it includes.

This is also apparent if we look more closely at Scott's analogy of the writer to a graphic artist, and consider what he means by 'copying from nature as she really exists in the common walks of life'. What he is drawing attention to when he compares Jane Austen's work to a Flemish painting after all, is the subject matter rather than the technique[115] and earlier in the review he complicates the relationship between graphic art and fiction-writing when he comments that 'something more than a mere sign-post likeness is . . . demanded'.[116] This pre-empts a fictional conversation which Scott was to insert into *The Bride of Lammermoor* (1819) between the 'author' Peter Pattieson and the sign painter Dick Tinto. Tinto, we are told, complains that Pattieson's novels contain too much dialogue, '"too much use of the *gob-box*"' (p. 10) and that as a result he has given his readers '"a page of talk for every single idea which two words might have communicated"' (p. 11). To this Pattieson responds that Tinto has '"confounded the operations of the pencil and the pen . . . painting . . . necessarily appealed to the eye . . . whereas poetry . . . lay under the necessity of doing absolutely the reverse, and addressed itself to the ear, for the purpose of exciting that interest which it could not attain through the medium of the eye"' (p. 11). While Tinto may protest that the same rules apply to both painting and fiction, Scott, via Pattieson, suggests otherwise: while sign-painting is an act of 'symbolical representation' (p. 5), the novel inhabits the 'talking world' (p. 14) and operates upon different principles. While Austen's work may be like Flemish painting (and it is a metaphor that he also uses in relation to De Foe) it does, and cannot, operate by the same methods, since fiction writing is compelled by different (and verbal) demands.

All this serves to imply that while Scott may seem to be advocating a straightforwardly mimetic style in fiction, he is simultaneously acknowledging that the linguistic basis of novel writing demands that its effects are achieved via more complex processes than mere imitation. Artifice (with all its nineteenth-century connotations of skill and craft) is a word that appears frequently in Scott's discussion of fiction; while metaphors from graphic art may recur in Scott's essays just as frequent are those which suggest that the author, operating within the 'talking world' is more akin to the master of an essentially 'dialogic' drama. 'A novelist, like the master of a puppet-show, has his drama under his absolute authority, and shapes the events to favour his own opinions' he writes in his essay on Robert Bage[117] and the metaphor of the puppet-show is also used in a comparison of Fielding and Smollett:

> Fielding pauses to explain the principles of his art, and to congratulate himself and his readers on the felicity with which he constructs his narrative, or makes his characters evolve themselves in its progress. These appeals to the reader's judgment, admirable as they are, have sometimes the fault of being diffuse, and always the great disadvantage, that they remind us we are perusing a work of fiction; and that the beings with whom we have been conversant during the perusal, are but a set of evanescent phantoms, conjured up by a magician for our amusement. Smollett seldom holds communication with his readers in his own person. He manages his delightful puppet-show without thrusting his head beyond the curtain.[118]

So too, in a discussion which in some ways pre-empts responses to Barthes's critique of realism, Scott also unpacks the ways in which even the reality effects[119] he finds in Austen and elsewhere are based in a highly skilled and controlled artifice. Scott alludes to this effect in his discussion of Richardson: 'by the circumstantial detail of minute, trivial, and even uninteresting circumstances', he writes, 'the author gives to his fiction an air of reality than can scarcely otherwise be obtained. In every real narrative, he who tells it, dwells upon slight and inconsiderable circumstances, no otherwise interesting than because they are associated in his mind with the more important events which he desires to communicate'.[120] However it is De Foe, he suggests, who is the master of this effect and he elaborates on this topic in his essay on that author.

For Scott, De Foe is one of the most compelling of novelists. Giving some insight into his own reading style, Scott comments that, unlike other novelists, De Foe's work compels us to 'read every sentence and word upon every leaf, instead of catching up as much of the story as may enable us to understand the conclusion'.[121] De Foe's skill, he suggests, lies in assuming 'the air of writing with all the plausibility of truth'[122] so that 'All the usual scaffolding and machinery employed in composing fictitious history are carefully discarded'.[123] 'The early incidents of the tale', for example, 'which in ordinary works of invention are usually thrown out as pegs to hang the conclusion upon' are here barely mentioned, and their details passed over without elaboration.[124] So too, the exactness and precision of the author adds to this plausibility effect so that Robinson Crusoe is delineated 'as acting and thinking precisely as such a man must have thought and acted in such an extraordinary situation'.[125] De Foe's writing style is described as contributing to this overall impression, so that his tale is told with 'the indifference of an old bucanier, and probably in the very way in which he may have heard them recited by the actors'.[126]

Again, initially what seems to appeal to Scott is a mimetic, or realistic mode. However, Scott's position here too is in fact more complex. His description of De Foe's style as one where the scaffolding and machinery of fiction 'are carefully discarded' is telling, for it implies that this so-called reality effect is in fact self-consciously wrought, a fact that is underlined by his suggestion that this is 'the last style which should be attempted by a writer of inferior genius; for though it be possible to disguise mediocrity by fine writing, it appears in all its native inanity, when it assumes the garb of simplicity'.[127] Indeed, the dangers of the 'plausible style', Scott concludes, are that the author 'debars himself from the graces of language, and the artifice of narrative'.[128] Along with later critics Scott acknowledges that the consequence of the 'authenticity effect' in eighteenth century fiction is, in fact, often simply to foreground the artifice involved in its creation.

Scott is acknowledging then that even the reality effect is composed with a great deal of artifice, implying that no sensible reader ever really believes but that the puppet-master, however well hidden, remains behind the scenes operating the strings. By doing so he is, as Levine argues, demonstrating that he is firmly grounded in an eighteenth-century concept of the novel where 'he sees fiction entirely as make-believe'.[129] The role of the novelist as it is described in these pieces is, in the end, an artificial and highly self-conscious one. As he outlines in his essay on Henry Fielding, the novelist is not, ultimately, like the graphic artist, or even the dramatist, for he cannot directly *show*, but can merely *tell*. The only tools he has available to him being, in the end, words:

It is the object of the novel-writer, to place before the reader as full and accurate a representation of the events which he relates, as can be done by the mere force of an excited imagination, without the assistance of material objects. His sole appeal is made to the world of fancy and of ideas, and in this consists his strength and his weakness, his poverty and his wealth. He cannot, like the painter, present a visible and tangible representation of his towns and his woods, his palaces and his castles; but, by awakening the imagination of a congenial reader, he places before his mind's eye, landscapes fairer than those of Claude, and wilder than those of Salvator. He cannot, like the dramatist, present before our living eyes the heroes of former days, or the beautiful creations of his own fancy, embodied in the grace and majesty of Kemble or of Siddons; but he can teach his reader to conjure up forms even more dignified and beautiful than theirs. The same difference follows him though every branch of his art. The author of a novel, in short, has neither stage nor scene-painter, nor company of comedians, nor dresser, nor wardrobe; words, applied with the best of his skill, must supply all that these can bring to the assistance of the dramatist. Action, and tone, and gesture, the smile of the lover, the frown of the tyrant, the grimace of the buffoon,—all must be told, for nothing can be shown.[130]

Given the complex critique of the novel and its relationship to 'reality' outlined in these pieces it is hardly surprising that Scott's own work does not follow any straightforwardly mimetic or representational style, but has, rather, as this study will demonstrate, an awareness of its own vexed position built into it, including the vexed nature of the medium in which it operates; namely language, or to borrow Scott's more simple terms, the 'poverty' of words. And this is, in fact, implied in those comments which Scott offers on his own fiction. Certainly, he famously differentiates his own style from Jane Austen's skill in 'copying from nature'. In his *Journal* for 14 March 1826 he comments:

Also read again and for the third time at least Miss Austen's very finely written novel of *Pride and Prejudice*. That young lady had a talent for describing the involvements and feelings and characters of ordinary life, which is to me the most wonderful I ever met with. The Big Bow wow strain I can do myself like any now going but the exquisite touch which renders ordinary common-place things and characters interesting from the truth of the description and the sentiment is denied to me.[131]

A similarly complex response to his own position as a novelist is also suggested in his own anonymous review of the first series of *Tales of My Landlord, The Black Dwarf* and *The Tale of Old Mortality*. The reflexive impulses lying behind this review have been well recognised, but so too, the praise which Scott gives to his own productions, while tongue in cheek, also alerts us in some ways to his thoughts upon his own style.[132] While Scott does indeed praise the Author of Waverley for offering depictions which are 'copied from nature' with an 'air of distinct reality'[133] he also draws attention once again to the artificial nature of these narratives by pointing out that 'his stories are so slightly constructed as to remind us of the showman's thread with which he draws up his pictures and presents them successively to the eye of the spectator'[134] so that '[p]robability and perspicuity of narrative are sacrificed with the utmost indifference to the desire of producing effect'.[135] *The Black Dwarf* is criticised for its 'utter improbability'[136] and for having a narrative which is 'unusually artificial',[137] and similar criticisms are levelled at *The Tale of Old Mortality* where Burley's change of heart is again described as 'improbable'.[138] Scott is also at pains to point out the ways in which the author has 'cruelly falsified history' and can only mitigate this by suggesting that he 'was writing a romance and not a history'[139] and that he has sacrificed the probable and natural to fulfil his overall aim of presenting 'the national cast, which it was chiefly his object to preserve'.[140] Scott's comments on *Tales of My Landlord* are of course a defence of his own style, so it is interesting to note that the grounds on which he defends his work are those which recognise that it does not offer the 'probable' or the 'natural' but is based, rather, on a style which values effect above a mimetic impulse, and which is prepared to acknowledge the presence of the 'showman's thread', the artifice behind the text.

Such reflections upon the craft of fiction are also embedded within the Waverley Novels themselves. This is most overt in Scott's 'Prefaces', particularly those written in the 1820s and thus contemporary with the *Novelist's Library* Introductions. Here the author uses those fictional narrators accrued as a result of his ostensible anonymity to offer a discussion of his own processes of creativity and it is hardly surprising that it is these prefaces which have gained most attention from those who recognise a 'reflexive and self-conscious' cast in Scott's work. As Patricia S. Gaston has recognised, these prefaces exhibit an essentially Quixotic impulse, which disrupts a realist trajectory in his fiction and leads to 'an almost inevitable confrontation with the text at hand as text'.[141] Gaston argues that whilst the Waverley novels themselves are essentially realistic because of their 'interpolation of historical fact' the prefaces draw attention to 'the impossibility of inscribing anything but forms of fiction within any narrative text'.[142] Similarly, Jerome McGann suggests that the prefaces 'establish the basic narrative terms of Scott's fiction' as essentially postmodern making 'the subject of tale-telling an explicit and governing preoccupation of the fiction'[143] while Levine argues that Scott's awareness that he was '"making things up"' reaches its logical conclusion in the disguises and 'self-reflexive games he intruded into the novels'.[144]

Fascinating though the Prefaces and paratextual materials are, however, a concentration on the most overt evidence of self-reflexivity within Scott's work is in danger of overlooking the fact that Scott's foregrounding of the fictionality of the novel form is much more widespread than this and both informs, and is at times the central preoccupation of, much of his art. Moreover, while several critics have observed this phenomenon in his work and drawn parallels with postmodern impulses few have actually explored the reasons for it. The present study will explore the extent to which it has its origins, like much postmodern self-reflexivity, in a growing and fundamental concern with the limitations of language as a transactional and referential medium and a consequent anxiety concerning its ability to inscribe both individual and collective experience. This anxiety is, I would suggest, manifested in his work from his poetry to his last novels and is, indeed, the tension that drives creativity throughout.

To suggest that an anxiety concerning the limits of language lies at the heart of Scott's work does, then, seems to be a line of enquiry that is worthy of pursuit. It is suggested by the 'self-reflexive and . . . experimental' tendencies that have been identified within it by criticism in recent years and is also prompted by a rewriting of the story of the novel that invites us to see its history as one of a general tendency to demonstrate an anxiety concerning language and its referential tensions. It is also a paradigm which is prompted by an increasing awareness of the implications of the Enlightenment context against which Scott's work should be set (particularly the 'radical' implications of Humean scepticism). Moreover, it is a critical position that is generated by Scott's own commentary on the novel form that places at its centre a discussion of how an art form grounded in the 'poverty' of words relates to the world. Levine argues that while Scott may have recognised a paradox at the heart of his own artistic medium, he 'misses what later novelists would see as opportunities to make the problem of fiction itself one of the novel's major preoccupations'.[145] The cornerstone of the present study, however, is the counter-claim that such scepticism concerning the communicative potentialities of language in fact runs throughout Scott's writing career and is a fundamental generator of creativity within it.

*Walter Scott and the Limits of Language*, then, suggests that in his early poetry and fiction Scott offers an exploration of the capacity of his chosen discourses to convey stories of both national and personal identity while even at this early stage demonstrating an anxiety about the potential of language as a communicative medium. In its discussion of *The Heart of Mid-Lothian* it will argue that Scott moves towards a growing and more fraught anxiety concerning the material substance of discourse, language itself, and the problematic nature of its referential impulses. By the time of the great Preface writing this anxiety has become overt, with texts such as *The Fortunes of Nigel* and *Peveril of the Peak* demonstrating a crisis in the capacity of language to communicate in any meaningful way, and an exploration of the novelistic implications of this. It will suggest that *Redgauntlet* and *Chronicles of the Canongate* offer a self-reflexive critique of how to continue in the face of this recognition, before demonstrating that Scott's late fictions, *Count Robert of Paris* and *Reliquiae Trotcosienses*, for example, suggestively prefigure the self-reflexive cast taken by late twentieth-century writing.

To suggest this is to risk the anachronistic fallacy of imposing a twenty-first century aesthetic upon a nineteenth-century writer. But to do so is not necessarily problematic; after all, as Brink comments, what we label Modernist or Postmodernist – an exploitation of the storytelling properties of language – 'has in fact been a characteristic of the novel since its inception'.[146] The danger of a study that draws such connections is that it elides difference, both cultural and philosophical. However, we should also recall that all categorisation of literature into periods or modes is in a sense limited. As John Barth reminds us '[a]ctual artists, actual texts, are seldom more than more or less modernist, postmodernist, formalist, symbolist, realist, surrealist, politically committed, aesthetically "pure", "experimental", regionalist, internationalist, what have you. The particular work ought always to take primacy over contexts and categories'.[147] While then, I have no wish to elide the difference between literatures from different periods, I agree with Barth that '*Whatever else it is about, great literature is almost always about itself*'.[148] A useful formulation is offered by Mieke Bal who comments: 'To claim that a phenomenon that becomes apparent in modern or contemporary literature can retrospectively be noticed in older literature is not to claim universal validity for that phenomenon. On the contrary, the modern case makes visible something that *could not be known* before'.[149] By identifying a scepticism towards the referential capacities of language in Scott's fiction, then, it is hoped that we may find fruitful things to say about Scott that will enhance our growing understanding of him as a writer who is relevant for the twenty-first century and whose moment has indeed once again arrived.

*Notes*

1  David Hewitt 'General Introduction', p. xi. This version of the 'General Introduction' appears in volumes published from 1999 onwards.
2  Graham Tulloch, 'Essay on the Text', *Ivanhoe*, pp. 424 and 449.
3  Janet Sorensen, '"Something Glee'd": The Uses of Language in Scott's Waverley Novels' in *Approaches to Teaching Scott's Waverley Novels* ed. by Evan Gottlieb and Ian Duncan (New York: The Modern Language Association of America, 2009), pp. 38–49 (p. 38).
4  See David Hewitt and Alison Lumsden, 'Essay on the Text', *The Heart of Mid-Lothian*, p. 513.
5  Ibid. p. 514.
6  Ibid. p. 513.
7  James Kirkton's *The Secret and True History of the Church of Scotland, from the Restoration to 1678*, ed. by C. K. Sharpe (London and Edinburgh: Longman, Hurst, Rees, Orme, and Brown, London; and John Ballantyne, Edinburgh, 1817).
8  To John Murray, March 1818, *Letters*, p. 5.108.
9  For a full account of the ways in which Scott draws on these sources see the Explanatory and Historical notes to *The Heart of Mid-Lothian*.
10 For a discussion of this see the Explanatory and Historical notes to *Peveril of the Peak*.
11 This is on p. 47 of the Edinburgh Edition. The change is discussed in the 'Essay on the Text', *The Heart of Mid-Lothian*, pp. 489–90.
12 'Essay on the Text', *The Pirate*, p. 399.
13 Ibid. p. 400.
14 'Essay on the Text', *Guy Mannering*, p. 372.
15 See 'Essay on the Text', *The Pirate*, pp. 403–4.
16 Jill Rubenstein, 'Scott Scholarship and Criticism: Where Are We Now? Where Are We Going?' in *Scott in Carnival: Selected Papers from the Fourth International Scott Conference Edinburgh, 1991*, ed. by J. H. Alexander and David Hewitt (Aberdeen: Association for Scottish Literary Studies, 1993), pp. 594–600 (p. 594).
17 Ibid. p. 595.
18 Ibid. p. 599.

19  Janet Sorensen, *The Grammar of Empire in Eighteenth-Century British Writing* (Cambridge: Cambridge University Press, 2000).
20  Jill Rubenstein, *Scott in Carnival*, p. 597.
21  Julian Meldon D'Arcy, *Subversive Scott: The Waverley Novels and Scottish Nationalism* (Reykjavik: University of Iceland Press, 2005).
22  Ibid. p. 19.
23  Ibid. p. 33.
24  J. H. Alexander and David Hewitt, 'Preface' in *Scott in Carnival*, pp. vii–viii (p. vii).
25  Fiona Robertson, *Legitimate Histories: Scott, Gothic, and the Authorities of Fiction* (Oxford: Clarendon Press, 1994) and Ian Duncan, *Modern Romance and Transformations of the Novel: The Gothic, Scott, Dickens* (Cambridge: Cambridge University Press, 1992).
26  Ina Ferris, *The Achievement of Literary Authority: Gender, History and the Waverley Novels* (Ithaca and London: Cornell University Press, 1991).
27  Catherine Jones, *Literary Memory: Scott's Waverley Novels and the Psychology of Narrative* (Lewisburg: Bucknell University Press, 2003).
28  Ian Duncan, *Scott's Shadow: The Novel in Romantic Edinburgh* (Princeton: Princeton University Press, 2007).
29  Julian Meldon D'Arcy, *Subversive Scott,* p. 34. D'Arcy is drawing here upon Roderick Watson's assumption that 'Polyphony and the potential for cultural and conceptual resistance may be one and the same thing'. See Roderick Watson, 'Postcolonial Subjects? Language, Narrative Authority and Class in Contemporary Scottish Culture', *The European English Messenger* 7:2 (1998), p. 30.
30  Judith Wilt, *Secret Leaves: The Novels of Walter Scott* (Chicago and London: University of Chicago Press, 1985).
31  Robert P. Irvine, *Enlightenment and Romance: Gender and Agency in Smollett and Scott* (Oxford and New York: Peter Lang, 2000).
32  Caroline McCracken-Flesher, *Possible Scotlands: Walter Scott and the Story of Tomorrow* (Oxford: Oxford University Press, 2005).
33  Ibid. p. 9.
34  Ibid. p. 107.
35  Andrew Lincoln, *Walter Scott and Modernity* (Edinburgh: Edinburgh University Press, 2007), p. 220.
36  See for example, Tara Ghoshal Wallace, *Imperial Characters: Home and Periphery in Eighteenth-century Literature* (Cranbury, NJ: Associated University Presses, 2010).
37  Jill Rubenstein, *Scott in Carnival*, p. 598.

38  Graham Tulloch provides an excellent account of the richness and complexity of Scott's vocabulary in *The Language of Walter Scott: A Study of his Scottish and Period Language* (London: André Deutsch, 1980). He does not, however, elaborate on the critical implications of this.

39  Dorothy J. Hale, 'Introduction' to 'Part III: Structuralism, Narratology, Deconstruction' in *The Novel: An Anthology of Criticism and Theory*, ed. by Dorothy J. Hale (Oxford: Blackwell Publishing, 2006), pp. 186–204 (p. 188). This volume will hereafter be referred to as Hale.

40  Roland Barthes, *Writing Degree Zero*, translated from the French by Annette Lavers and Colin Smith (London: Jonathan Cape, 1967), p. 9.

41  Ludwig Wittgenstein, *Tractatus Logico-Philosophicus*, translated by D. F. Pears and B. F. McGuinness (1921; London and New York: Routledge, 1997), p. 57.

42  See Hale, 'Introduction' to 'Part III: Structuralism, Narratology, Deconstruction', p. 189. The term 'narratology' was coined by Tzvetan Todorov in 1971.

43  Hale, 'Introduction' to 'Part III: Structuralism, Narratology, Deconstruction', p. 190.

44  Ibid. p. 196.

45  Jacques Derrida, *Writing and Difference*, translated by Alan Bass (London: Routledge and Kegan Paul, 1979), pp. 280 and 279.

46  '[T]he term "language-*game*" is meant to bring into prominence the fact that the *speaking* of language is part of an activity, or of a form of life'. Ludwig Wittgenstein, *Philosophical Investigations*, translated by G. E. M. Anscombe (1953; Oxford: Basil Blackwell, 1989), p. 11.

47  See André Brink, *The Novel: Language and Narrative from Cervantes to Calvino* (Basingstoke: Macmillan Press, 1998), p. 15.

48  André Brink argues that amongst the diverse body of work that has been labelled as the postmodernist novel 'the one common feature is a foregrounding of language'. See André Brink, p. 3.

49  Jill Rubenstein, *Scott in Carnival*, p. 595.

50  George Levine, *The Realist Imagination: English Fiction from Frankenstein to Lady Chatterley* (Chicago and London: University of Chicago Press, 1981), pp. 92 and 87.

51  See David Daiches, 'Foreword' to the Edinburgh Edition of the Waverley Novels.

52  See *Scott: The Critical Heritage* ed. by John O. Hayden (London: Routledge and Kegan Paul, 1970). *The Reception of Scott in Europe* ed. by Murray Pittock (London and New York: Continuum, 2006) also enhances our

understanding of the extent of Scott's influence on the development of the European novel.

53   *The Novel*, ed. by Franco Moretti, 2 vols (Princeton and Oxford: Princeton University Press, 2006). Moretti's collection will hereafter be referred to as Moretti.

54   John Barth, 'The Literature of Exhaustion' in *The Friday Book: Essays and Other Nonfiction* (New York: G. P. Putnam's Sons, 1984), pp. 61–76 (p. 71). I will return to John Barth's discussion of what this exhaustion means later in this study.

55   Hale, 'Introduction', p. 2.

56   Víktor Shklovsky, 'Sterne's *Tristram Shandy*: Stylistic Commentary' in Hale, pp. 31–53 (p. 34).

57   J. Hillis Miller, 'Reading Narrative' in Hale, pp. 242–56 (p. 252).

58   Jack Goody, 'From Oral to Written: An Anthropological Breakthrough in Storytelling' in Moretti, pp. 1.3–36 (p. 33).

59   Luiz Costa Lima, 'The Control of the Imagination and the Novel' in Moretti, pp. 1.37–68 (p. 53).

60   Catherine Gallagher, 'The Rise of Fictionality' in Moretti, 1.336–63 (p. 337).

61   John Brenkman, 'Innovation: Notes on Nihilism and the Aesthetics of the Novel' in Moretti, pp. 2. 808–38 (pp. 810–11).

62   Ian Duncan, *Scott's Shadow*, pp. 28–9.

63   Ibid. p. 87 and p. 92.

64   Andrew Lincoln, *Walter Scott and Modernity*, p. 6.

65   André Brink, *The Novel*, p. 1.

66   Ian Duncan, *Scott's Shadow*, p. 29.

67   Ibid. p. 124.

68   Ibid. p. 133.

69   See Cairns Craig, *Associationism and the Literary Imagination: from the phantasmal chaos* (Edinburgh: Edinburgh University Press, 2007).

70   Susan Manning, *Fragments of Union: Making Connections in Scottish and American Writing* (Basingstoke: Palgrave, 2002).

71   Ibid. pp. 61–2.

72   David Hume, 'The Sceptic' in *Selected Essays*, ed. by Stephen Copley and Andrew Edgar (Oxford: Oxford University Press, 1993), pp. 95–113 (p. 99).

73   Ibid. p. 101.

74   David Hume, 'Of the Standard of Taste' in *Selected Essays*, pp. 133–54 (p. 134).

75   Ibid. p. 136.

76   Ibid. p. 137.

77  Cairns Craig, 'Coleridge, Hume, and the Chains of the Romantic Imagination' in *Scotland and the Borders of Romanticism*, ed. by Leith Davis, Ian Duncan and Janet Sorensen (Cambridge: Cambridge University Press, 2004), pp. 20–37 (p. 34).

78  Terence Penelhum, *David Hume: An Introduction to his Philosophical System* (West Lafayette, IN: Purdue University Press, 1992), p. 10. Penelhum notes that 'both men have the same deflationary objective of offering us release from the never-ending uncertainties of philosophical reflection'.

79  Susan Manning, *Fragments of Union*, p. 35.

80  Janet Sorensen argues that the obsession of Scottish Enlightenment thinkers with language arises in part from their awareness of 'the performative and learned quality of speaking and developing an ear for a polite version of one's "native" language'. See *The Grammar of Empire*, p. 152.

81  James Burnet, Lord Monboddo, *Of the Origin and Progress of Language*, 2nd edition, 6 vols (Edinburgh: J. Balfour and T. Cadell, 1774–1809), p. 1.385.

82  Adam Smith, 'Considerations Concerning the First Formation of Language' in *The Scottish Enlightenment: An Anthology*, ed. by Alexander Broadie (Edinburgh: Canongate Classics, 1997), pp. 695–714 (p. 697).

83  Henry Home, Lord Kames, *Elements of Criticism*, 4th edition, 2 vols (Edinburgh: A. Kincaid and J. Bell, 1769), p. 2.24.

84  Ludwig Wittgenstein, *Philosophical Investigations*, p. 118.

85  James Burnet, Lord Monboddo, *Of the Origin and Progress of Language,* p. 2.195.

86  Ibid. p. 3.41.

87  Ibid. p. 2.8–9.

88  Ibid. p. 4.16–17.

89  Ibid. p. 1.460.

90  Henry Home, Lord Kames, *Elements of Criticism*, p. 2.18–19.

91  Ibid. pp. 2.516–17.

92  Ibid. p. 2.517.

93  Ibid. p. 2.517.

94  Adam Smith, 'Considerations Concerning the First Formation of Language', p. 703.

95  Hugh Blair, *Lectures on Rhetoric and Belles Lettres*, new edition, 3 vols (Edinburgh: Bell and Bradfute, 1811), pp. 1.7–8.

96  Ibid. p. 2.427.

97  James Burnet, Lord Monboddo, *Of the Origin and Progress of Language*, p. 6.15.

98   Ibid. p. 6.91.

99   Ibid. p. 6.15.

100  George Campbell, 'The Philosophy of Rhetoric' in *The Scottish Enlightenment: An Anthology*, pp. 685–96 (p. 691).

101  Ibid. p. 691.

102  Ibid. p. 686.

103  Henry Home, Lord Kames, *Elements of Criticism*, p. 2.517.

104  David Hume, Letter to John Home, Sept 20 1775 in *Well Temper'd Eloquence,* ed. and selected by Ingrid A. Merikoski (Edinburgh: David Hume Institute, 1996), pp. 38–9.

105  Ioan Williams, 'Introduction' in *Sir Walter Scott On Novelists and Fiction*, ed. by Ioan Williams (London: Routledge and Kegan Paul, 1968), pp. 1–12 (p. 1).

106  These introductions originally appeared in volumes of *Ballantyne's Novelist's Library* between 1821 and 1825. The series was intended as a means of reprinting work by the most esteemed novelists. The introductions are reprinted in Scott's *Prose Works* volumes 3 and 4. George Goodin comments that along with Scott's prefaces, reviews and articles, these pieces show that Scott 'is a great critic of fiction' with 'an immense erudition comparable to that of giants of scholarship such as Erich Auerbach': 'Scott's Narratology' in *Scott in Carnival,* pp. 40–9 (p. 41).

107  Walter Scott, 'Henry Fielding' in *Prose Works,* pp. 3.77–116 (p. 81).

108  Walter Scott, 'Samuel Richardson' in *Prose Works*, pp. 3.3–76 (p. 38).

109  Walter Scott, '*Emma*: a Novel' in *Sir Walter Scott on Novelists and Fiction*, ed. by Ioan Williams, pp. 225–36 (p. 230). This review originally appeared in the *Quarterly Review*, xiv (1815–16).

110  Ibid. pp. 226–7.

111  Ibid. p. 235.

112  Ibid. p. 228.

113  Ibid. p. 228.

114  Ibid. p. 231.

115  Ioan Williams recognises that the analogy between Flemish painting and poetry and art had been well rehearsed in the eighteenth century, but by applying it to the novel Scott adds a new and problematic dimension to it. See 'Introduction', p. 8.

116  Walter Scott, '*Emma*: a Novel', p. 231.

117  Walter Scott, 'Robert Bage' in *Prose Works*, pp. 3.441–64 (p. 464).

118  Walter Scott, 'Tobias Smollett' in *Prose Works*, pp. 3.117–90 (p. 178).

119  'The Reality Effect' is the name of an essay by Roland Barthes, originally published in *Communications* (1968) and reprinted in Hale, pp. 229–34.

120 Walter Scott, 'Samuel Richardson', pp. 70–1.

121 Walter Scott, 'Daniel De Foe' in *Prose Works*, pp. 4.228–81 (p. 261).

122 Ibid. p. 274.

123 Ibid. p. 274.

124 Ibid. p. 274.

125 Ibid. p. 275.

126 Ibid. p. 276.

127 Ibid. p. 265.

128 Ibid. p. 265.

129 George Levine, *The Realist Imagination*, p. 86.

130 Walter Scott, 'Henry Fielding', pp. 82–3.

131 *Journal*, p. 114.

132 Ina Ferris demonstrates that in this review Scott is inserting himself into a contemporary debate concerning the rival claims of formal historiography and historical fiction.

133 Walter Scott, 'Tales of My Landlord' in *Prose Works*, pp. 19.1–86 (p. 2).

134 Ibid. p. 3.

135 Ibid. p. 3.

136 Ibid. p. 24.

137 Ibid. p. 27.

138 Ibid. p. 58.

139 Ibid. p. 55.

140 Ibid. p. 11.

141 Patricia S. Gaston, *Prefacing the Waverley Novels: A Reading of Sir Walter Scott's Prefaces to the Waverley Novels* (New York: Peter Lang, 1991), pp. 6 and 16.

142 Ibid. p. 17.

143 Jerome McGann, 'Walter Scott's Romantic Postmodernity' in *Scotland and the Borders of Romanticism*, ed. by Leith Davis, Ian Duncan and Janet Sorensen (Cambridge: Cambridge University Press, 2004), pp. 113–29 (p. 119).

144 George Levine, *The Realist Imagination*, p. 88.

145 Ibid. p. 90.

146 André Brink, *The Novel*, p. 7.

147 John Barth, 'The Literature of Replenishment: Postmodernist Fiction' in *The Friday Book*, pp. 193–206 (p. 200).

148 John Barth, 'Historical Fiction, Fictitious History, and Chesapeake Bay Blue Crabs, or, About Aboutness' in *The Friday Book*, pp. 180–92 (p. 191).

149 Mieke Bal, 'Over-writing as Un-writing: Descriptions, World-Making and Novelistic Time' in Moretti, pp. 2.571–610 (p. 581)

# Chapter 1

# 'Living in a World of Death':

# Scott's Narrative Poems

The main focus of this study is Scott's fiction. However, it is worth beginning any exploration of it by taking a step backwards to consider his early narrative poetry since it is here that Scott formulates his first theories on the nature and purpose of literature, the role of the modern writer and the relationship of both to history and national identity. If Scott's fiction has undergone something of a renaissance in recent years his poetry, sadly, remains neglected. There is no modern edition of the poetry and very little criticism.[1] Many reasons for this neglect might be proposed. Among them, there is the simple fact that long narrative poems are out of fashion. In addition, Scott dismissed his own poetic career as eclipsed by the work of Byron, a perception which has to some extent become embedded in modern constructions of Romanticism.[2] Perhaps above all, however, the surface simplicity of Scott's narrative poetry and its romance modes and themes has led to virtual neglect when compared to his fiction; while Nancy Moore Goslee suggests that developments in narrative theory clear the way for new responses to Scott's poems they have remained relatively untouched by readings in modern critical terms.[3] Yet Scott's poetry lends itself to such analysis since it is in fact far more complex than its seemingly narrative driven cantos initially imply. They are vexed by questions of form and genre and as such not only reveal the relationship of the modern poet to history and society but also gesture towards an anxiety concerning the nature of the poetic medium which foreshadows Scott's later, more troubled relationship with language.

One of the most immediately striking aspects of the poetry is the way in which Scott explores within it the role of the poet and his relationship to modern society, issues clearly relevant not only for the poems themselves but for his writing in general. His idea of the poet is foregrounded in the title of his first long poem *The Lay of the Last Minstrel*. While several critics suggest the critical distance that Scott places between the minstrel and himself there is clearly a sense in which Scott here at least potentially aligns the role of poet with the evocative one of 'minstrel', a notion that he in fact revisits in his major narrative poems. Recent criticism has recognised this aspect of Scott's work, highlighting the role he played in integrating the concept of the bard into constructions of Romanticism and noting that the identification of poet with minstrel carries with it a host of overt and latent connections that cluster around the term linking it to this bardic, or minstrel, tradition.[4] The *OED* defines the term minstrel in several ways. In its earliest use the term denotes a servant or functionary but by the end of the sixteenth century it had assumed its more familiar use of 'a person employed by a patron to provide entertainment by singing, playing music, storytelling, juggling etc.' By Scott's time it had also acquired the more elevated and specific function of 'a singer or musician of the medieval period, *esp.* one who sings heroic or lyrical poetry'.[5] This more elevated function was in part created by Scott himself and by Thomas Percy in his 1765 'Essay on the Ancient Order of English Minstrels'.

Clearly, one of the main purposes of the minstrel in the *Lay* is simply to 'provide entertainment'. His audience as it is imagined in the poem is predominantly female and he sings to them of, among other things, love, his 'dearest theme' (3.1). His request to the Duchess that he might play is couched in the simple terms of entertainment: 'That, if she loved the harp to hear, / He could make music to her ear' (Introduction), a description which, perhaps, emphasises musical rather than verbal entertainment.[6] However, as the *Lay* progresses it is clear that the minstrel's function also incorporates the more elevated role of a singer of heroic poetry and serves a number of other purposes crucial to our understanding of what this figure represents for Scott. In his introduction to the *Minstrelsy of the Scottish Border* Scott represents the role of the bard in 'recounting the exploits of their forefathers, recording their laws and moral precepts, or hymning the praises of . . . deities'[7] and the role of the minstrel in this poem similarly involves this social function of preserving traditional values by the recording of heroic and chivalric mores. As such, social function also incorporates the resonant role of chronicler, with all the implications for recording the past that this carries with it. In his 'Essay on Romance' Scott reinforces the connection between early romance poetry (mediated via minstrels) and historical record when he suggests that 'Romance and real history have the same common origin'[8] and it is clear that this is how the minstrel in the *Lay* perceives his role; in the introduction to the poem we are told that as soon as his physical needs were supplied the minstrel's pride began to rise and he started to speak of the past:

> Of good Earl Francis, dead and gone,
> And of Earl Walter, rest him God!

A braver ne'er to battle rode:
And how full many a tale he knew
Of the old warriors of Buccleuch; (Introduction)

In the fourth canto the minstrel also suggests that the version he gives of the past is an accurate one. Describing his training as a bard he gives an account of his own teacher and the rigidity with which he has insisted upon passing on such details as the rules of combat with scrupulous veracity:

I know right well, that, in their lay,
Full many minstrels sing and say,
    Such combat should be made on horse,
On foaming steed, in full career,
With brand to aid, when as the spear
    Should shiver in the course:
But he, the jovial Harper, taught
Me, yet a youth, how it was fought,
    In guise which now I say;
He knew each ordinance and clause
Of Black Lord Archibald's battle-laws,
    In the old Douglas' day.
He brook'd not, he, that scoffing tongue
Should tax his minstrelsy with wrong,
    Or call his song untrue: (4.34)

As this implies, veracity is clearly one of the key elements in bardic recitation. As Scott comments '[t]he Historical Ballad relates events, which we either know actually to have taken place, or which, at least, making due allowance for the exaggerations of poetical tradition, we may readily conceive to have had some foundation in history'.[9] This is significant in enhancing our understanding of what this figure represents for Scott. Writing in the long shadow of an age obsessed with the role of historiography (only a generation before Hume had famously described his own as the historical age and Scotland as the historical nation) Scott's comment offers an interesting intervention, for it reinforces the significance of 'story' (here presented in its most Romantic form as 'lay') as a significant part of the historical record, a concept which was to form the backbone of all of his subsequent creative work.[10] Re-calling the past, re-telling it, and by implication recording it and passing it on to another generation are presented, therefore, as key aspects of the minstrel's function, a fact reinforced by his recounting of the *Lay* proper of a sixteenth-century event to a seventeenth-century audience.

All this is self-evident and accords with Katie Trumpener's assessment of the role of the bard figure in nation formation in post-Union Britain. 'For nationalist antiquaries' she writes, 'the bard is the mouthpiece for a whole society, articulating its values, chronicling its history, and mourning the inconsolable tragedy of its collapse'.[11] As several critics have recognised, in using the minstrel in his poetry in this way Scott is inserting himself into a debate concerning the relationship between poetry and history and indeed the different forms that historiography may take. For many critics Scott's scholarly paratexts (the notes, glosses, introductory essays etc. that accompany the narrative poems) suggest that he is engaging with this subject by offering a mediation between poetic account and antiquarianism. Interesting though this may be, however, it is not the subject of this study, which is less concerned with the form of history that Scott is offering than with the process by which the past can be rendered via the fraught medium of language.

Any suggestion that the minstrel simply offers an unmediated version of the past is complicated by Scott's remark that our understanding of the relationship between the ballad and history must take into account 'the exaggerations of poetical tradition' and by his 1830 'Introductory Remarks on Popular Poetry' where he adds that while lays may be of interest to the 'general historian', 'poets were a fabling race from the very beginning of time, and so much addicted to exaggeration, that their accounts are seldom to be relied on without corroborative evidence'.[12] It is clear, therefore, that if ballads do form part of the historical record it is not a straightforward one. What is perhaps more interesting than a recognition that Scott sees the minstrel as contributing to a record of the past, consequently, is the *process* by which the minstrel communicates his information. In the *Lay* he does not simply record the past, but, far more significantly, his method of story-telling involves re-creating the past, and in doing so, eliding the passage of time so that it appears to collapse in on itself to dissolve the gulf between what has gone before and the time of story-telling. Catherine Jones has written convincingly on the role of different types of memory in Scott's work and the ways in which these are used collectively to provide a version of the past filtered through various systems of commemoration.[13] In the *Lay* the minstrel combines various forms of memory and imagination to offer a new version of historical events as 'Each blank, in faithless memory void, / The poet's glowing thought supplied' (Introduction). Memory and imagination, consequently, operate together not only to record the past but to create a version of it.

J. H. Alexander has drawn attention to the extent to which metaphors articulating the flux of time pervade *The Lay of the Last Minstrel*.[14] Certainly, one of its key themes is the passage of time, and the inevitable teleological movement this brings from life to death. This preoccupation haunts the opening of the fourth canto, for example, as the minstrel begins with a meditation on the passage of time, juxtaposing the apparently changeless face of nature with the constant flux of human experience:

> Sweet Teviot! on thy silver tide,
>     The glaring bale-fires blaze no more;
> No longer steel-clad warriors ride
>     Along thy wild and willowed shore;
> Where'er thou wind'st by dale or hill,
> All, all is peaceful, all is still,
>     As if thy waves, since Time was born,
> Since first they rolled their way to Tweed,
> Had only heard the shepherd's reed,
>     Nor started at the bugle-horn.
>
> Unlike the tide of human time,
>     Which, though it change in ceaseless flow,
> Retains each grief, retains each crime,
>     Its earliest course was doomed to know;
> And, darker as it downward bears,
> Is stained with past and present tears.
>     Low as that tide has ebbed with me,
> It still reflects to memory's eye
> The hour, my brave, my only boy,
>     Fell by the side of great Dundee.  (4.1–2)

However, what this passage also suggests is that while human time may be a 'ceaseless flow', what we might call *emotional* time (the time of personal remembrance) is not linear, but rather, retains the imprint of 'past and present tears' through 'memory's eye'. While Enlightenment historiography offers an essentially teleological view of historical development, here recollection and imagination operate almost in opposition to the passage of time, so that it folds back upon itself to hold all emotional response in a kind of continuum or co-existence.

Katie Trumpener describes a similar process at work in one of the most evident precedents for all Romantic bardic poetry, the poems of Ossian:

> Describing the actions of three generations of bards and warriors, Ossian's poems let the time of action and of memory overflow into one another, creating a complex temporality of bardic repertoire and performance that both constitutes history and stands outside historical time . . . Left in a present that is empty, he revives the past to fill it; unable to see the landscape in front of his blind eyes, he re-creates a mental landscape of memory and voice, a past composed of earlier bardic songs.[15]

Coining the term 'retrojection' to describe this technique, Trumpener observes that Macpherson employs it to create 'an almost seamless dissolve between the narrative frame of a particular poem and the epic material (or bardic recitation) at its core'.[16] In essence, this process is how the *Lay* also functions, for its effect is to recreate an emotional response on the part of its listeners (and in turn its readers) so that they are invited to engage with the events described as if they were part of their present experience. For example, the minstrel moves from the description of his son's death evoked above: 'Enough—he died the death of fame; / Enough—he died with conquering Graeme' (4.2) swiftly back into the events of his tale which, while presented in the past tense and of course located in the past, are offered with a new immediacy as each of the next two cantos opens with the word 'Now', as though demanding that the reader's emotional attention is transferred from the 'present' (the son's death) to the past, presented 'now' with a new emotional intensity. The minstrel's lay, consequently, serves both to deflect grief away from the present but also to transfer emotional response onto the past so that 'The present scene, the future lot, / His toils, his wants, were all forgot; / Cold diffidence, and age's frost / In the full tide of song were lost' (Introduction). His audience, as a result of this process, experience the events of the past as if they were recalled from the grave:

Marvelled the Duchess how so well
His legendary song could tell—
Of ancient deeds, so long forgot;
Of feuds, whose memory was not;
Of forests, now laid waste and bare;
Of towers, which harbour now the hare;
Of manners, long since changed and gone;

> Of chiefs, who under their gray stone
> So long had slept, that fickle Fame
> Had blotted from her rolls their name,
> And twined round some new minion's head
> The fading wreath for which they bled—
> In sooth, 'twas strange, this old man's verse
> Could call them from their marble hearse. (4.32)

The *OED*'s definition of the term 'minstrel' also emphasises, however, that the earliest meanings of the term includes that of a *servant* or *functionary*. While part of the minstrel's service in the *Lay* may be the recording and re-creating of the past Scott also suggests that he, and indeed this process of recreating the past, may serve another purpose. Penny Fielding observes that 'Scott himself was not averse to exploiting the authoritative persona of the bard for openly political ends' and it is clear that one of the functions of recreating the past in the poem is, for this minstrel at least, one of re-awakening a sense of national identity.[17]

This idea is hardly a surprising one in relation to Scott and is of course famously reiterated at the end of Canto 5 and the opening of Canto 6 when the minstrel proclaims:

> Breathes there the man, with soul so dead,
> Who never to himself hath said,
>     This is my own, my native land!
> Whose heart hath ne'er within him burned,
> As home his footsteps he hath turn'd,
>     From wandering on a foreign strand! (6.1)

This statement is given in response to a question by his audience: 'they bade him tell, / Why he, who touched the harp so well, / Should thus, with ill-rewarded toil, / Wander a poor and thankless soil, / When the more generous southern land / Would well requite his skilful hand' (5.30). The minstrel's response implies that he who feels no sense of national pride is 'doubly dying' for 'concentered all in self' he lacks social responsibility and will remain unsung in poetry (6.1). A sense of national identity and a place in poetry thus become conjoined, a notion reiterated in the next stanza, where poetic sensibility and a sense of Scottish national identity are presented as confluent, and also linked, crucially, to an understanding that place (a well-known and identifiable landscape) is linked to event as it is inscribed in a knowledge of the country's past:

O Caledonia! stern and wild,
Meet nurse for a poetic child!
Land of brown heath and shaggy wood,
Land of the mountain and the flood,
Land of my sires! what mortal hand
Can e'er untie the filial band,
That knits me to thy rugged strand!
Still, as I view each well known scene,
Think what is now, and what hath been,
Seems as, to me, of all bereft,
Sole friends, thy woods and streams were left;
And thus I love them better still,
Even in extremity of ill. (6.2)

In the *Lay* then, the role of the minstrel is that of entertainer, but it is also that of chronicler, of re-creator of the past through story so that time may collapse upon itself and so that a knowledge of that past, 'what is now, and what hath been', may inspire a sense of national pride and national identity. It is, Ian Duncan has suggested, this social aspect of Scott's poetry that has caused him to fall out of the Romantic canon yet in spite of what seem to be clear resonances with the role that Scott apparently adopted for himself as a writer we should be cautious in assuming that the role of the minstrel can be straightforwardly mapped onto that of modern poet and author.[18] In fact, for several critics the minstrel is, to some extent at least, set in binary opposition to the figure of the poet. Penny Fielding, for example, sees a tension between the oral and the written operating within Scott's work, with the modern day poet, whose medium is print culture, being set in opposition to the medieval minstrel or bard who is a transmitter of oral messages, here given cultural and political significance both in Scott's work and in Romantic literature more generally. Nancy Goslee also sees a tension of this sort operating in the *Lay* so that the performance of it 'demonstrates the tension between oral and written text',[19] the latter demanding a kind of corrective.[20]

More recently, however, Maureen McLane argues that 'the minstrel is both like and unlike Scott' and to read the opposition of minstrel and poet in straightforward binary terms is problematic and cannot be entirely sustained by a close reading of the poem.[21] In spite of an apparent schism between bard and poet there are many aspects of the *Lay* which suggest that minstrel and modern day poet serve similar functions, and that their poetry operates by parallel processes. This is implied by the very title of the poem, *The Lay of the Last Minstrel*. In his 1830 introduction to the poem Scott comments that he 'introduced the Old Minstrel, as an appropriate prolocutor, by whom the lay might be sung, or spoken, and the introduction of whom betwixt the cantos, might remind the reader at intervals, of the time, place, and circumstances of the recitation. This species of *cadre*, or frame, afterwards afforded the poem its name of "The Lay of the Last Minstrel."'[22] This seems to imply that the title refers entirely to the fictional minstrel. In reality, however, the title is more complex than this since it is given to the poem as a whole, not only to the interpolated lay 'proper' which opens with 'Canto First'. As a consequence it is unclear who the title refers to and it thus serves to deconstruct any straightforward opposition between minstrel and poet. While the most obvious interpretation is that the title refers to the teller of the tale of Branksome Tower this is problematised by the word 'of' which is ambiguous here. Prepositions formed a particularly interesting category of semantic unit for Enlightenment commentators since they are evidence of a contingent rather than simply referential model of language. Adam Smith, for example, comments:

> It is, perhaps, worth while to observe that those prepositions, which in modern languages hold the place of the ancient cases, are, of all others, the most general, and abstract, and metaphysical; and of consequence, would probably be the last invented. Ask any man of common acuteness, What relation is expressed by the preposition *above*? He will readily answer, that of *superiority*. By the preposition *below*? He will as quickly reply, that of *inferiority*. But ask him, what relation is expressed by the preposition *of*, and, if he has not beforehand employed his thoughts a good deal upon these subjects, you may safely allow him a week to consider of his answer.[23]

In Scott's poem the non-specificity of the preposition 'of' (defined by *OED* as expressing both a sense of source or origin and the meaning 'concerning' or 'about') raises doubts about who the minstrel actually is.[24] If we understand it in the sense 'about' then he is the wanderer who turns up at Newark. If we understand it in the sense of source, however, it implies that the poem is by the 'minstrel' and thus the term also embraces the modern narrator who provides the introduction to the poem and who intervenes from time to time in the course of its telling. As McLane comments the poem thus operates both as 'a lay sung by him [the minstrel], but also, by virtue of Scott's astonishing poetic and historiographic fluencies, a lay about him'.[25] This question produced by semantic ambiguity is further complicated by the fact that at the end of the introduction the wandering minstrel is also given the alternative title of 'latest minstrel' as he begins his song, thus suggesting that he is only one in a line of his kind that may, indeed, ultimately lead to the present poet.

The title of the poem thus creates some elision between minstrel and the modern poet and this elision is reinforced, or perhaps further complicated, by the fact that the lay itself is not placed within inverted commas; while it may represent the speech of a character within the poem – the latest minstrel – this is never signalled via punctuation.[26] And more significantly, this lack of grammatical clarity creates a situation where, at the beginning and ends of cantos, there is a further slippage between the voices of the minstrel himself and that of the modern day speaker. A good example of this can be found if we look again at the close of Canto 3 and the opening of Canto 4. Ostensibly, the minstrel's lay ends with the couplet 'So passed the anxious night away, / And welcome was the peep of day' (3.31) and the nineteenth-century poet's voice provides the framing narrative which takes the reader back out of the seventeenth-century to comment and reflect on the audience's relationship to the minstrel. This frame is apparently reinforced by the fact that in this instance the Master of Song's response '"Aye! once he had – but he was dead!"' is placed within inverted commas (3.31). However, while the lay appears to begin again with the opening of 'Canto Fourth' and the words 'Sweet Teviot' the first two stanzas do not form part of the sixteenth-century story and the reflections which are made, concerning the passing of time as flux and flow, and the role of 'Memory's eye' are located far more in nineteenth-century sensibilities that those of the earlier period. The structure of the stanzas also offers little clue as to who the speaker may be for while these reflections do not follow the modern narrator's couplets which close Canto 3, neither do they mirror the form of the later stanzas where the tale of border warfare is recounted.

There is, then, an elision of minstrel's voice and poet's voice at the opening and closing of each canto, so that it is not altogether clear whether we as readers are being addressed by poet or bard. This modulation of seventeenth-century and nineteenth-century voices essentially means that the poem as a whole – *The Lay of The Last Minstrel* – mirrors the effects of the interpolated tale within it in that it serves, like the minstrel's tale, to fold time in upon itself, so that the different time-frames of the poem come to co-exist. In this sense at least, minstrel and poet share the same function; that of re-creating and re-telling the past so that it can be experienced and emotionally engaged with afresh by the audience. While it is in one sense true that the sixteenth-century story is told by the minstrel it is being 'simultaneously relayed' by the nineteenth-century poet who is the modern carrier of the tale – one of the future bards who will sing of the heroism of those involved in it.

In his 1805 headnote to the *Lay* Scott states that 'The Poem now offered to the Public is intended to illustrate the customs and manners which anciently prevailed on the Borders of England and Scotland'.[27] As such, he is claiming a similar role for himself as modern poet to that suggested by his own descriptions of the minstrel. Through a poetic slight-of-hand in the matter of voice, poet and minstrel come to share the function of re-creating the past and making it live again. Moreover, it would seem to be the case that, for Scott at least, the modern day poet shares with his minstrel brother the function of re-inscribing the past in order to reawaken national consciousness. If there is an elision of the two voices at the opening of Canto 4 this is also the case at the close of Canto 5 and opening of Canto 6, those stanzas which deal with the relationship of poetry to national identity. Again, there is some slippage between the end of the minstrel's lay and the narrating frame that surrounds it. Here, this effect is reinforced by the content of the narrator's stanza, for it describes the seeming echoes of the requiem for Musgrave resonating in the minstrel's song, as if repeating down the centuries. Their resonance for the nineteenth century is once more reinforced by the use of the word 'Now' which here again serves to dissolve time; this is also amplified by the rhyme scheme, which in this instance is shared by the surrounding stanzas of the 'lay' and by the repetition of the phrase 'minstrel's wail' (5.30) which further elides the speaking minstrel with a minstrel referred to by him at the close of the canto. As time frame and voice collapse here, the question put to the minstrel concerning his decision to remain in Scotland and his famously patriotic response may as well be put to the speaker of the poem as a whole, and is in a sense responded to by him. Unlocking and recovering a sense of national pride via an account of the events of the nation's past is, then, a task shared by both minstrel and poet, a topic which, of course, has a long and vexed history in Scott criticism.

Scott's second, and without doubt his most ambitious poem, *Marmion*, also offers the reader a self-reflexive contemplation of the role of the poet. Again, the poem is marked by the use of a dual time-frame[28] and part of its function is a re-inscribing of the events of the past – this time the historical Battle of Flodden – and the reawakening via this account of an increasingly complex version of national identity. In this instance, however, the role of the minstrel is replaced by the far more sophisticated frame supplied by the Introductory Epistles where, in a more directly self-reflexive way than in his other poems, Scott explores the role and function of the modern poet and his relationship both to his art and to society so that the epistles become both a justification of the poet as Scott defines the role and of the form of poetry he has chosen to write.

On *Marmion*'s first appearance it was the Introductory Epistles which caused most confusion to Scott's readers. His friend George Ellis, for example, recognised that the epistles were to some extent a replacement of the minstrel frame present in the earlier poem, but expressed disappointment at the exchange. Interestingly, he complained that this frame – unlike that of the minstrel – created a disruption in the experience of reading the tale:

> The personal appearance of the Minstrel who, though the last, is by far the most charming of all Minstrels, is by no means compensated by the idea of an author, shorn of his picturesque beard, deprived of his harp, and writing letters to his intimate friends. These introductory epistles indeed, though excellent in themselves, are in fact only interruptions to the fable, and accordingly, nine readers out of ten have perused them separately either before or after the poem; and it is obvious that they cannot have produced, in either case, the effect which was proposed, viz that of relieving the reader's attention, and of giving variety to the whole.[29]

As J. H. Alexander and other commentators have recognised, however, the epistles operate not only for 'relieving the reader's attention' but are also concerned with 'an investigation of the nature and status of Scott's art' and the function of the poet in the modern world.[30] The epistles, Alexander argues, are in one sense those parts of the poem written by Scott, while in the Tale of Flodden Field (the sub-title of the poem) the speaker is 'generally the minstrel, though in a very half-hearted and spasmodic way when compared with *The Lay of the Last Minstrel*'.[31] However, as we have seen with the *Lay*, this distinction is to some extent a false one and it is evident that, while re-cast in quintessentially Romantic terms, the function of the poet as it is outlined in the epistles is in many ways similar to that of the minstrel as it is outlined in the earlier poem.[32]

As we might expect, the theme of the first epistle, dedicated to W. S. Rose, is the need to record the past; to provide a testament to deeds of valour, even those of the relatively recent past, so that they might not be forgotten: 'Say to your sons,—Lo, here his grave' (Introduction, Canto 1). The modern day poet, like the minstrel, can be the one to record such deeds via his 'Border Minstrel's rhyme'. While the speaker here suggests that this chosen theme may be more suitable for stories from the past, 'the ancient shepherd's tale' in the tradition of the 'fair fields of old romance', the implication is that, nevertheless, by recording the past the poet may also comment on the heroism of his own day: if time can be collapsed or telescoped via poetry then distinctions between times become artificial:

> But thou, my friend, cast fitly tell,
> (For few have read romance so well)
> How still the legendary lay
> O'er poet's bosom holds its sway;
> How on the ancient minstrel strain
> Time lays his palsied hand in vain;
> And how our hearts at doughty deeds,
> By warriors wrought in steely weeds,
> Still throb for fear and pity's sake; (Introduction, Canto 1)

The second epistle, dedicated in this instance to John Marriott, continues this theme and here reiterates the relationship between place and poetry as the speaker recounts how, in earlier days, they were recognised as intrinsically linked in his mind, landscape prompting poetry and poetry evoking landscape:

> We marked each memorable scene,
> And held poetic talk between;
> Nor hill, nor brook, we paced along,
> But had its legend, or its song. (Introduction, Canto 2)

By the third epistle Scott more explicitly expresses the relationship of the modern poet and the minstrel as he offers the plea 'in the minstrel spare the friend'. In this epistle he offers a discussion of poetic types, and suggests that his own chosen mode, contrary to his friend William Erskine's advice, is to 'ramble on through brake and maze, / With harpers rude of barbarous days' (Introduction, Canto 3); an essentially Romantic mode rather than a classical form. Interestingly, in the light of the discussion above, his justification for the form he chooses – and by implication the role he maps out for the poet – involves both its ability to recapture the past and the ways in which such verse, or Romantic story, inspires an understanding of national identity which causes the deeds of the past to collide, or elide, with the national concerns of the present:

Old tales I heard of woe or mirth,
Of lovers' sleights, of ladies' charms,
Of witches spells, of warriors' arms;
Of patriot battles, won of old
By Wallace wight and Bruce the bold;
Of later fields of feud and fight,
When, pouring from their Highland height,
The Scottish clans, in headlong sway,
Had swept the scarlet ranks away. (Introduction, Canto 3)

Such experiences cause the young poet both to 'mimic ranks of war' and to trace the heroism of the past in those around him in 'each kind familiar face'. A similar sentiment is expressed in the fifth canto, where poetry (or at least poetry as it functions here) is used to redeem or recapture time and make 'the gentle poet live again'. The elision between poet and minstrel also continues here where the 'minstrel lessons' he requests of his friend George Ellis are to help him to write a poetry which 'charm[s], instruct[s], and mend[s]' (Introduction, Canto 5). This 'northern strain', however is described not as formal or classical, but again as essentially Romantic:

Come, listen!—bold in thy applause,
The Bard shall scorn pedantic laws;
And, as the ancient art could stain
Achievements on the storied pane,
Irregularly traced and planned,
But yet so glowing and so grand;
So shall he strive, in changeful hue,
Field, feast, and combat, to renew,
And loves, and arms, and harpers' glee.
And all the pomp of chivalry. (Introduction, Canto 5)

In the last epistle, that to Richard Heber, Scott reiterates his choice of mode and once again positions his art in opposition to classical literature stating that to do so has a national or patriotic dimension since 'All nations have their omens drear' (Introduction, Canto 6). Both his themes, and his form, it seems, are chosen because they are appropriate for Scotland.

As in the *Lay* the version of the poet that is presented in *Marmion* is one whose function is to recapture and retell the past so that by doing so he may invigorate a sense of national pride and consciousness. In this poem, however, the ways in which the recounting of past events may inspire respect for the 'heroism' of the present day is more fully iterated than in his earlier work as the framework provided by the epistles encourages the reader to draw parallels between the heroism of former days and that of the recent past, with the poet acting, in both instances, as a testament-bearer for these events.

Scott returns to the relationship between poet and minstrel in his third long poem *The Lady of the Lake*. While this poem deals far less overtly with the subject of the role of the poet or minstrel than the *Lay* it is evident that Scott is reiterating both the function of the minstrel in society and the ways in which this can be mapped onto the role of his modern counterpart. In this instance the voices of the poet and that of the minstrel are more straightforwardly elided, since the poem opens with an invocation to the 'Harp of the North' to 'wake once more' (Introduction, Canto 1). As Trumpener notes, the harp is resonant with meaning since '[a]s a bardic instrument, the cherished vehicle of Irish, Welsh, and Scottish nationalism, and then as the emblem of a nationalist republicanism, the harp stands for an art that honors the organic relationship between a people, their land, and their culture'.[33] Here, the speaker of the poem refers back to the 'earlier lay' and takes on the mantle of the minstrel to wake the silence of the harp:

> O wake once more! how rude soe'er the hand
>   That ventures o'er thy magic maze to stray;
> O wake once more! though scarce my skill command
>   Some feeble echoing of thine earlier lay:
> Though harsh and faint, and soon to die away,
>   And all unworthy of thy nobler strain,
> Yet if one heart throb higher at its sway,
>   The wizard note has not been touch'd in vain.
> Then silent be no more! Enchantress, wake again! (Introduction, Canto 1)

As in *The Lay of the Last Minstrel* the function of minstrelsy here is both to reinscribe the past and to reawaken a sense of national pride, and again the modern poet re-enacts this function via the subject matter of the poem which in this instance is a recognisable historical event, the feud between the Highland clans and the Douglasses, and the Stewart kings. McLane comments that 'with eighteenth-century Britain in mind, we can see that minstrelsy began – or was revived – as a way of talking about the historical and cultural situations of poetry'[34] and here too, there are self-reflexive references to the functions of minstrelsy which reiterate the roles that Scott is mapping out for both minstrel and poet. One such instance of this, for example, can be found late in the poem when dying Roderick Dhu commands Allan to describe the battle which has taken place in his absence:

"Strike it!—and then, (for well thou canst,)
Free from thy minstrel-spirit glanced,
Fling me the picture of the fight,
When met my clan the Saxon might.
I'll listen, till my fancy hears
The clang of swords, the crash of spears!
These grates, these walls, shall vanish then,
From the fair field of fighting men,
And my free spirit burst away,
As if it soared from battle fray."—
The trembling bard with awe obeyed,—
Slow on his harp his hand he laid;
But soon remembrance of the sight
He witnessed from the mountain's height,
With what old Bertram told at night,
Awakened the full power of song,
And bore him in career along;—
As shallop launched on river's tide,
That slow and fearful leaves the side,
But, when it feels the middle stream,
Drives downward swift as lightning's beam. (6.14)

The function of poetry here, clearly, is to allow the Chieftain to experience vicariously the battle he has not seen: by 'flinging [him] the picture' the minstrel can allow Roderick to almost experience the battle so that 'grates, walls shall vanish' and 'his spirit burst away, / As if it soared from battle fray'. Similarly, through memory ('remembrance of the sight') and testimony ('what old Bertram told at night'), the minstrel is liberated to give an account of the battle both to Roderick Dhu and, of course, via the nineteenth-century mediator, to the reader.

These reflections on poetry reiterate an idea of the poet as recorder of the past and also demonstrate its ability to make that past come to life. As Wittgenstein states, 'man learns the concept of the past by remembering'[35] and the poet, as he is described here, contributes to that act of remembering through his verse. By suggesting that poetry can thus recapture and 're-imagine the past' Scott ascribes a significant power to it and, by implication, to the language from which it is constructed. Indeed, several critics have read the role of the poet in Scott's poems as offering an example of romance transformation. J. H. Alexander and Nancy Moore Goslee, for example, argue that Scott's model of poetry can be seen as a kind of transforming 'magic' which seeks to redeem time and even in a sense defeat death via the power of the word – the act of poetry. Goslee, for example, argues that in the *Lay* Scott writes 'a book of magic that escapes the grave'[36] and argues that through the 'redemptive conversion of minstrel memory'[37] the minstrel 'cancels intervening time' by virtue of his art.[38] She elaborates on this process, describing the model of poetry that Scott is presenting here as a kind of magic:

> In Scott's poems, the transformation and use of magical codes to project a nostalgic harmony that is also heuristically prophetic is extremely important. One of the ways Scott accomplishes this transformation and projection is to shift, while still reporting their magic, from the incantatory, performative codes of his enchanters to the magical code of the poet, and especially of the writer. Describing poetry as magic seems at first glance so hackneyed an idea as to be a cliché. Yet we take such claims with great seriousness when we read the high romantics, and Scott intends this transformation of powers more seriously than he admits. His poems are riddled with metaphors, symbols, and signs of the rival magical powers of singing minstrel and of written text, of codes acceptable to writer and reader that evoke older magical conflict. Codes, scrolls, books, and documents are crucial to the transformation of his plots. Moreover, his conversion of sung narrative to printed document makes acceptable an older magic by transforming it to the modern poet's writing.[39]

While less overtly Romantic in his language than Goslee, Alexander also reads the *Lay* as essentially a poem about rejuvenation, if only a temporary one. Drawing attention to the extent of word play on the themes of life and death and the liminal state between them Alexander suggests that the *Lay*'s 'deepest underlying theme is thus man's attempt to avoid death, his encounter with death, and his learning to live in the face of death'.[40] Similarly, he recognises in *Marmion*'s epistles a movement from decay towards rejuvenation, suggesting that through the redemptive power of poetry Scott explores a way to move from despondency at time passing towards an acceptance of this as the inevitable state of the human condition.

These essentially optimistic readings of Scott's major poems, and of his understanding of the role of language, are appealing and are also to an extent convincing. Hinging upon Scott's punning of the relationship between the terms 'glamour' and 'grammar' (magic and language) Goslee reads Scott's poetry in terms of a dominant trajectory towards rejuvenation and such a reading can clearly be justified. In the *Lay*, for example, the minstrel, by the act of recitation, transforms himself from a man 'infirm and old' with 'withered cheek, and tresses gray' and isolated from the community, to one who is revitalised, once more a vital part of the community and who can by virtue of his verse, appear to redeem time:

> There sheltered wanderers, by the blaze,
> Oft heard the tale of other days;
> For much he loved to ope his door,
> And give the aid he begged before.
> So passed the winter's day—but still,
> When summer smiled on sweet Bowhill,
> And July's eve, with balmy breath,
> Waved the blue-bells on Newark heath;
> When throstles sung on Harehead-shaw,
> And grain waved green on Carterhaugh,
> And flourished, broad, Blackandro's oak,
> The aged Harper's soul awoke!
> Then would he sing achievements high,
> And circumstance of Chivalry,
> Till the rapt traveller would stay,
> Forgetful of the closing day;
> And noble youths, the strain to hear,
> Forsook the hunting of the deer;
> And Yarrow, as he rolled along,
> Bore burden to the Minstrel's song. (6.31)

In support of such readings Alexander reiterates an essentially redemptive impulse in Scott's work concluding that 'Scott is not Beckett, and he allows the Minstrel to end his days in acceptance of the kindliest aspect of natural time, the regular succession of winter and summer'.[41]

However, while such readings are convincing, even here, in Scott's early poetry, we can see indications that this redemptive reading of it may be only partly satisfactory. Andrew Lincoln suggests that the presence of the minstrel figure in the poem is a marker of Scott's particularly sceptical form of Romanticism and, indeed, Scott is rather more like Beckett in his critique of the transformative power of language than recuperative readings would imply; while the minstrel's poetry may, in one sense, reinvigorate the past it cannot, finally, bring the dead back to life.[42] After all, the point of closure of the *Lay* is not the minstrel's happy re-situation within the community, but rather, somewhere in the time frame of the nineteenth-century poet when 'Hushed is the harp—the Minstrel gone' (6.31). Like the characters in Keats's 'Eve of St Agnes' the minstrel and all others in the *Lay* are long dead 'gone—aye, ages long ago'.[43] They are located, as Coleridge puts it in 'Christabel', in 'a world of death',[44] divorced at least for the present from 'that dreadful day' when 'heaven and earth shall pass away' and the dead be reawakened (6.32). Indeed, the implication of the 'Dies Irae' which ends the *Lay* can only be that the poet's magic of reawakening the dead is at best only a partial magic; the poet may allow time to collapse upon itself but there is a sense in which this is only a 'magician's trick'. As Alexander acknowledges, the minstrel's 'Indian summer at the end of the final canto' can only be 'a brief repose before death'.[45]

Most pertinent for the present study, however, is the possibility that the in-built scepticism towards its own strategies which might be said to haunt the end of the *Lay* is built upon a wide-spread interrogation of the power of poetry and indeed, the limits of language that runs throughout Scott's major poems. Several critics, such as Fielding and Goslee, have recognised such a critique operating within them. Fielding, for example, reads this opposition between minstrel and poet as part of Scott's attempt to set up a false opposition between the written and the oral, with the written privileged. However, just as Scott elides the distinction between minstrel and poet in these poems, so too the opposition between oral and written is, as Fielding ultimately recognises, merely socially constructed and ultimately collapses in Scott's poetry so that it offers an altogether more comprehensive critique of the limitations of all language, both written and oral, as a source of authority, or as a way of either describing or knowing the world.

J. H. Alexander implies this when he draws attention to the complex use of pun and word play in Scott's poetry, suggesting that, for example, 'The verbal texture of *The Lay of the Last Minstrel* is made up of strands which are in themselves commonplace but which Scott combines into an intricately patterned structure of a powerful and complex originality'.[46] In support of this argument he lists the various ways in which the concept of death and indeed the words 'dead' and 'death' are revisited and explored in the poem. He also finds a similar complexity at work in *Marmion* as Scott revisits and re-echoes such key terms as 'chivalry', 'honour', 'courtesy' and 'nobility', interrogating the layers of meaning and ambiguity which cluster around these ideas. For example, Alexander argues that 'In many ways the most complex of these qualities associated with chivalric virtue is faith, which constantly shifts its meaning, so that it rarely has the same significance in any two occurrences'.[47] He cites as an instance the ways in which two shades of meaning in the word 'faith' are demonstrated in

'L'Envoy'. Alexander's observations concerning Scott's poetry are convincing and re-reading it while alert to such punning and repetition of key words has the effect of encouraging the conclusion that Scott is, in fact, raising epistemological questions in his poetry, questioning the stability of language, and by implication its ability to communicate in any clearly referential or fixed way.

As with Scott's critique of the nature of the minstrel / poet it is in *The Lay of the Last Minstrel* that he offers his most overt engagement with the nature of language and the limitations of its power. As most readers of the poem recognise, the magical book which Deloraine recovers from the grave of Michael Scott is in many ways a kind of palimpsest of Scott's own act of writing and a metaphor for the power and purposes of poetry. Nancy Goslee, for example, notes that the goblin page's 'first action is to open a book. He thus claims a role in opening Scott's own book for interpretation; and a part of that interpretation, in turn, leads to a discovery of the ambiguous power of reading'.[48] While, as Goslee suggests, there is certainly some implication that this tension involves an opposition to the power of orality, the role of the book in the poem is part of a more general critique of the power of language, both oral and written. What is clear is that, however it is read, the status of the book in the *Lay* and by implication, the status of words or language more generally, is problematic. It is described as a 'mighty book' 'iron clasped' 'that never mortal might therein look' (2.15 and 2.21). It is connected both with the magic of the Lady of Branksome Tower who conjures up unearthly voices (1.18) and with the magic of the wizard Michael Scott who, by words alone, has cleft the Eildon hills. The book, then, is both powerful, and potentially dangerous: '"If thou readest thou art lorn! / Better hadst thou ne'er been born"' (1.23). To speak the words it contains is also problematic and sinful:

> "Some of his skill he taught to me;
> And, warrior, I could say to thee,
> The words that clove Eildon hills in three,
>   And bridled the Tweed with a curb of stone:
> But to speak them were a deadly sin;" (2.13)

However, the book presumably also has a potential for good, since the Lady of Branksome Hall sends William of Deloraine to fetch the 'treasure of the tomb' (1.22) in her hour of need.

The ambivalent attitude to language expressed via Michael Scott's book in the poem is significant since in the *Lay* its power is clearly very closely aligned to that of poetry itself. As discussed earlier, the power of the minstrel's art is presented as in many ways transformative; a kind of magic which can potentially redeem time, create a reality almost as vivid as lived experience, and awaken national sentiment. So too, Michael Scott's book also has the power to perform this magic. Its main function as it is used by the goblin page is to transform, although the status of that transformation (here called delusion we should note) is clearly ambiguous:

> The iron band, the iron clasp,
> Resisted long the elfin grasp:
> For when the first he had undone,
> It closed as he the next begun.
> Those iron clasps, that iron band,
> Would not yield to unchristened hand,
> Till he smeared the cover o'er
> With the Borderer's curdled gore;
> A moment then the volume spread,
> And one short spell therein he read.
> It had much of glamour might,
> Could make a ladye seem a knight;
> The cobwebs on a dungeon wall,
> Seem tapestry in lordly hall;
> A nut-shell seem a gilded barge,
> A sheeling seem a palace large,
> And youth seem age, and age seem youth—
> All was delusion, nought was truth. (3.9)

If then, the power of Michael Scott's book and the power of language more generally are being aligned in the *Lay* this is clearly problematic. If the language of the 'mighty book' has the potential for both revealing truth and for deceiving so too, this implies, does poetry. However, Scott also explores a more fundamental limitation of linguistic power; while the status of the book is at best ambiguous in places the *Lay* also questions what, if anything, it can actually achieve. Thematically, a great deal seems to be made of the book. The ride of William of Deloraine through the night to fetch it from Michael Scott's grave is one of the most memorable and engaging pieces of writing in the poem. However, having built up the status of the book in this dramatic way, and after implying that it will be the vehicle to resolve the love dilemma that is central to the plot of the poem, Scott rather interestingly *deflates* the status of the book. Although retrieved by Deloraine it falls not into the possession of the Lady of Branksome Tower but, rather, into that of the mischievous Goblin Page Gilpin Horner, in whose hands its power is clearly limited.

As a consequence and in spite of its dangerous potential the actual uses to which the book is put in the poem prove fairly ineffectual; in reality, little comes of it other than mischief-making. The clasps are closed to Gilpin Horner (3.9) and he learns only one spell, that of transformation. His use of it is only to swap places with the young Lord of Branksome Tower by leading him into the wood in the guise of 'some comrade gay' and then scowling at the 'startled child' (3.12 and 3.13) causing him to run away. While the subsequent capturing of him by the English army is of structural importance to the plot of the poem it is not hard to see how this element of the plot could have been achieved without the aid of a magic book or even a goblin page. For all the dramatic effect with which Michael Scott's book is initially presented it is finally unclear what it actually *does* in the poem. While the Goblin's cry of '"Found, Found, Found"' and his strange disappearance at the end of the poem may imply that the book and the power of its words are still 'out there' it is, nevertheless, difficult to see what the importance of this can be. Moreover, while both book and the words it contains are presented here as dangerous and taboo, this is not the only book to be mentioned in the poem. The magic book is clearly juxtaposed with the holy book used at the burial of the knights at Roslin Abbey (6.23) and that used by the Holy Fathers as they come to Melrose to sing the 'Dies Irae': 'The holy fathers, two and two, / In long procession came; / Taper, and host, and book, they bare, / And holy banner, flourished fair / with the Redeemer's name' (6.31). Compared to this book, which in theological terms has the power to genuinely bring about a Christian redemption and transformation (although about which we can never have any direct knowledge), Michael Scott's book, here aligned with the power of poetry, can only ever be a kind of 'rough magic' which like Prospero's, may finally have to be abjured.

Taken in this way, then, the book in the *Lay* and its magic 'gammarye' seem to imply that the power of words, and in turn that of poetry, may, to some extent be to transform, but that the status of such transformation is at best ambiguous and possibly trivial. This reading of the role of the book in the *Lay* is also supported if we consider the ways in which the power of language is presented elsewhere in his poems. In fact, throughout Scott's poetry language is presented as a tool which can reconcile, restore and redeem but also as one which can beguile, delude and deceive.[49] And there are, perhaps most interestingly of all, many places in the poems where language seems to rupture and disintegrate, simply failing to communicate in any meaningful way.

In his *Journal* Scott notes that after he has suffered a stroke, his handwriting seems to stammer, as if there is a gap between mind and pen.[50] There is a sense in which, however, there is always a stammer between mind and pen in Scott, or what we can see as a kind of fissure between what the writer wishes to communicate and what he actually can communicate; a rupture which is in fact signalled as early as Scott's poems where the persona of the minstrel repeatedly allows him to draw attention to the limits of what can actually meaningfully be achieved via language. This becomes evident if we look closely at the references to language and its communicative capacities in, for example, *The Lady of the Lake*.

In *Fragments of Union* Susan Manning suggests that one legacy of Hume's influence on the Scottish and American writing she discusses is 'the representation in language of elements of experience that resist articulation in words' so that it 'interrupts the coherent telling of experience'.[51] Celeste Langan also comments that the very nature of poetry, and its 'residual sound effects of meter and rhyme . . . seems to threaten the Enlightenment ideal of transparent communication'.[52] Indeed, there is a sense in which the whole plot of *The Lady of the Lake* relies upon such interruption and upon what is not said rather than what is said. The main example of this is King James and his decision not to reveal his identity but to travel to the Highlands under the guise of the 'Knight of Snowdoun, James Fitz-James' (1.29). This failure to name himself, is, it is clear, made possible by the fact that Highland hospitality demands that a stranger is made welcome, without the need to enquire who he actually is: 'And every courteous rite was paid, / That hospitality could claim, / Though all unasked his birth and name' (1.29). Nevertheless, this act of not naming is crucial to the plot of the poem, the injury of Roderick Dhu, and its eventual denouement as the king reveals himself in order to grant Ellen her boon. Moreover, while this act of leaving things unsaid has structural implications in the poem it is only one extreme example of non-communication. In fact there are many instances in *The Lady of the Lake* where language breaks off at crucial moments. Many of these are related to the character of Ellen Douglas who at several key points in the poem is literally lost for words. Our introduction to Ellen at stanza 17 of the first canto, for example, finds her with 'lips apart' but saying nothing and she is described as being 'In listening mood'. The first words she utters in the poem (in a voice described as 'soft') are borne away on the gale and fail to reach those for whom they are intended:

> Impatient of the silent horn,
> Now on the gale her voice was borne:—
> "Father!" she cried; the rocks around
> Loved to prolong the gentle sound.
> And while she paused, no answer came,—
> "Malcolm, was thine the blast?" the name
> Less resolutely uttered fell,
> The echoes could not catch the swell. (1.20)

Later, as the king departs, Ellen is again rendered silent. While she 'sate and smiled' she offers no words of parting, but instead 'one courteous parting sign she made' (2.6). Again, confronted by her father and her lover we are told that Ellen once more cannot say what she feels but speaks instead with a 'faultering tongue' (2.22) and a few stanzas later, as she tries to question her father, her speech is broken off and her anxieties go largely un-articulated:

> And, "O my sire!" did Ellen say,
> "Why urge thy chase so far astray?
> And why so late return'd? And why"—
> The rest was in her speaking eye. (2.26)

Finally, at the denouement of the poem, Ellen is once more rendered speechless. As she discovers the true identity of James Fitz-James 'No word her choking voice commands' (6.27) and she is incapable of requesting the freedom of her lover Malcolm Graeme:

> Blushing, she turned her from the King,
> And to the Douglas gave the ring,
> As if she wished her sire to speak
> The suit that stained her glowing cheek.— (6.29)

Ellen is not the only character in the poem who seems to be silenced at crucial points. There are other moments where the silence of characters is notable and at times significant in the development of the plot. Following the 'blunt speech' (2.30) in which Roderick seeks to resolve the situation by marrying Ellen, Malcolm for example, is 'eager to speak' but is prevented from doing so 'ere / His tongue could hurry forth his fear' by the intervention of Douglas (2.32). Roderick himself fails to offer a word of parting to Ellen at their last meeting (2.35) while the minor characters in the poem are also characterised by what goes unsaid. Brian's mother, for example, has 'locked her secret in her breast, / And died in travail, unconfessed' (3.5) while Blanche of Devon fails to say what she wishes on her deathbed ('"It was not what I meant to tell . . ."' (4.24)) but imparts her sad history through the medium of song, her dying words being represented as broken, interrupted and somehow failing to communicate: '"They watch for thee by pass and fell . . . / Avoid the path . . . O God! . . . farewell."' (4.27).

This failure to articulate in *The Lady of the Lake* also extends to the poet or minstrel himself who at crucial points in the poem is also rendered speechless or chooses not to communicate all that he may know. The poem opens with an address to the 'harp of the north' and a request that its mute voice 'silent be no more':

> O minstrel harp, still must thine accents sleep?
> Mid rustling leaves and fountains murmuring,
> Still must they sweeter sounds their silence keep,
> Nor bid a warrior smile, nor teach a maid to weep? (Introduction, Canto 1)

The speaker here describes his art as 'rude' and 'Some feeble echoing of thine earlier lay' and there are times where he seems to deliberately draw attention to the limits of his own art. At stanza 1.6, for example, he states that '"Twere long to tell what steeds gave o'er, / As swept the hunt through Cambus-more"' and this tale is therefore given in what must be an abbreviated form. A little later the speaker here, like the minstrel in the *Lay*, seems reluctant to speak of love, and only comments 'O need I tell that passion's name!' (1.19). The poem ends, too, with a marked lack of communication. The actual conclusion of the narrative is abrupt to say the least, and we are aware that there is much that is left unsaid (we have no idea, for example, what is to become of Ellen and Malcolm Graeme) and the 'coda' by the narrating poet is simply, as this absence implies, a retreat into silence; a farewell to the 'Harp of the North' and a realisation that it is 'silent all'.

If there are moments of failure in linguistic communication in this poem there are also several places in it where we are reminded of the significance of non-verbal communication. For example, the poem opens with a description of the 'deep-mouthed blood-hound's heavy bay' and of the 'clanging hoof and horn' and there are many examples in the poem of descriptions of the sounds of nature, of echoes, and of music, such as the pibroch at 2.16. Most significantly, the description of the fiery cross in the poem gives a clear example of a form of communication used by a non-literate culture, where symbol, rather than words, is used to muster the clans:

> Fast as the fatal symbol flies,
> It arms the huts and hamlets rise;
> From winding glen, from upland brown,
> They poured each hardy tenant down.
> Nor slacked the messenger his pace;
> He shewed the sign, he named the place,
> And, pressing forward like the wind,
> Left clamour and surprise behind. (3.14)

Such aspects of the poem are a reminder that language is not the only medium of communication and, as we have seen already, that it is at times an inadequate one, or one that can fail at crucial moments. It is perhaps tempting to see these ruptures or failures in speech as making some kind of political statement related, potentially, to Scott's agenda of reawakening national identity in the poem. One could, for example, make a convincing case that Ellen's inability to communicate or to speak for herself arises out of her peripheral status as a woman. A similar argument could be extended to suggest that such ruptures are representative of the silencing of Highland culture in nineteenth-century Scotland; certainly when the Highlanders are given 'lines' in the poem they often communicate in Gaelic – such as in the refrain to the boat song (2.19) – thus speaking in a medium which renders them essentially silenced since they cannot be understood by the majority of Scott's readership. While these arguments could be made, however, they clearly also form part of a more general questioning of language taking place in this poem.

When language is foregrounded in this poem it has, as in *The Lay of the Last Minstrel* a problematic status. At times language can be a powerful medium such as when the men from the south recognise the power of naming in Highland culture:

> "We Southern men, of long descent;
> Nor wot we how a name—a word—
> Makes clansmen vassals to a lord:" (6.11)

Such power, however, is again presented as potentially dangerous, as Brian the Hermit illustrates. Born as a result of his mother's failure to speak out about her condition, Brian, we are told, mixes 'heathen lore' among 'the charms he muttered o'er' (3.4). Like the Goblin Page he has looked into the 'sable-lettered page' and there found 'food for the fever of his mind' in the form of 'magic, cabala and spells' (3.6). Similarly, the curses of the women on those who invoke the power of the fiery cross are described as a kind of dark 'babbling', 'stammered slow' (3.10) to which nature does not give the echo of the 'deep Amen' (3.11). Some uses of language may be powerful, then, but also dangerous. Elsewhere, characters such as Blanche use a kind of wild language which is to feature in Scott's later fiction, which is simultaneously on the periphery of communication, but powerful in its effect.[53]

As in the earlier poem language also has a potentially transformative power although again the status of this is at times ambiguous. It is through the power of re-naming, or finally declaring himself, that the king gives up his 'name which veils [his] power' and 'Snowdoun's Knight is Scotland's King!' (6.3) However, as in the *Lay*, such transformations can also be deceptive; even the power of the harp of the north is described as a 'magic maze'; something which both transforms and ensnares. James, similarly, is described as having speech which 'flowed fair and free, / In phrase of gentlest courtesy' (1.21) and while this may be a mark of his nobility, it is also symptomatic of the act of deception which is at the heart of the poem. On the other hand the 'blunt speech' of Roderick Dhu is also problematic: while he may claim that his temper does not allow for 'glozing' (or deceitful) words (2.28) nevertheless his true feelings towards Malcolm Graeme are not revealed via his 'action, word, or eye' but in 'Secret parley' (2.27). In spite of his 'blunt speech' to Ellen he immediately retracts his words with the suggestion that 'I meant not all my heat might say' (2.30). Finally, just as it is crucial to the plot of the poem that James goes un-named through most of it, so too it is vital to its denouement that the king acknowledges that his bad opinion of Douglas was based on 'slanderous tongue' (6.27), a false use of language. In this poem words do not render experience transparently and the very nature of the abrupt conclusion to the poem, which is based on a discrepancy between what James says and what his actions actually demonstrate (thus confusing many readers as to what actually happens to Graeme at the end of the poem), illustrates that words are not always the most reliable form of communication. As James discovers at the end of the poem, words in *The Lady of the Lake* can be fickle things; the acclamation, or shouts of the crowd mean nothing; the words of this 'many-headed monster-thing' are 'Fantastic, fickle, fierce, and vain' and 'fickle as a changeful dream' (5.30). In this poem, then, language clearly has limits; what is not said can be as powerful as what is said, and when words are spoken they are often spoken to deceive rather than to reveal. Poetry, made up of such words, is no more than a 'magic maze' that has only silence at its centre.

It is these early signs of his dis-ease with his own medium which generates poetic experimentation in Scott's poetry. The innovative nature of Scott's poetry has long been recognised. Generic experimentation was, of course, a preoccupation of the Romantic period, but even if we take this into account Scott's poems seem to raise particular problems in terms of the forms in which they are operating, since at times the poems seem to modulate between different genres, cutting across recognisable categories. As J. H. Alexander notes, 'we have still no agreed title to designate the genre to which Scott's longer poems belong – if indeed they all belong to the same genre, and if they do not themselves constitute a unique genre, so it will come as no surprise to find that the question of kind was a major area of debate for their first reviewers'.[54] Several reviewers were to find this disconcerting and struggled with the question of how his poems were to be categorised in generic terms. Jeffrey, for example, originally defined the *Lay* as 'such a romance as we may suppose would have been written in modern times' but by the publication of *Marmion* had lost patience with the quirkiness of Scott's form stating that its mixture of romance and verse epistles was like building 'a modern abbey, or an English pagoda'.[55] Defending the poem from this attack Lord Minto again draws attention to the mixed genre of the poem by pointing out that the genre of it was not defined. It was not 'Epic, Heroick, Historical, descriptive or any other'.[56] In modern times, Nancy Goslee maintains that what Scott is writing is essentially romance but admits that within this category his work remains problematic, suggesting, for example, that in *The Lady of the Lake* Scott explores an uneasiness about writing in this mode and that 'the poem traces the meaning romance as a genre carries in at least three different historical periods: the medieval, the Renaissance, and his own'.[57]

It is hardly surprising that both contemporary and modern commentators have had such difficulties in categorising the form of Scott's poems for a reader does not have to look far to see that one of the things which marks them is the fragmented nature of the narrative style. In *The Lady of the Lake*, for example, even if we leave aside the various styles which are incorporated into the main body of narrative, we can see that Scott interpolates into the poem a direct evocation of medieval romance (1.22), songs of various sorts (1.31, 2.2, 3.23, 4.22, 6.5), a boat song (2.19), curses (3.9), a coronach (3.16), an Ave Maria (3.29), a prophecy in the form of a dialogue (4.1), a ballad (4.12), a minstrel's tale

(6.15), a lament (6.22), and a lay (6.24). Interestingly too, if one looks at the distribution of these examples, one can see the concentration of them in the final canto; just as the minstrel competition at the end of *The Lay of the Last Minstrel* causes that poem to dissolve into a polyphony of stories, so too *The Lady of the Lake* splinters into a cacophony of voices (or perhaps babble) at its conclusion, as if Scott is searching for the best voice with which to bring his narration to a close, or, perhaps, prefiguring his later work by subverting the very notion of closure in language.

This feature of Scott's poetry was to bring criticism. One early commentator on the *Lay*, Scott's friend John Stoddard, objected to this aspect of the poem, claiming that it drew attention to the artificiality of the whole production:

> The main defect (if I may dare to use such an expression) is a want of interest in the *tale*—I mean regular, permanent, continued interest—This is made up by the spirit & variety of the pictures—Noble indeed they are; but for want of what I once called a 'cementing subterraneous unity', they seem rather *too* much at variance with each other, like the scenes of a showman's box.[58]

Jeffrey similarly attacked the poem for its lack of unity. But these early reviewers perhaps missed the point. While many arguments could be made to explain Scott's restlessness with poetic form one reason may be a deep seated anxiety concerning the limits of the 'blunt tool' of language and a consequent search for a form of words which might somehow, nevertheless, communicate.

In his poetry, then, Scott offers us, through his presentation of the minstrel, a meditation on the role of the poet and his relationship to society. He suggests that while poetry has a function in recording history, it does so by seemingly dissolving boundaries of time, so that the past can be recaptured and revisited. In this he seems to credit poetry, and by implication language, with the ability both to communicate something of the past, and in turn to transform our relationship to it. By 1830, however, he was to write that the bard's role is one of 'embodying and detailing circumstances, which can only place before the eyes of others a scene which only exists in his own imagination', thus expressing a far more limited view of what poetry can achieve.[59] There are, however, indications that Scott, even as he was writing his great poems, was already well aware of this limitation. Not only does it erupt into the poems at key moments but, it may be argued, it also evident in the restlessness of poetic form which marks his major poems, and indeed the whole of his writing career.

David Hewitt, writing primarily of Scott's novels and of his tendency to add notes and prefaces, reminds us that in Scott's work:

> Writing is laid down in layers, comment commenting on commentary. The provision of such varied evidence, presented in such a complex way, and in each case over many years, implies that he is never absolutely confident that truth can be captured in a particular form of words; it is as though he were constantly trying to work out the relationship of the literary artifact to what it conveys.[60]

Such exploration of form and its relationship to meaning is indeed a hallmark of Scott's fiction. In the remainder of this study it will be argued that this unceasing restlessness arises in part precisely from Scott's scepticism about the communicative capacity of language and his anxious awareness that, as a result, literary production, perhaps all linguistic production, however 'redemptive' or 'transformative' in its thematic strategies, is no more than a 'magic maze'. It is hardly surprising, therefore, that at the height of his poetic career Scott should shift his attention away from the narrative poem to something altogether different, the novel.

*Notes*

1 Notable exceptions to this are Penny Fielding in *Writing and Orality: Nationality, Culture, and Nineteenth-Century Scottish Fiction* (Oxford: Clarendon Press, 1996), Nancy Moore Goslee in *Scott the Rhymer* (Lexington: University Press of Kentucky, 1988), Susan Oliver, *Scott, Byron and the Poetics of Cultural Encounter* (Basingstoke: Palgrave Macmillan, 2005), the work of J. H. Alexander discussed in the chapter and most recently Maureen N. McLane, *Balladeering, Minstrelsy, and the Making of British Romantic Poetry* (Cambridge: Cambridge University Press, 2008). Several interesting chapters and articles on Scott's poetry have also recently appeared and are listed in the bibliography.

2 Duncan Wu's *Romanticism: An Anthology* (3rd edition; Oxford: Blackwell Publishing, 2006), for example, contains none of Scott's poetry. While extracts were present in the 1994 first edition these were removed in later editions.

3 Nancy Moore Goslee, *Scott the Rhymer*, p. 3.

4 Both Katie Trumpener and Maureen N. McLane provide excellent accounts of the role which minstrelsy plays in the construction of Romanticism.

5 *Oxford English Dictionary*, On-line edition (http://www.oed.com/ accessed 1 August 2010).

6  In 'Introductory Remarks on Popular Poetry' in *Poetical Works,* pp. 1.50–51 Scott discusses whether minstrels would always have used words to accompany their music.

7  Walter Scott, 'Introduction' to *Minstrelsy of the Scottish Border*, 2 vols (Kelso: James Ballantyne for T. Cadell and W. Davis, Strand, London, 1802), pp. 1.i–cx (p. xci).

8  Walter Scott, 'Essay on Romance' in *Prose Works*, p. 6.134.

9  Walter Scott, 'Introduction' to *Minstrelsy of the Scottish Border*, p. xcvii.

10  For an excellent account of how Scott disrupts the idea of historiography by adding the element of fiction to it see Ina Ferris, *The Achievement of Literary Authority*.

11  Katie Trumpener, *Bardic Nationalism: The Romantic Novel and the British Empire* (Princeton: Princeton University Press, 1997), p. 6.

12  Walter Scott, 'Introductory Remarks on Popular Poetry', p. 14.

13  See Catherine Jones, *Literary Memory*.

14  J. H. Alexander, *'The Lay of the Last Minstrel': Three Essays* (Salzburg: Institut für Englische Sprache und Literatur Universitat Salzburg, 1978), p. 176.

15  Katie Trumpener, *Bardic Nationalism*, p. 76.

16  Ibid. p. 104.

17  Penny Fielding, *Writing and Orality*, p. 46.

18  Leith Davis, Ian Duncan and Janet Sorensen in *Scotland and the Borders of Romanticism*, p. 5.

19  Nancy Moore Goslee, *Scott the Rhymer*, p. 23.

20  Ibid. p. 20.

21  Maureen N. McLane, *Balladeering, Minstrelsy, and the Making of British Romantic Poetry*, p. 131.

22  Walter Scott, 'Introduction' to *The Lay of the Last Minstrel* in *Poetical Works*, pp. 6.5–31 (p. 29).

23  Adam Smith, 'The First Formation of Languages', p. 705.

24  *Oxford English Dictionary*, On-line edition (http://www.oed.com/ accessed 1 August 2010).

25  Maureen N. McLane, *Balladeering, Minstrelsy, and the Making of British Romantic Poetry,* p. 157. This point has also been made by Celeste Langan. See 'Understanding Media in 1805: Audiovisual Hallucination in *The Lay of the Last Minstrel*' in *Scott, Scotland and Romantic Nationalism*, Special ed. *Studies in Romanticism* 40:1 (Spring, 2001), ed. by Ian Duncan, Ann Rowland and Charles Snodgrass, pp. 49–70 (p. 54).

26  This is certainly true of the first edition, the 1830 edition and all modern editions. The absence of a manuscript for *The Lay of the Last Minstrel* makes

it unclear whether it appears in print as Scott intended but it is hoped that further editorial work on the poem may yet cast further light on this issue.

27 Walter Scott, *The Lay of the Last Minstrel*, headnote.

28 In fact *Marmion* as a whole operates within many different time-frames. The dual time frame referred to here means only the framing epistles as opposed to the story time of the poem.

29 George Ellis in J. H. Alexander, *The Reception of Scott's Poetry by His Correspondents: 1796–1817*, 2 vols (Salzburg: Institut für Anglistik und Amerikanistik Universitat Salzburg, 1979), p. 2.284.

30 J. H. Alexander, *'Marmion': Studies in Interpretation and Composition* (Salzburg: Institut für Anglistik und Amerikanistik Universitat Salzburg, 1981), p. 3.

31 Ibid. p. 95.

32 For a full discussion of *Marmion* as a meditation on the role of the Romantic poet see Ainsley McIntosh, *'Marmion; A Tale of Flodden Field': A Critical Edition* (Unpublished PhD thesis, University of Aberdeen, 2009).

33 Katie Trumpener, *Bardic Nationalism*, p. 19.

34 Maureen N. McLane, *Balladeering, Minstrelsy, and the Making of British Romantic Poetry*, p. 119.

35 Ludwig Wittgenstein, *Philosophical Investigations*, p. 231.

36 Nancy Moore Goslee, *Scott the Rhymer*, p. 40.

37 Ibid. p. 27.

38 Ibid. p. 24.

39 Ibid. p. 12.

40 J. H. Alexander, *'The Lay of the Last Minstrel': Three Essays*, p. 50.

41 Ibid. p. 102.

42 Andrew Lincoln, *Walter Scott and Modernity* (Edinburgh: Edinburgh University Press, 2007), p. 36.

43 John Keats, 'The Eve of St. Agnes' (1820). Jane Millgate comments that the poem is thus 'the dramatisation of a delay that can have but one outcome. History is a process from which no one is immune'. Jane Millgate, '"Naught of the Bridal": Narrative Resistance in *The Lay of the Last Minstrel*', *Scottish Literary Journal*, 17.2 (November, 1990), pp. 16–26 (p. 23).

44 Samuel Taylor Coleridge, 'Christabel: Part 2' (1800).

45 J. H. Alexander, *'The Lay of the Last Minstrel': Three Essays*, p. 37.

46 Ibid. p. 2.

47 J. H. Alexander, *'Marmion': Studies in Interpretation and Composition*, p. 60.

48 Nancy Moore Goslee, *Scott the Rhymer*, p. 18.

49 Goslee draws attention to the theme of forgery in *Marmion* suggesting that it operates as a metaphor for Scott's anxiety about the authority of the written word.

50  See Scott's entry for 1 January 1831: *Journal*, p. 621.

51  Susan Manning, *Fragments of Union*, p. 13. Lucinda Cole and Richard G. Swartz also recognise this 'trope of inarticulation' as a recurring feature in Romantic poetry. See '"Why Should I Wish for Words?": Literacy, Articulation and the Borders of Literary Culture' in *At the Limits of Romanticism: Essays in Cultural, Feminist, and Materialist Criticism*, ed. by Mary A. Favret and Nicola J. Watson (Bloomington and Indianapolis: Indiana University Press, 1994), pp. 143–69 (p. 147).

52  Celeste Langan, 'Understanding Media in 1805: Audiovisual Hallucination in *The Lay of the Last Minstrel*', p. 50.

53  Blanche is perhaps the first woman in a Scott tradition which includes such characters as Elspat Muckebackit, Meg Merrilies, Madge Wildfire, Ulrika and Norna of the Fitful Head, among others. All of these characters adopt a kind of 'outlawed language' which is nevertheless crucial in revealing key elements of the plots of the novels they inhabit.

54  J. H. Alexander, *Two Studies in Romantic Reviewing: Edinburgh Reviewers and the English Tradition: The Reviewing of Walter Scott's Poetry 1805–1817* (Salzburg: Institut für Englische Sprache und Literatur Universitat Salzburg, 1976), p. 245.

55  Ibid. p. 248 and p. 251.

56  J. H. Alexander, *The Reception of Scott's Poetry by His Correspondents: 1796–1817*, 2 vols (Salzburg: Institut für Anglistik und Amerikanistik Universitat Salzburg, 1979), p. 33.

57  Nancy Moore Goslee, *Scott the Rhymer*, p. 67.

58  Alexander, *The Reception of Scott's Poetry by His Correspondents: 1796–1817*, p. 23.

59  Walter Scott, 'Introductory Remarks on Popular Poetry', p. 10.

60  David Hewitt, 'Walter Scott' in *The History of Scottish Literature*, ed. by Cairns Craig, 4 vols (Aberdeen: Aberdeen University Press, 1988), pp. 3.65–85 (p. 69).

# Chapter 2

# Speaking my Language:

# *Waverley, Guy Mannering* and *The Antiquary*

As has been shown in the previous chapter in Scott's early narrative poems he searches for a means to recover the past while simultaneously voicing a concern about poetry itself as a medium for locating and reinvigorating it. It is hardly surprising, therefore, that in 1814, arguably at the height of his poetic career, he should turn to the newer form of the novel in order to explore the ways in which the past can be recovered and mediated to a modern audience through its discourses.[1] This chapter will explore the ways in which, in his early fiction, Scott simultaneously looks back to his eighteenth-century predecessors and reinvents the novel form as he searches for a way to locate his stories of Scotland's past and personal identity within language.

If Scott's major poems were recognised as generically experimental at their time of publication, in the modern period much more has been made of the innovative nature of Scott's first novel *Waverley*. Ina Ferris, for example, notes:

> A historically central and theoretically exemplary instance of generic innovation, the narratives of the Author of Waverley represent not simply the invention of a new novelistic form, the classical historical novel celebrated by Georg Lukács, but also a (less analyzed) crucial alteration of the generic hierarchy in place at the turn of the nineteenth century.[2]

Fiona Robertson also notes that 'originality' was one of the features observed upon the publication of *Waverley*[3] citing in particular, Jeffrey's famous review of the novel where he praises it for being 'true to nature' and suggests that 'the way in which [manners and customs] are here represented must satisfy every reader . . . that the delineation has been made from actual experience and observation'.[4] However, Robertson argues that this critical positioning of Scott's fiction has 'its own unformulated agenda, which at its most simple is the denial of significant influence from earlier fiction' (in Robertson's study its connections to the Gothic) and there is certainly a danger in positioning Scott only in this way.[5] While the innovative nature of *Waverley* is beyond dispute, rethinking the 'tidy little story' of the novel that sees its narrative as a trajectory from realism to modernism to postmodernism encourages us to revisit Scott's first work of fiction. In doing so we recognise that what is too often overlooked is the extent to which it not only marks the beginning of what might be regarded as the modern novel, but also looks backwards to its predecessors, engaging with the debates which vexed the early practitioners of the form in English.

The Introduction to this study outlines Scott's comments on his fictional predecessors in the series of essays which formed the introductions for *Ballantyne's Novelist's Library*. Several questions recur in this discussion, including, most importantly, the extent to which the novel is an 'imitative' form, the ways in which the novelist balances 'the limits between the concentric circles of probability and possibility' (as well as those which are 'copied from nature') and perhaps most significantly the function of 'artifice' in negotiating this mix. All of these concerns are ones which are firmly situated in the eighteenth-century where, as George Levine notes, the novelist was in no doubt that what he was writing was 'make-believe'.[6] As John Barth notes 'all the inventors of the English novel seem to share' a 'spookily contemporary sense . . . of the documentary nature of their enterprise: novels in the form of journals, of letters, of diaries, of confessions – of almost anything except novels, as if to say, "It is not life we imitate, but writing: life's enscripted epiphenomena."'[7]

One of the novelists Barth categorises in this way is Fielding and Scott repeatedly turns to him when discussing these questions, employing him as something of a sounding board in his discussion of other novelists. This is hardly surprising, for in the introductory chapters or prefaces to each book the Fielding of *Tom Jones* is quintessentially concerned with the questions that vex the eighteenth-century novel. In the preface to Book 8 for example, Fielding engages with a discussion of the nature of the marvellous, exploring the relationship between the possible and the probable and how this relates to the art of novelistic composition. 'First then', he writes, 'I think, it may very reasonably be required of every writer, that he keeps within the bounds of possibility; and still remembers that what it is not possible for man to perform, it is scarce possible for man to believe he did perform'.[8] The problem for Fielding, however, is that the novelist is essentially 'a historian of human nature' 'obliged to record matters as he finds them; though they may be of so extraordinary a nature as will require no small degree of historical faith to swallow them'.[9] Human nature, in short, is not always probable and it is the novelist's role to balance what is likely to be believed with what Robert Louis Stevenson was later to call the 'mingled tissue' of human experience,[10] treading a tightrope between what Fielding calls the marvellous, and a far more pernicious condition which he terms the incredible:

> To say the truth, if the historian will confine himself to what really happened, and utterly reject any circumstance, which, tho' never so well attested, he must be well assured is false, he will sometimes fall into the marvellous, but never into the incredible. He will often raise the wonder and surprize of his reader, but never that incredulous hatred mentioned by Horace. It is by falling into fiction therefore, that we generally offend against this rule, of deserting probability, which the historian seldom if ever quits, till he forsakes his character, and commences a writer of romance. In this, however, those historians who relate publick transactions have the advantage of us who confine ourselves to scenes of private life. The credit of the former is by common notoriety supported for a long time; and public records, with the concurrent testimony of many authors, bear evidence to their truth in future ages . . .
>     . . . But we who deal in private characters, who search into the most retired recesses, and draw forth examples of virtue and vice, from holes and corners of the world, are in a more dangerous situation. As we have no publick notoriety, no concurrent testimony, no records to support and corroborate what we deliver, it becomes us not only to keep within the limits of possibility, but probability too; and this more especially in painting what is greatly good and amiable.[11]

When we consider this debate as a crucial element of the discussion concerning the novel form which takes place within *Tom Jones* it is not hard to draw a line between Scott and Fielding. Ina Ferris acknowledges this connection and draws attention to one of the ways in which *Waverley* makes an overt gesture towards its fictional predecessor, by a reference not to *Tom Jones* but *Joseph Andrews*: 'Drawing on *Joseph Andrews*, Scott's narrator authorizes his text by declaring in a well-known passage that "the object of my tale is more of a description of men than manners."' However, for Ferris, this recognition is used to differentiate Scott from the earlier novelist: 'But the buried citation is ambiguous' she continues:

> For the realist text must separate itself from all rivals—even canonical ones. Scott may establish his allegiance to the canonical line of novel writing, but he distinguishes himself from it all the same. His point in the opening chapter is indeed the Fieldingesque point that the novelist concentrates on

what is common (the human nature of "men") rather than what is particular (the cultural variable of "manners"). His wording, however, inverts that of Fielding, who had written that "I describe not men, but manners; not an individual, but a species." The generic point is ostensibly the same, but the formulation turns Fielding on his head, prefiguring the way in which Scott's nineteenth-century historical mode of fiction will overturn the hierarchy of men and manners affirmed by Fielding's eighteenth-century satiric fictions.[12]

While such observations are valid, they lead us to overlook the extent to which *Waverley* is not only an innovative novel but one which is in many ways exploring the same questions as those which had concerned the generation before. This is significant, for it reminds us that in spite of its now iconic status as a first novel *Waverley* is something of an apprentice piece and consequently incorporates within itself an investigation of the process of *how* to write a novel, posing questions about the nature of the discourse by which the form operates and its relationship to both history and personal identity. In other words, it is far more *explorative* (and therefore self-reflexive) about its own practices than readings of it only in terms of innovation allow. As a novel which both looks forward to what the form will become in the nineteenth century, and backwards towards what its eighteenth-century predecessors had already achieved, *Waverley* also inserts itself into an on-going theoretical dialogue; indeed it occupies a pivotal space in the development of novelistic theory and practice.

Perhaps more than any of its other more polished successors *Waverley* concerns itself with a discussion of the nature of the novel form. Scott does this with what George Levine describes as a 'self-conscious clumsiness'[13] via a narrator who is in many ways similar to that found in Fielding's Prefatory Chapters. While Scott's narrator in *Waverley* is more firmly embedded within his narrative than Fielding's he assumes, more than any of Scott's subsequent narrators (with the possible exception of Chrystal Croftangry in *Chronicles*) a character in his own right, and it is a character which discusses the novel form, what can be achieved within it, and the relationship of its own discursive practices to those of personal subjectivity and history.

This is implied from the outset via *Waverley*'s famous opening chapter on the subject of the name of his hero. As many critics have recognised, the narrator's statement that he wishes to choose an 'uncontaminated name' for his protagonist, one 'bearing with its sound little of good or evil, excepting what the reader shall be hereafter pleased to affix to it' is in many ways a marker of the author's desire to establish new ground, moving away from the preoccupations of his eighteenth-century predecessors (p. 3). However this opening chapter can be seen to be in dialogue with these fictional forerunners, since repeatedly the author teases his reader with the suggestions that this novel might become a Fieldingesque novel, before defeating this expectation and moving into altogether different terrain. Certainly, the description of Sir Everard and his way of life which is offered in the second chapter of the text appears to locate the novel reader in a familiar landscape, that of the eighteenth-century rural squire:

> For it may be observed in passing, that instead of those mail-coaches, by means of which every mechanic at his six-penny club may nightly learn from twenty contradictory channels the yesterday's news of the capital, a weekly post brought, in those days, to Waverley-Honour, a Weekly Intelligencer, which, after it had gratified Sir Everard's curiosity, his sister's, and that of his aged butler, was regularly transferred from the hall to the rectory, from the rectory to Squire Stubbs at the Grange, from the Squire to the Baronet's steward at his neat white house on the heath, from the steward to the bailiff, and from him through a huge circle of honest dames and gaffers, by whose hard and horny hands it was generally worn to pieces in about a month after its arrival. (p. 8)

The community described here locates the reader very much in an eighteenth-century context, what Garside calls in his Edinburgh Edition Essay 'the somnambulant English country-house situation'[14] and this is compounded as we learn of Sir Everard's thwarted romance with Lady Emily, of the inclinations of the 'list of the beauties who displayed their hebdomadal finery at the parish church of Waverley' (p. 20) including the 'passable' Miss Caecilia Stubbs, who have set their affections at the novel's hero, and of the rivalry and political differences between the baron and his brother. Repeatedly the reader's expectations are raised that he or she is about to read a type of novel with which he or she is familiar; for example, in tracing the sources for the novel Garside notes that 'a predominantly literary foundation seems to underlie Scott's charac-terisation' in the novel, with 'a conscious reworking of the characters' of sentimental fiction and 'burlesque character names . . . in the tradition of the comic novels of Fielding and Smollett'.[15] On the other hand, as we are told that the hero steals away from the family legends recounted by his aunt to 'indulge the fancies they excited' in 'the corner of the large and sombre library, with no other light than was afforded by the decaying brands of its ponderous and ample hearth' (p. 18) the reader's expectations are again raised as the narrator hints that the basis for this novel may in fact lie in Gothic fiction.

These expectations are, of course, raised only that they might be thwarted, as the Author of Waverley maps out an altogether different kind of text in which his subject becomes not the domestic life of an eighteenth-century country household, or the Gothic adventures of a romantic young man, but, rather, the altogether more revolutionary topic of the relationship of the individual to the forces of history and the ways in which historical process may be explored through such an approach.[16] However, while this may seem to establish the key distinction between Scott's novel and those that have gone before, *Waverley* as a text does not altogether abandon the questions concerning form which vex its eighteenth-century predecessors, but in fact constantly revisits them, exploring their relevance for this new form of fiction.

Such questions are signalled by the ways in which *Waverley* constantly sets up dynamics between itself and other forms of discourse. Most overt of these is the comparison of the literary text with that of pictorial art, as the novel draws attention to the ways in which it is operating (via the written word) in contrast to the ways in which other forms of art convey meaning. Most famously, this comparison occurs as Waverley arrives at Tully-Veolan and the narrator offers the reader a 'chapter of still life' (p. 38) which gives a detailed depiction of what Waverley observes as he approaches the Baron's mansion. This strategy (of offering a scene through the eyes of a character who is observing it) is one which Scott exploits throughout his fiction, but here it is also being used to draw our attention to the fact that we are not observing a painting of Scotland, but, rather, having it described to us in words. In the Introduction it was noted that Scott at times draws analogies between the author and the graphic artist, but here, as he explores the ways in which he will move beyond the parameters of the eighteenth-century form, he seems to draw our attention to the difference between them, for this is a description of Scotland not as it is offered by the narrator, but as 'Waverley had conjured up'; in fact it is a static view of Scotland which the whole dynamic of the novel is to argue against as it demonstrates a country in turmoil and rebellion rather than one captured in still life. And the comparison between 'still life' painting and a dynamic, fluid discourse grounded in words (that is the novel) is also reiterated by the painting that closes this novel. Many critics have, of course, drawn attention to this painting of Waverley and Fergus that is the 'one addition to this fine old apartment' (p. 361). Most see it as an inadequate conclusion to the text, and some go so far as to read it as a metaphor for the ways in which Scott himself reduces the actual dynamism and trauma of the Jacobite Rising to a static work of art, history 'aestheticized' as Levine puts it.[17] Claire Lamont argues that via this motif 'Scott is trying to keep Culloden in the background, but it will not stay there, and we despise Waverley with his paintings and his furniture'.[18] However, what most critics overlook is that the painting, which is like one by 'Raeburn himself, (whose Highland chiefs do all but walk out of the canvas)' (p. 361) may well be *intended* to be an inadequate conclusion to what has gone before. What is being offered here is an ironic comment on the inability of graphic art to adequately convey the complexities of experience and the on-going tensions which persist in society in spite of the progress of history: the key words here are surely 'do all but'; graphic art cannot keep the past alive, this seems to suggest, and that role may lie, instead, with the far more 'debatable' and lively form of the printed word.

This reading of what is occurring in the text is also supported if we consider the extent to which the novel has embedded within it a self-reflexive impulse to draw attention to its own status as a printed – and indeed fictional – document, as its narrator foregrounds questions of form. As we have already seen, Scott suggests that Fielding's technique has the consequence of reminding us that we are observing a puppet-show, a 'set of evanescent phantoms, conjured up by a magician for our amusement'. However, while this is levelled at Fielding as something of a criticism in opposition to Smollett, there is an extent to which Scott's narrator in *Waverley* serves a similar function via his repeated and frequently obtrusive observations on the nature of his chosen form.

Jerome McGann has noted the ways in which Scott's later novels, such as *Ivanhoe*, draw attention to the fictional apparatus of text.[19] However, this tendency is evident as early as *Waverley*. Often this occurs in what seems like relatively straightforward ways. At the end of the second chapter, for example, as he begins to offer reflections on Waverley's education, the narrator states 'But more of this in a subsequent chapter' (p. 12). The opening of the second volume, in a similarly self-reflexive vein, is reminiscent of those discussions posed by Fielding which, according to Scott himself, serve the function of disrupting the narrative:

Shall this be a short or a long chapter?—This is a question in which you, gentle reader, have no vote, however much you may be interested in the consequences; just as probably as you may (like myself) have nothing to do with the imposing a new tax, excepting the trifling circumstance of

> being obliged to pay it. More happy surely in the present case, since, though it lies within my arbitrary power to extend my materials as I think proper, I cannot call you into Exchequer if you do not think proper to read my narrative. (p. 121)

Such questions concerning the relationship of the writer to his readers are also punctuated by more overtly self-reflexive observations concerning the textuality of print.[20] In the sixth chapter, for example, Scott's narrator reminds us of the physical nature of print, and the extent to which the publishing industry is governed by practical considerations.[21] As the publisher approached by Mr Pembroke reminds us, the printed text is governed by 'pages so many, paper so much, letter-press' keeping on the 'windy side' of the law and within the civility of the mob (p. 31).

The craft of the author is, then, a business, and is governed by practical considerations as much as any trade, an issue that the Author of Waverley was to return to more frequently as his career developed.[22] Moreover, the writer is, like other craftsmen, governed by rules and skills; crafts which must be learned. Just as the author of *Waverley* reflects upon the nature of his craft, then, he is also engaged in a debate concerning the rules by which it might proceed. For example, there are points in this novel where we can see the author working out, almost as he writes, the extent to which what he wishes to convey can be contained by that old question for the eighteenth-century novelist: what is probable? As Waverley approaches the cave of Donald Bean Lean, the narrator comments:

> At the bottom of the descent, and, as it seemed, by the side of a brook, (for Waverley heard the rushing of a considerable body of water, although its stream was invisible in the darkness,) the party again stopped before a small and rudely-constructed hovel. (p. 189)

This passage is interesting for it conveys an anxiety about the limits of what can be legitimately conveyed by the narrator. While the omniscient narrator of *Waverley*, who can make a chapter short or long at his own whim, can describe a brook to us in this scene if he so wishes it is clear that he is only eager to do so if he can suggest that Waverley, through whom so much of the text is in fact focalised, can comprehend its presence. As in *The Lady of the Lake*, then, meaning is conveyed both by what is said, and by what must remain silent.

Similar anxieties are voiced in the text concerning the far more ancient question of the unities of time, again apparently raised so that the narrator may draw attention to the artificiality of the narrative, which does not treat all time equally, but, on the contrary, manipulates it so that it may move at different rates:

> But, ere entering upon a subject of proverbial delay, I must remind my reader of the progress of a stone rolled down hill by an idle truant boy (a pastime at which I was myself expert in my more juvenile years:) it moveth at first slowly, avoiding by inflection every obstacle of the least importance; but when it has attained its full impulse, and draws near the conclusion of its career, it smokes and thunders down, taking a rood at every spring, clearing hedge and ditch like a Yorkshire huntsman, and becoming most furiously speedy in its course when it is nearest to being consigned to rest for ever. Even such is the course of a narrative, like that which you are perusing; the earlier events are studiously dwelt upon, that you, kind reader, may be introduced to the character rather by narrative, than by the duller medium of direct description; but when the story draws near its close, we hurry over the circumstances, however important, which your imagination must have forestalled, and leave you to suppose those things, which it would be abusing your patience to narrate at length. (p. 353)

The author, then, controls what may be communicated to the reader and what can be left out, the pace at which information is revealed, and the extent to which the reader may be kept in the dark. Elsewhere the narrator informs us that he has left some details unexplained 'according to the custom of story-tellers . . . for the purpose of exciting the reader's curiosity' (p. 329). Examples such as these suggest that in this, his first novel, the Author of Waverley is experimenting with what can be legitimately achieved in the form, examining the extent to which he wishes to adopt the models proposed by his fictional predecessors, and the extent to which he wishes to break away from them. The cumulative effect of such reflections is not only to suggest that such eighteenth-century questions are still very much at the forefront of the mind of the Author of Waverley, but to produce a tantalisingly 'modern, self-reflexive' text where, in spite of Jeffrey's claims that the author is drawing from nature, the puppet-master seems very much on show, foregrounding the constructed nature of his text, and in places its very material nature as a piece of print.

In spite of the dialogue it is setting up here with the texts that have gone before it, however, *Waverley* does without doubt mark a point of departure for the novel and the concerns with form which vex its pages are fundamentally linked to the nature of that departure. Scott's main preoccupation in *Waverley* is with the relationship between history and story and the extent to which the past can be communicated via the discourse of the novel. As John Barth puts it '[t]here are obvious differences in the way history and fiction are about what they're about'.[23] This difference has already been explored in Scott's poetry and becomes increasingly important in his fiction. This aspect of Scott's novelistic craft has been well documented, but what is of note in the context of this study is the extent to which, even at this early stage in Scott's career, the debate is grounded in a recognition of the relationship between discourse and meaning framed within specifically linguistic terms. This is evident if we revisit the first chapter of the novel where, in the famous opening lines, Scott overtly explores the relationship between word and meaning:

> The title of this work has not been chosen without the grave and solid deliberation which matters of importance demand from the prudent. Even its first, or general denomination, was the result of no common research or selection, although, according to the example of my predecessors, I had only to seize upon the most sounding and euphonic surname that English history or topography affords, and elect it at once as the title of my work, and the name of my hero. (p. 3)

Again Scott is overtly entering into a dialogue with the novels which have gone before, signalling both that he has looked to their example concerning how to choose a name for his work, and that he will not entirely follow their practice. His reasons for such deliberation, he continues, lie in the fact that names, like all words, are not neutral entities, but carry with them a cluster of (here overtly inter-textual) meanings which will haunt the reader's understanding of the text and his or her expectations: 'But, alas! what could my readers have expected from the chivalrous epithets of Howard, Mordaunt, Mortimer, or Stanley, or from the softer and more sentimental sounds of Belmour, Belville, Belfield and Belgrave, but pages of inanity, similar to those which have been so christened for half a century past?' (p. 3). He chooses, therefore, what he calls 'an uncontaminated name, bearing with its sound little of good or evil' (p. 3).

This opening paragraph of Scott's first novel signals an awareness of the problematic nature of language, the fact that words carry with them, as Derrida would put it, traces of earlier meaning which consequently resist any purely referential function, positing, instead, clusters of pre-existing connotations that pull against any form of 'uncontaminated' discourse. This is, ironically, reinforced by the choice of 'Waverley' itself which, Claire Lamont informs us, is not entirely uncontaminated since it refers both to a Cistercian house in Surrey and, more significantly, to a character in an earlier novel, Charlotte Smith's *Desmond* (1792).[24] As Garside points out in his edition of the novel 'There is some possibility that Scott was aware of the Abbey through its connection with Charlotte Smith: both through her choice of Waverley as the surname for one of the characters in her novel *Desmond* (1792), and by virtue of her own residence at Tilford, near Farnham, in later life'.[25] But whether or not he was aware of these traces is not the issue; the fact that they can be uncovered by future readers (or indeed recognised by his contemporaries) reinforces the point that no name is neutral or 'uncontaminated'.[26]

This point is crucial to our understanding of *Waverley*, for, as this opening paragraph would suggest, it is deeply concerned with the question of the ways in which discourses operate, and the extent to which they can be 'translated' or understood by those who stand outside of them. In his 'Postscript, which should have been a Preface' Scott outlines something of his intention in this respect, commenting that 'it has been [his] object . . . to describe these persons, not by a caricatured and exaggerated use of the national dialect, but by their habits, manners, and feelings; so as, in some distant degree, to emulate the admirable Irish portraits drawn by Miss Edgeworth' (p. 364). He elaborates on this process in a famous statement from the 'General Preface':

> I felt that something might be attempted for my own country, of the same kind with that which Miss Edgeworth so fortunately achieved for Ireland— something which might introduce her natives to those of the sister kingdom, in a more favourable light than they had been placed hitherto, and tend to procure sympathy for their virtues and indulgence for their foibles.[27]

Here, then, writing of his intentions for *Waverley* nearly fifteen years after its publication, Scott is suggesting that his purpose in writing it was essentially one of 'translation', of making accessible the discourse of one nation (Scotland) to another (England).[28]

Indeed, the need for such translation is demonstrated throughout *Waverley*, and is the impulse behind Scott's strategy of choosing an English hero to journey into Scotland; by doing so Scott can recapture the 'otherness' of his own nation as it is viewed through Waverley's eyes, and consequently carry out his act of translation as he interprets his experiences both for his hero, and of course for his imagined English readership. This process is illustrated in Waverley's first arrival at Tully-Veolan. As already indicated, what is notable about this passage is the extent to which Scott takes the opportunity to denote the 'otherness' of a

'Scottish Manor House Sixty Years Since'. To Waverley, all is strange, and this affords Scott the opportunity of describing the village in great detail. What is of most interest here, however, is that in spite of the overtly pictorial nature of this introduction to Scotland for his assumed readership, its alterity is, in fact, described in specifically linguistic terms. This need for translation is signalled in the chapter when our attention is drawn to the fact that the whole scene defies definition within English linguistic terms: 'to say the truth, a mere Englishman, in search of the *comfortable*, a word peculiar to his native tongue, might have wished the clothes less scanty, the feet and legs somewhat protected from the weather, the head and complexion shrouded from the sun' (p. 35). To an English outsider, then, the scene can only be described by what it is not, and it is clear that on other levels too, it requires an almost literal act of translation for its English audience – both Waverley himself and Scott's reader. Each village in Caledonia, we are told, maintains a relay of 'curs, called *collies*' (p. 35); the cottagers grow a crop of '*kale* or colwort' (p. 36) and, as he enters Bradwardine's estate, we are informed that opposite the garden there is a 'narrow meadow, or *haugh*, as it was called' (p. 40). As Waverley enters Scotland, then, both he and the readers of the text are literally learning the language, the novel highlighting the act of translating one national discourse into another.[29]

The act of translation which takes place in the novel becomes even more acute as Scott has his hero enters the Highlands, an arena other not only to his English readers but also to many Scots. The following passage, for example, exemplifies the extent to which Scott is offering an act of simultaneous translation in his text, as linguistic mis-match is used not only to illustrate the otherness of the Highlands, but also to produce humour, and to introduce the reader to Highland culture so that he or she, like Waverley, may more fully understand it and, we might imagine, 'sympathise' with it to borrow Scott's concept from the General Preface. '"Ah! if you Saxon Duinhe-wassal (English gentleman) saw but the chief himself with his tail on!"' states Evan Dhu:

> "With his tail on?" echoed Edward in some surprise.
> "Yes—that is, with all his usual followers, when he visits those of the same rank. There is," he continued, stopping and drawing himself proudly up, while he counted upon his fingers the several officers of his chief's retinue; "there is his *hanchman*, or right-hand man, then his *bhaird*, or poet; then his *bladier*, or orator, to make harangues to the great folks whom he visits; then his *gilly-more*, or armour-bearer, to carry his sword, and target, and his gun; then his *gilly-casflue*, who carries him on his back through the

sikes and brooks; then his *gilly-comstraine*, to lead his horse by the bridle in steep and difficult paths; then his *gillie-trusharnish*, to carry his knap-sack; and the piper and the piper's man, and it may be a dozen young lads beside, that have no business, but are just boys of the belt to follow the laird, and do his honour's bidding." (p. 81)

There is no need to labour what is happening here and this act of translation in turn acts as a metaphor for how the novel as a whole is operating, suggesting that through the novel form the reader may be brought to understand not just the discourse of Scottish culture (thereby learning to sympathise with its foibles) but more tellingly the contingent and 'fraught' nature of linguistic signification itself.[30] While another culture may be alien or other, Scott, prefiguring Wittgenstein in his later work, seems confident that it may be at least 'sympathised with' by learning its grammar, the rules by which it operates.[31] Ina Ferris draws attention to this aspect of the text and suggests that in Scotland:

> Waverley comes to discern not simply the duplicity of words, the slipperiness of the signifier, but also the distinctiveness and relativity of signifying systems. One of his first lessons, for example, is that 'in Scotland a single house was called a *town*, and a natural fool an *innocent*' . . . Thus begins his education in the historical variability of language, and it is followed by a whole series of lessons on words, clothes, foods, and other symbolic cultural practices . . . Waverley discovers the cultural, psychological, and political power of signs.[32]

In *Waverley*, then, Scott is apparently optimistic about the ability of the novel form to educate his readership about the nature of Scottish culture. However, just as an anxiety about language erupts into his poetry his first novel is similarly vexed concerning acts of communication. Scott's novel of simultaneous translation is, in fact, cut across by the fact that repeatedly in this text, plot is generated by Waverley's *failure* to understand what is going on around him; in Humean terms Waverley *lacks* the necessary sympathy to understand another culture, the ability to interpret what the events he experiences mean. This confusion is also overtly linguistic and is signalled early in the novel and revisited throughout its pages. Waverley's first blunder arises from his failure to understand the insult which Balmawhapple makes to the Hanoverian dynasty, because it is couched in terms of a linguistic code or riddle: "'to the little gentleman in black velvet who did such service in 1702'". Waverley, we are informed, 'was not at that moment clear-headed enough to remember that King William's fall, which occasioned his death, was said to be owing to his horse stumbling at a mole-hill' (p. 52). Waverley's failure to de-code this series of linguistic signs has long-term implications, but it is only one in a series of failures to understand language which cause Waverley's troubles. The most obvious example of this occurs at Glennaquoich, where Waverley's difficulties become more acute as the medium of communication is Gaelic. Here, again, Scott seems initially to imply that while Waverley may not understand the language he can, nevertheless, understand part of what is being communicated. As he listens to Fergus's bard, Waverley conjectures as to what is being said:

> He seemed to Edward, who attended to him with much interest, to recite many proper names, to lament the dead, to apostrophize the absent, to exhort and entreat and animate those who were present. Waverley thought he even discerned his own name, and was convinced his conjecture was right, from the eyes of the company being at that moment turned towards him simultaneously. (p. 105)

However, Waverley's 'conjecture' (a loaded term in the eighteenth-century context of the novel) is problematic, since it only allows him to discern part of the truth. While he has, indeed, been mentioned in the song, he fails to recognise that what has been communicated to the clan is his proposed role in a Jacobite Rising. Waverley is being used as a pawn in Fergus's political intrigues but his failure to fully understand the language results in his failure to recognise this, with disastrous results. And significantly, Flora's 'translation' of the poem in turn offers no enlightenment, since it too is an act of manipulating language, a performance of translation that 'draws attention to Flora's own pragmatic (rather than strictly mimetic) understanding of translation'.[33] The crucial stanzas which refer to Waverley's proposed part in the uprising are interrupted by the appearance of Fergus's dog, and offered to him only in humorous paraphrase couched in the language of Flora's charm. What is not said, however, or what is not translated, becomes a crucial aspect of the plot and the means by which Waverley can be tricked into involvement in the rising. So too, Waverley's failure to understand Gaelic at the stag-hunt almost costs him his life: 'The word was given in Gaelic to fling themselves upon their faces; but Waverley, upon whose English ears the signal was lost, had almost fallen a sacrifice to his ignorance of the ancient language in which it was communicated' (p. 124). Fergus may intervene to save his life, but again his injury, which necessitates his absence from his regiment, is crucial to his joining with Charles Stewart. More significantly, his failure to understand the words of the 'ancient language' also stands for his failure to recognise that he has been present not only at a stag-hunt but at a gathering of the clans, signifying what is, in fact, a failure to understand in any real sense, the discourse of the culture in which he has been placed.

Such ignorance is a marker of Waverley's character throughout the text. While at one level this may appear to be a novel about 'learning a language' at another it is a text about the total failure of the protagonist to do so. Even at a late stage in the novel, when the rising has failed, Waverley seems oblivious to the reality of the event in which he has been embroiled: '"Why did the Highland Chiefs consent to this retreat, if it is so ruinous?"' Waverley asks Fergus. The more realistic and level headed Fergus, who fully understands the stakes of the game they have been involved in, replies, '"The Hanoverian ministers always deserved to be hanged for rascals, but now, if they get the power in their hands,—as soon or late they must—since there is neither rising in England nor assistance from France,—they will deserve the gallows as fools if they leave a single clan in the Highlands in a situation to be again troublesome to government"' (p. 293).

This reading of *Waverley* implies that while at one level it is a novel about the translation of one culture so that another may understand it, thus reflecting the role proposed for the minstrel in the narrative poems, it also, like so many of Scott's texts, offers a counter-narrative whereby it implies a recognition that such translation may be impossible, that it is, in fact, impossible to 'learn a language' sufficiently to ever fully comprehend another discourse. While Scott may provide both Waverley and his readers with an on-going gloss to Scottish and Highland culture, he also suggests that much remains which is left unsaid, or at least not understood. Read in this way, it is hardly surprising that in spite of the apparent eighteenth-century conventionality of the conclusion of the novel with the marriage of Rose and Waverley, much about this ending has to be left unsaid: 'We will not attempt to describe the meeting of father and daughter', the narrator tells us, 'for my part I cannot conceive how so important an affair could be communicated in so short a space of time' (p. 338). At the conclusion of the text, the narrator chooses, then, to 'hurry over circumstances', and by a further process of what we might call negative narration leaves much that cannot be articulated. In place of words, however, the Author of Waverley leaves us with the painting of Fergus and Waverley that, for so many critics, stands as a synecdoche of the meeting of cultures, and the fixing of this meeting in the frozen time of pictorial art. As Caroline McCracken-Flesher puts it, for many critics 'The tartan-clad Englishman who looms from his portrait in the novel's last chapter is held to figure Scott's British-oriented nostalgia and prefigure a Scotland locked in the romance of the past through England's cultural and economic dominance'.[34] As Cairns Craig concludes, the painting suggests that Fergus's political vitality has been 'framed and removed from the flow of events'.[35]

However, McCracken-Flesher also suggests that this painting may be reclaimed for a more subversive and progressive reading of the text. 'We have', she writes, 'privileged the tale over its telling and locked ourselves out of the lively process of negotiation by which Scott narrates a nation's future'.[36] Indeed, in the light of the discussion of the limitations of pictorial art, and indeed of the substitution of any one sign for another which have taken place in this text, it seems likely that we are being encouraged to read this painting ironically. In spite of its attempts at translation, *Waverley* also hints at the possibility that it is impossible to completely learn a language, substituting one set of signs for another; if this is the case, synecdoche itself is always deceptive: the part cannot stand for the whole for the whole can never be fully represented by anything other than itself.

*Waverley* then, at one level does offer Scott's readership an opportunity to learn the language of Scottish culture thus reflecting an eighteenth-century desire to 'imitate life' and even a nineteenth-century concern with how this may be done 'realistically'. However even here, in this first novel, Scott seems to hint at a much more modern awareness of the extent to which this enterprise may be problematic. It is, then, perhaps hardly surprising that in his next two novels, *Guy Mannering* and *The Antiquary*, he should engage more overtly with the question of how the discourse of the novel operates and what, if anything, can be communicated by it.

## *Voices at Play:* Guy Mannering *and* The Antiquary

In spite of having to some extent established the blueprint for the historical novel in *Waverley* Scott's next two novels, while still clearly set in the past and engaging with how we may understand it, do not engage directly with a recognisable historical event such as the Jacobite Rising, but, rather, with questions of how forms of discourse relate to meaning and our understanding of the past.

The second novel by the Author of Waverley, *Guy Mannering* (1815), has received less critical attention than some of his other, more overtly Scottish and more straightforwardly historical, novels. As P. D. Garside, its editor for the Edinburgh Edition puts it, 'Scott's "tale of private life" is singularly devoid of the concrete historical details found in *Waverley* (1814), and lacks too the connection with a public incident (the feared invasion of 1794) evident in its immediate successor, *The Antiquary* (1816).'[37] Set, as Garside argues, in 1782, and looking backward to a period approximately seventeen years before the main action, the novel is located amid no major political event and while located in Scotland, its Scottishness is not particularly foregrounded. Similar observations can be drawn regarding *The Antiquary*, for while it does have the feared French invasion referred to by Garside as a backcloth to its action, this appears almost incidental, and impinges only on the novel in terms of minor farce. Rather, these are novels which deal with, as Scott acknowledges, personal past, the methods by which this can be known, recovered and assimilated, and, perhaps most significantly for the purposes of the enquiry here, limitations governing the extent to which it can ever be fully understood. Also linked to the debates of Scott's own time and the generation before concerning the nature of historiography, these novels take as their subject matter the collision between official forms of understanding the past and alternative epistemes of story, personal recollection and folk memory.

Nevertheless in their opening pages both *Guy Mannering* and *The Antiquary* seem to be following a pattern established by their predecessor. Both novels open with what appears to be a young English male protagonist arriving in Scotland, and *Guy Mannering* at least seems to suggest that it is offering the opportunity for the 'translation' of culture suggested in *Waverley*. As Julian D'Arcy observes,[38] it confronts the reader with a similar set of linguistic puzzles: '"But what must I do then, good dame? for I can't sleep here upon the road all night?"' asks Mannering:

> "Troth, I ken na, unless ye like to gae doun and speer for quarters at the Place. I'se warrant they'll take ye, whether ye be gentle or semple."
>
> "Simple enough, to be wandering here at such a time of night," thought Mannering, who was ignorant of the meaning of the phrase, "but how shall I get to the *place*, as you call it?"
>
> "Ye maun haud *wessel* by the end o' the loan, and take tent o' the jaw-hole."

"O, if you get to *easel* and *wessel* again, I am undone!—Is there no boy that could guide me to this *place*?" (pp. 5–6)

Again, similarly, the young protagonist of *The Antiquary*, like Edward Waverley, meets an older, slightly eccentric character early in the text who takes him under his wing.

However here the parallels between *Waverley* and the subsequent novels cease for, as Scott himself suggests, these are novels of private life rather than 'national tales' and their plots are built around what D'Arcy calls the 'more "traditional" romance plot of a lost heir reclaiming his inheritance',[39] as both characters seek (at times unbeknown to themselves and those around them) for the key to their lost identities. In this sense, these texts appear to be on fairly familiar novel terrain as the form builds on its romance origins and evolves towards its more socialised nineteenth-century guise. However, what is interesting about them is not the recovery of lost identity *per se*. As Jane Millgate observes of *Guy Mannering* there is in fact little suspense in its plot but rather, 'the dynamic of the novel inheres, in fact, not in whether Bertram will win Julia Mannering but in how his identity will be established'.[40] In other words, these texts are novels not about *what* can be recovered from the past but about the *means* by which we can recover it, the extent to which it can be *knowable* via such knowledge and, ultimately, the implications of this knowledge for the present and for our current constructions of the self; questions crucial for the historical novelist.

What is most relevant here is the ways in which Scott responds to these questions in these early fictions, for he suggests that an understanding of the past is only possible via a wide, and at times seemingly conflicting, range of discourses. This is foregrounded very clearly in *Guy Mannering* for it is a text that is peopled by characters who communicate via non-standard forms of language.[41] While the novel lacks the representation of Gaelic found in *Waverley* and elsewhere in Scott's work this is replaced here by the language of gypsies and smugglers and by the strange idiolect of Dominie Sampson. *Guy*, in fact, is the first in a series of Scott's novels which incorporate into them the use of cant language, and there are well over thirty words listed in the notes and glossary derived from thieves' cant alone, along with words based in Scots, Dutch, German, Latin, French, Cumbrian and with nautical origins. It is hardly surprising that Garside should draw attention to the 'amazing . . . polyphonic variety' in this text and this polyphony is a marker of the range of discourses that are at play within it.[42] It is equally unsurprising that much of this complexity was obfuscated by the first edition. As Garside notes '[a] common failure is non-recognition of idiomatic expressions and / or their needless syntactical smoothing out . . . A similar flattening effect is found in the representation of Sampson's biblical rhetoric . . . the cant-derived talk of the gypsies . . . and Hattaraik's German-Dutch pidgin English'. Phrases such as Meg's 'fremit giberish' (replacing the first edition's 'French gibberish') are restored in the Edinburgh Edition, however, thus giving a full sense of Scott's linguistic complexity.[43]

This is even more evident in *The Antiquary*. As has been frequently discussed in this novel Scott appears to set official, 'Enlightenment' models of the past (expressed in Oldbuck himself and his constant allusion to historical sources) in opposition to folk memory (represented by Edie and the interpolated tale), and its counterpart, oral culture (expressed via Elspat Mucklebackit whose fragmentary, associative and rambling narrative of what has occurred in the novel's 'backstory' unlocks the key to Lovel's real identity).[44] The revisionist reading of this interplay is that through this oppositional arrangement Scott both satirises the antiquarian pursuits in which he himself was engaged, and simultaneously challenges any straightforwardly empirical model for understanding the past via his debunking of Oldbuck's position by Edie Ochiltree and his famous claim that he 'mind[s] the bigging' of the shelter which Oldbuck has interpreted as being a Roman praetorian. (p. 30) As Julian D'Arcy comments, 'It is Edie's Scottish voice which can prove to be more incisively accurate and subversive than the antiquarian's'.[45]

However, the discussion of what discourse actually means and how it in turn conveys meaning in *The Antiquary* is more complex than these oppositional readings imply. Certainly, there is not just one opposition being offered here, but many; Oldbuck's methods of understanding the past are in fact set against not only the discourse of Edie's folk memory, but also that of his fellow antiquarian Wardour, the oral recollections of Elspat and, via his relationship with his Highland nephew Hector McIntyre, the type of collective 'memory' or relic represented by the Ossian cycle and constructed (or reconstructed) by James Macpherson. And while less overtly set in opposition to Oldbuck other voices are also at play in this text which serve to problematise any simple binary construction of how it is operating. The interpolated tale of Martin Waldeck as it is recounted by Isabella Wardour, the voices of the gossips at the local post office and even the testimony of half effaced tomb stones and sea-chests operate to create a polyphony of voice, and one which, at times, offers a kind of female or feminised discourse in opposition to the Antiquary with his aversion to the babbling of 'womankind'. Similarly, the genre of the novel itself, which veers between historical novel, domestic fiction, romance and Gothic narrative, offers an internal structural polyphony that resists meaning within any one frame of reference.

What is significant, however, is not only that the novel contains within it a polyphony of voices (reminiscent of the ways in which the poetry splinters into multiple strands and genres), but also that Scott resists reasserting any definite sense of hierarchy upon these competing utterances within the text. While Edie may appear to get the better of Oldbuck, we should recall that it is never made clear which of these authorities is correct. Similarly, as Sheena Sutherland has convincingly demonstrated, both Wardour's and Oldbuck's uses of the authorities to which they appeal is flawed by the fact that both misquote the sources upon which they set such store.[46] It should be remembered that while Oldbuck's opinion may seem the more valid on the Ossian controversy, nevertheless, this was a real and genuine debate at the time at which the novel was set, with greater authorities than Hector McIntyre supporting the authenticity of the poems. Caroline McCracken-Flesher suggests that what is actually being explored here is, as in *Guy Mannering*, the problematics inherent in telling a coherent tale,[47] and Catherine Jones similarly recognises the fragmentary nature of these two novels:

> Within each text, the fragmentary is formally and thematically crucial. In *Guy Mannering* for example, Scott maximizes disjunction by juxtaposing different discourses, genres, and conventions in a narrative that is temporally fractured following the violent abduction of the heir of Ellangowan. Each character possesses a fragment of the past, which requires coordination and unraveling for the story's resolution and the restoration of the lost heir . . . The past is made whole and a future is imagined in which society is brought together under the rightful heir.[48]

However, while it is tempting to see these shards of narrative resolving themselves into some coherence at the end of these texts in fact what is being posited is not a binary relationship, which reorganises itself into a status quo or hierarchy, but rather a kind of mosaic or kaleidoscope of discourse, where meaning resides, rather, in the shifting patterns and contingent relationship of the fragments of meaning which constitute the past and both personal and national identity. Significantly, the key to Lovel's identity is unlocked through a range of apparently contradictory and conflicting discourses. While on the one hand Elspat's rambling tale of Eveline Neville and the machinations of Lady Glenallan, which itself operates by strange disjunctions and incoherences, may seem to be privileged over Oldbuck's antiquarian searches it becomes apparent, as Julian D'Arcy argues, that 'no one individual has the complete knowledge, overview, or even understanding of this tragic story'.[49] Indeed, Oldbuck's documents and legal searches, collected many years earlier, are ultimately as crucial to an understanding of Lovel's identity as Elspat's rambling, and ultimately unverifiable, tale. No one discourse, these novels suggest, can offer the resolution of identity, but rather our understanding of the past remains contingent, pieced together, as McCracken-Flesher puts it, out of 'bits and pieces'.[50]

Constructed as the past is from the 'bricolage' of language these early novels suggest that it can only ever be partially recovered. While both *Guy Mannering* and *The Antiquary* conclude with the restoration of their young heroes to their rightful identities in neither instance can time be redeemed and the denouement of each is something of an anti-climax where Scott, in a pattern which is to become familiar in his fiction, offers a kind of fracturing of discourse at the end of his tale rather than a conclusion; much is deferred or, as in *Waverley*, left unsaid. While loose ends may appear to be tied up at the end of *Guy Mannering*, the past and all it has cost cannot be erased. Neither Bertram's mother or father live to see the restoration of their son, and his surrogate mother, Meg Merrilies, dies at the moment of his restoration, suggesting that his coming into his estate marks the beginning of a new era rather than the redemption of an old. Similarly, while the various strands of narrative which combine to offer the secret to Lovel's identity in *The Antiquary* offer a resolution of sorts, again, narrative cannot completely erase the horror of Elspat's story and the tragedy of Eveline Neville. Elspat, who tells her tale 'like the dead speaking to the living' (p. 214), dies (as does Meg in *Guy Mannering*) in the act of recounting her story, as if in order for reconciliation to be reached at the conclusion of these texts certain of their many voices have to be silenced. So too, no act of narration, however powerful, can restore dead Steenie to his family. As Meiklebackit tells Oldbuck, it is as if different rules apply for the ordinary people of the novel: '"It's weel wi' you gentles, that can sit in the house wi' handkerchers at your een when ye lose a friend; but the like o' us maun to our wark again, if our hearts were beating as hard as my hammer"' (p. 267). The implication is that while the romance trajectory of the main plot of this novel may bring a restoration of sorts, there is also another discourse operating to undermine it where time cannot be so miraculously recuperated.

As in Scott's poems and in *Waverley*, anxiety about the possibility of recovering the past rests in part at least upon the unreliable and slippery nature of language, which itself always has ruptures and slippages within it which resist meaning being closed into fixed sequence. *The Antiquary* is full of references to the unreliable nature of language and much of its plot hinges on such discrepancies in the meaning of words. At one level, this appears to be used simply for comic effect, but linguistic play also has implications for the development of plot. Edie Ochiltree, for example, dupes the aptly named Dousterswivel by a linguistic trick. Mocking this swindler by a play on his name, calling him, humorously, 'Dusterdivel' (p.196), 'Dousterdrivel' and 'Dustanshovel' (p. 203) Edie also bemuses him with the indeterminate story of the riddle of Misticot's grave and persuades him that the word 'Search' on the buried chest is an imperative rather than the name of ship (p. 197). Significantly, too, an early argument in the text between Wardour and Oldbuck concerning the derivation of the one word remaining in the language of the Picts appears to be simply an opportunity to satirise the absurdity of antiquarian pursuits. However, Lovel, who has not understood a word of the conversation, offers the following comment, suggesting that the exchange perhaps has other implications:

> "The Piks, or Picts," said Lovel, "must have been singularly poor in dialect, since in the only remaining word of their vocabulary, and that consisting only of two syllables, they have been confessedly obliged to borrow one of them from another language; and methinks, gentlemen, with submission, the controversy is not unlike that which the two knights fought, concerning the shield that had one side white and the other black. Each of you claim one-half of the word, and seem to resign the other. But what strikes me most, is the poverty of the language which has left so slight vestiges behind it." (p. 49)

Lovel's implication seems clear. One word is not enough to construct a narrative and as such it is impossible to offer any coherent story of the 'Piks, or Picts' whose very name is lost in the mists of time. Rather, language, in all its poverty, operates by being contingent; via the construction of (often competing and sometimes irreconcilable) discourses.

Scott's early fiction, then, suggests that just at the point when he appears to be producing the template for the historical novel he is simultaneously problematising any straightforward version of it. Presenting the form as a kind of dialogue between past and present, and between different discourses of national identity, he suggests that any such acts of 'simultaneous translation' are necessarily compromised, and that, by definition they leave much unsaid. If we recognise that *Waverley* is not only an iconic novel but also a kind of 'learning curve' for its author we can see that in it he discovers that the past cannot be known via the narratorial authority of a text like *Waverley* nor can it be recovered by the 'poverty' of a language monolithically constructed (like that of the Picts). In *Guy Mannering* and *The Antiquary* he investigates whether a kaleidoscope of competing discourses offers a more fruitful way of recovering the past, but this too is limited. Exploring how such choruses recover and communicate the past and negotiate possible versions of it for the future, these texts suggest that all that can ever really be reiterated by the novel is a range of competing discourses, which, in their polyphony, in turn open up fissures where any notion of a 'correct' version collapses and disappears and where certain voices within it (Meg, Elspat, Flora and Fergus all stand as examples) must be silenced.

It is hardly surprising, therefore, that in the novels that follow Scott continues to explore the fraught question of the role of discourse in constructing identity, to search for new ways to recover the past within it, and to offer an increasing and ever more vexed awareness of the limits of language.

*Notes*

1 Recent scholarship has demonstrated that Scott began writing *Waverley* around 1808 and continued in 1810. This is contemporaneous with the composition of *Marmion* and *The Lady of the Lake* and therefore the shift from poetry to fiction did begin at the height of Scott's poetic career. See P. D. Garside 'Essay on the Text', *Waverley*, p. 367.

2 Ina Ferris, *The Achievement of Literary Authority*, p. 1.

3 Fiona Robertson, *Legitimate Histories*, p. 28.

4 Francis Jeffrey, review of *Waverley* from the *Edinburgh Review*, November, 1814 in *The Critical Heritage*, pp. 79–84 (pp. 79 and 81).

5 Fiona Robertson, *Legitimate Histories,* p. 51.

6 George Levine, *The Realist Imagination*, p. 60.

7   John Barth, 'The Self in Fiction, or, "That Ain't No Matter. That Is Nothing."' in *The Friday Book*, pp. 207–14 (p. 209).
8   Henry Fielding, *The History of Tom Jones*, ed. by R. P. C. Mutter (London: Penguin, 1985), p. 323.
9   Ibid. p. 325.
10  Robert Louis Stevenson, 'Books Which Have influenced Me' in *Essays Literary and Critical*, The Works of Robert Louis Stevenson, Tusitala Edition, vol. 28 (London: William Heinemann, 1923), p. 65.
11  Henry Fielding, *Tom Jones*, pp. 325–6.
12  Ina Ferris, *The Achievement of Literary Authority*, p. 96.
13  George Levine, *The Realist Imagination*, p. 88.
14  P. D. Garside 'Essay on the Text', *Waverley*, p. 509.
15  Ibid. p. 519.
16  This is of course the classic Lukáscian reading of Scott's fiction. See Georg Lukács, *The Historical Novel*, translated by Hannah and Stanley Mitchell (Lincoln, NE and London: University of Nebraska Press, 1983).
17  George Levine, *The Realist Imagination*, p. 104.
18  Claire Lamont, 'Introduction' in Walter Scott, *Waverley*, ed. by Claire Lamont (Oxford: Oxford University Press, 1986), pp. vii–xx (p. xiv).
19  See Jerome McGann, 'Walter Scott's Romantic Postmodernity', p. 125.
20  Celeste Langan comments that in this passage 'the question of mastery, of sovereignty and subjection, is linked to language, and our attention is directed to the difference made by the "virtual" speech act of writing'. See '"The Poetry of Pure Memory": Teaching Scott's Novels in the Context of Romanticism' in *Approaches to Teaching the Waverley Novels*, pp. 67–76 (p. 73).
21  This can be seen as part of Scott's conversation with the subject of books in this novel as he explores how he may offer his 'book' on the subject of Scottish history and how it relates to other discourses.
22  Scott was to revisit the idea of writing as trade in the later Prefaces and he confronts it head-on in *The Betrothed* (1825).
23  John Barth, 'Historical Fiction, Fictitious History, and Chesapeake Bay Blue Crabs, or, About Aboutness' in *The Friday Book*, pp. 180–92 (p. 181).
24  See Walter Scott, *Waverley*, ed. by Claire Lamont, p. 411, note to Vol. 1, p. 3, line 14.
25  See P. D. Garside 'Essay on the Text', *Waverley*, p. 509 and the note to 3.22 on p. 525.
26  The novel is located in Scott's library at Abbotsford although that does not necessarily meant that he had read it. See J. G. Cochrane, *Catalogue of the Library at Abbotsford* (Edinburgh: Bannatyne Club, 1838), p. 333.

27  'General Preface', Walter Scott, *Waverley Novels*, 48 vols (Edinburgh: Cadell and Company, 1829–33), p. xiii.

28  The need for such 'translation' in fiction is also reiterated by Scott in the General Preface by his reference to Joseph Strutt's *Queen-Hoo-Hall*, a text to which he refers elsewhere in his fiction. For Scott this text fails because it does not offer an act of translation but rather Strutt '[renders] his language too ancient, and [displays] his antiquarian knowledge too liberally' (General Preface, p. xvi). I will return to this in Chapter 4. Both Ina Ferris and James Buzard have drawn attention to the ways in which *Waverley* operates as an act of translation with Buzard viewing this as an act of cultural imperialism and Ferris suggesting that as a form of 'national tale' *Waverley* offers a kind of residual resistance to such assimilation. See James Buzard, 'Translation and Tourism: Scott's *Waverley* and the Rendering of Culture', *Yale Journal of Criticism* 8 (1995), pp. 31–59 and Ina Ferris, 'Translation from the Borders: Encounter and Recalcitrance in *Waverley* and *Clan-Albin*', *Eighteenth-Century Fiction* 9.2 (1997), pp. 203–22.

29  Janet Sorensen suggests that 'the creative borrowings of alternative linguistic communities demonstrate the limits of official languages': *The Grammar of Empire*, p. 27.

30  As Ferris suggests the national tale 'tends to thematize the problem of translation itself, so blocking any sense of transparent access to the represented culture': 'Translation from the Borders: Encounter and Recalcitrance in *Waverley* and *Clan-Albin*', pp. 208–9.

31  See Ludwig Wittgenstein, *Philosophical Investigations*, p. 116.

32  Ina Ferris, *The Achievement of Literary Authority*, p. 103.

33  Ina Ferris, 'Translation from the Borders: Encounter and Recalcitrance in *Waverley* and *Clan-Albin*', p. 218.

34  Caroline McCracken-Flesher, *Possible Scotlands*, p. 17.

35  Cairns Craig, *Out of History: Narrative Paradigms in Scottish and English Culture* (Edinburgh: Polygon, 1996), p. 39.

36  Caroline McCracken-Flesher, *Possible Scotlands*, p. 18.

37  P. D. Garside, 'Historical Note', *Guy Mannering*, p. 496. Garside quotes Scott's own description of his novel in *Letters*, p. 4.13.

38  Julian Meldon D'Arcy, *Subversive Scott*, p. 75.

39  Ibid. p. 75.

40  Jane Millgate, *Walter Scott: The Making of the Novelist* (Toronto: University of Toronto Press, 1984), p. 69.

41  Ina Ferris draws attention to John Wilson Croker's early review of the novel that suggestively comments that the work 'would be on the whole improved,

by being *translated into English*': 'Translation from the Borders: Encounter and Recalcitrance in *Waverley* and *Clan-Albin*', pp. 212–13.

42  Robert P. Irvine comments, for example, that 'The interpenetration of the classes, the multiplicity of voices that so offends Mannering, is a principal feature of Scott's text itself, as it is of all the Waverley Novels'. *Enlightenment and Romance: Gender and Agency in Smollett and Scott* (Oxford and New York: Peter Lang, 2000), p. 117.

43  See P. D. Garside, 'Essay on the Text', *Guy Mannering*, p. 423.

44  Several critics, including Jane Millgate and Julian D'Arcy, have written on this aspect of the novel.

45   Julian Meldon D'Arcy, *Subversive Scott*, p. 91.

46  See Sheena Sutherland, *Scott's Voices: An Analysis of Discourse Competition in the Waverley Novels* (Unpublished PhD thesis, University of Aberdeen, 1997).

47  Caroline McCracken-Flesher, *Possible Scotlands*, p. 16 and p. 46.

48  Catherine Jones, *Literary Memory*, pp. 132–3.

49  Julian Meldon D'Arcy, *Subversive Scott*, p. 92.

50  Ibid. p. 34.

# Chapter 3

# 'Last Confessions and Dying Words':
## *The Heart of Mid-Lothian*

Scott's early fiction incorporates within it an exploration of the ways in which the novel form may be deployed to offer narratives of both national and personal identity. However, while these early novels by the Author of Waverley may exhibit an anxiety concerning what can be communicated via the discourse (or discourses) from which the novel is constituted his seventh novel, *The Heart of Mid-Lothian*, manifests an increasingly fraught relationship to the specific linguistic materials upon which narrative discourse rests, demonstrating an acute anxiety concerning the limits of language's referential potentialities.

*The Heart of Mid-Lothian* is ostensibly less concerned with the recovery of the past, whether national or personal, than Scott's earlier fiction. It deals with no major historical event and if we follow its carefully controlled time scheme its protagonist Jeanie Deans is already at least thirty-three by the time the main action begins. 'Approaching to what is called in females the middle age' (p. 84) she shows, as Jane Millgate notes, none of the tendencies towards waywardness, fancy and rebellion attributed to Scott's more youthful (frequently male) heroes.[1] Certainly, *The Heart of Mid-Lothian* can barely be called a historical novel in the conventional sense and it does not follow the template set out by Scott in *Waverley* or followed in later works such as *The Tale of Old Mortality*, *Rob Roy* or *Redgauntlet* where the protagonist is caught up in a major historical moment and required to align himself with the political events that shape the force of history. While the Porteous Riots are an historical event in the sense that they did occur they are not of the same magnitude as the Jacobite Risings or the Covenanting Wars and they are, in any case, only tangential to the story of Jeanie and Effie Deans. Nevertheless there is a sense in which *The Heart of Mid-Lothian* remains consummately concerned with how to capture the past and how to communicate the processes by which memorialisation operates. The opening of the novel signals this. In spite of the fact that its primary concern is the story of Jeanie and Effie the novel begins with an account of the Porteous Riots and the circumstances which led to the trial and murder of John Porteous. While this may be a minor incident in Scottish history, opening the novel in this way locates it in a very specific historical period (thirty years after the Union) and as Scott dovetails Jeanie's narrative with it he ensures that his novel is also one that deals with the discontent that marked the period as well as providing a record of Helen Walker's walk to London. There is a sense in which this is clearly a novel about the state of the nation, a commentary on what has been lost and gained since "'Scotland was Scotland'" (p. 38).

There is also another sense in which this text operates as a historical novel, however. As David Hewitt and myself argue in the 'Historical Note' to the Edinburgh Edition, while the ostensible time scheme covers the point from Effie's arrest and the Porteous Riots up until Jeanie's settling at Roseneath, the birth of her children and the death of Staunton at the hands of the Whistler, the discourse time is in fact far longer since 'David Deans stretches the story well back into the seventeenth century. He is said to have been present at Talla-linns (178.9), a historic gathering which took place in 1682, and to have at least witnessed the murder in the same year of Trooper Francis Gordon'.[2] The much-debated final volume of the novel also extends the period covered to 1751, beyond the 1745 Rising. As a result, this is a novel not only about a specific event in Scottish history but also one about a span of Scottish history which covers the period from the unsettled times of the Covenanting Wars through the discontent of the mid eighteenth century and on towards the period when Scotland began to assume its modern and settled place within the union. In a sense this is a novel about the working out of the great debates on sovereignty that shaped Scottish history in the seventeenth and eighteenth centuries: '*The Heart of Mid-Lothian*', we argue, 'is more of a chronicle than any other Scott novel, and when viewed this way it appears that while David Deans is not the primary focus of our interest, the revolution seen in his life and lifetime is at least one of the underlying subjects of the fiction' (p. 598). While the question of how to recover the past in discourse may not be as overt as in Scott's earlier work, therefore, it is clear that it is still one with which Scott is wrestling, and which informs this text.

If *The Heart of Mid-Lothian* is not an historical novel in the conventional sense, neither does it overtly take the question of personal growth and recovery of identity as its subject matter. Whereas anonymity surrounds the male protagonists of *Guy Mannering* or *The Antiquary* there is no mystery concerning Jeanie Deans's identity and while the novels discussed above broadly follow the pattern of *bildungsroman* this is not an appropriate description of *The Heart of Mid-Lothian*. As Millgate notes, Jeanie 'has no need to search for a father or an identity – her paternity and her selfhood are never in doubt'[3] Again, however, while in this novel questions of personal identity may not be approached as directly as in other of Scott's texts, it remains a subject with which *The Heart of Mid-Lothian* is in fact consummately concerned. Underpinned narratologically by disguises, changes of name, and veiled identities, it is a novel which offers some of Scott's most complex interrogations of the nature of identity and the ways in which this is positioned within discourse. Where *The Heart of Mid-Lothian* differs most significantly from Scott's earlier fiction, however, is in the fact that the exploration of the relationship between discourse and meaning and the concomitant anxiety concerning language hinted at in Scott's earlier work now assumes a central position. As such it is particularly pertinent to the present discussion for in it we see Scott moving from an underlying interest in the *best* form of discourse through which to articulate identity (both national and personal) towards a more overt and increasingly profound engagement with the role and limitations of language in the very construction of such discourses.

This is signalled by the generic complexity of the novel. While Scott's work is often difficult to categorise in generic terms and at times swithers between different modes and genres, *The Heart of Mid-Lothian* provides an extreme example of this in that it operates narratologically by offering a series of generically various texts.[4] The first volume, for example, which includes the Porteous riots and the 'back-story' to the Deans family, seems to locate the reader in the terrain of the historical novel. The second volume, which deals with Jeanie's meeting with Staunton at Muschat's Cairn and the trial of Effie, is apparently situated in both Gothic and legal terms. The third, which involves Jeanie's walk to London, the various trials she meets with along the way and her pleading before the Queen, seems to belong in the terrain of the romance quest, a feature signalled by the frequent references to *Pilgrim's Progress*, while the last volume, where the Deans family is relocated at Roseneath, may be loosely described as pastoral, although elements of romance transformation persist in, for example, Effie's translation into a member of the aristocracy.[5] The stretching out of the time scheme of the novel via this final volume also contributes to its final status as chronicle.

The generic complexity of *The Heart of Mid-Lothian*, then, contributes to a sense of its concern with different forms of discourse. This is also signalled more locally within the text by the ways in which alternative forms of discourse are embedded within it. An example of this may be found if we consider the many letters that appear within its pages. The appearance of letters within a novel looks back, of course, to the epistolary form so common in the eighteenth century and in this sense they introduce yet another generic category into this text. However, letters may also be posited as repositories of personal identity – sites where the self is potentially offered in its most intimate textual form – and as such alert the reader to the concern with the relationship between identity and forms of discourse being explored here. There are many letters in this fiction, some of which are quoted directly to the reader, others simply reported. Jeanie writes five, David one, Effie two and Staunton at least three. There are also numerous brief notes and communications. It is, however, Jeanie's letters that are of most significance, although Effie's and Staunton's are also revealing.

Jane Millgate describes Jeanie's letters as 'masterpieces of persuasive rhetoric' (as we have seen, a loaded word in the context of eighteenth-century discussions of language), suggesting that in them she re-harmonises her relationships with Reuben and her father, relationships ruptured by Jeanie's radical act of taking power into her own hands.[6] Jeanie's letters are certainly significant, although perhaps less for the reasons proposed by Millgate than because they reveal fundamental concerns about the ways in which the construction of identity via linguistic frameworks is being explored in this text; while Blair may have argued that 'true rhetoric and sound logic are very nearly allied', Scott seems to be suggesting a more complex relationship between identity and forms of discourse here.[7]

Jeanie writes two sets of letters, the first during her rest day at York with Mrs Bickerton, and the second from London after she has successfully gained Effie's pardon. In the first set she excuses her bad orthography and spelling by stating 'excuse bad spelling and writing, as I have ane ill pen' (p. 252). Scott elaborates on this topic by adding that to the 'southron' the orthography may 'require a better apology', stating in mitigation, however, that 'Jeanie Deans wrote and spelled fifty times better than half the women of rank in Scotland at that period' (p. 252). In her second letter to Butler Jeanie states again that she 'is not a 'great pen-woman' and excuses her orthography this time by the lateness of the hour, and the experiences she has undergone in London; 'It is a muckle place, and I hae seen sae muckle of it, that my poor head turns round' (p. 352). For many readers of what was the standard text of the novel Jeanie's words have seemed strange, since while here Jeanie writes in a Scots dialect, her spelling does not seem idiosyncratic to the extent that these disclaimers would imply. The Edinburgh Edition of the Waverley Novels, however, returned to the manuscript versions of Jeanie's letters and reinstated many of the orthographical features found there and, consequently, the full force of Jeanie's words comes into play.[8] Here, her letters are indeed full of idiosyncrasies such as the spellings 'Deuke', 'muckell', 'cristian', 'pardun', 'instriments' and 'orguns' to name only a few. Jeanie's orthography emerges, consequently, as highly disruptive, breaking through the 'polite style' of the rest of the narrative. The first letter which Jeanie writes from London is brief, and while orthographically it is less disruptive than her others it is also problematic. Addressed to George Staunton it opens with the words 'to prevent farder mischieves, whereof there hath been enough, comes these' (p. 349). It is signed, enigmatically, 'ye ken wha'. In this letter it is the tone which seems odd, prompting readers to ask why Scott frames Jeanie's letter to Staunton in this cloak-and-dagger form, as if his protagonist has somehow suddenly slipped out of *The Heart of Mid-Lothian* and into the world of Gothic fiction or melodrama.

An explanation for these letters may be found by reference to Scott's working methods. In the Introductory Epistle to *The Fortunes of Nigel* Scott writes of the 'demon on his pen' which detracts from his plans for authorial control and design to dictate instead a process of Romantic generation, a process by which the work itself apparently takes on organic form to develop under the author's hands (p. 10). There is plenty of evidence for this process at work in *The Heart of Mid-Lothian*. The character of Reuben Butler, for example, begins life in the manuscript as the generic schoolmaster Tawse (the Scots word for belt, used in schools in place of the English cane), a companion to his senior 'Whackbairn'. As Scott writes, however, the character, and his role in the fiction, develops, and as he becomes more complex he is suitably re-named. It is a similar process of organic generation which operates in Jeanie's letters. Writing in the character of a Scottish peasant, for example, Scott slips into an orthographical style appropriate to her. Writing to Staunton, Jeanie responds in a way suitable to the Byronic character he has created for himself, 'the character of Macheath under condemnation,' as he portrays himself, 'a fine, gay, bold-faced ruffian' (p. 301).

These letters, then, restored to reflect Scott's intentions in the Edinburgh Edition, exemplify Scott's working methods, and the ways in which the 'demon on his pen' takes over at key moments in the text. Interesting though this might be, however, their *critical* significance here lies in the fact that they exemplify interludes in the text where alternative discourses (and as discussed above, even alternative genres) break through what we might categorise as the dominant Enlightenment episteme of this fiction to disrupt its narrative form. Seen in this way, the letters emerge not only as potential sites of disclosure or repositories of identity, but also as examples of sites where alternative styles, genres and forms of narrative come into play allowing a space for competing discourses within the novel to come to the fore, disrupting narrative homogeneity, and adding to the polyphonic aspect of the narrative which has been identified in *Guy Mannering* and *The Antiquary*. Such modulation is, however, only part of a much deeper concern with discourse which runs throughout this novel, and which is intrinsic to the discussion of language operating within it.

*The Heart of Mid-Lothian* is not simply a virtuoso display of polyphony; it is in fact a novel that is vexed by the ways in which different discourses operate, and it is a symptom rather than an outcome that so many different kinds of discourse – those of the law, religion and national identity, as well as those suggested by the generic categories of romance and pastoral identified above – are operating within its pages. This is signalled early in the novel in a number of key exchanges that serve to foreground some of the discourses at play. For example, one of the most significant dialogues in the novel operates on national terms and is that between the Scottish and English nations. Scott draws our attention to these alternative voices repeatedly in the early scenes, and indeed the terms of the union are given as a justification for Wilson's and Robertson's act of felony. 'Smuggling was almost universal in Scotland in the reigns of George I. and II.', the narrator tells us, 'for the people, unaccustomed to imposts, and regarding them as an unjust aggression upon their ancient liberties, made no scruple to elude them wherever it was possible to do so' (p. 22). In this context, Wilson's stealing back the smuggled goods that have been appropriated from him takes on the power of a political action, for it is in defiance of the 1707 Acts of Union. A similar dialogue is also found in the early conversations of the novel, for the pardon of Porteous is seen as an assault by London upon the people of Edinburgh and of Scotland in general. '"I am judging," said Mr Plumdamas, "that this reprieve wadna stand gude in the auld Scots law, when the kingdom was a kingdom"':

> "I dinna ken muckle about the law," answered Mrs Howden; "but I ken, that when we had a king, and a chancellor, and parliament-men o' our ain, we could aye peeble them wi' stanes when they were na gude bairns—But naebody's nails can reach the length o' Lunnon."
> "Weary on Lunnon, and a' that e'er came out o't!" said Miss Grizell Damahoy, an ancient seamstress; "they hae ta'en awa' our parliament, and

they hae oppressed our trade. Our gentles will hardly allow that a Scots needle can sew ruffles on a sark, or lace on an owerlay." (p. 37)

An apparent competition between the dominant discourse of union, and the marginal one of separate Scottish identity, is thus posited in the opening scenes.

Another set of voices put into play in the opening of the novel involves a dialogue between masculine and feminine discourses figured in particular in the exchanges between Bartoline and Mrs Saddletree. 'This good lady' we are told 'was in the habit of letting her husband take his way, and go on improving his stock of legal knowledge without interruption, but, as if in requital, she insisted upon having her own will in the domestic and commercial departments which he abandoned to her' (p. 38). Subtly figured is a seeming opposition between 'masculine' forms of knowledge and those which are the domain of womanhood. Bartoline may (or may not) know a great deal about the law and the workings of the Scottish court, but when it comes to common sense, or domestic understanding, it is Mrs Saddletree who has the upper hand; while she '"wad hae had the truth o' her situation out o' her [Effie]"', Mr Saddletree has no understanding of this, a feminine arena of experience and '"might be in a lying-in hospital, and ne'er find out what the women cam there for"' (p. 44).

The law and the legal system by which it operates are also shaping epistemes in this text and in the opening pages the conversations between these minor characters also set up an apparent opposition between the letter of the law, and what the Duke of Argyle is later to call its 'spirit'. It is Saddletree, of course, who is the champion of its letter; he has all the statutes at his 'finger-ends' and is capable of outlining the law under which Effie is to be condemned. It is, however, the women (and again a masculine/ feminine opposition comes into play) who argue for its spirit, immediately recognising the fundamental flaw of justice at the heart of this statute. '"So that," said the good woman, "unless puir Effie has communicated her situation, she'll be hanged by the neck, if the bairn was still-born, or if it be alive at this moment?"'(p. 47).

If we consider the opening of the novel by taking note of the apparent binaries being posited within it it is tempting to see the narrative of *The Heart of Mid-Lothian* as a working out of these competing discourses and to read it as a novel apparently concerned with the question of where 'truth' or 'identity' may ultimately be located; in Union Britain or its margin Scotland, in masculine or feminine models for interpreting experience, in the letter of the law or in its spirit. Jeanie's refusal to lie under oath may, consequently, be seen as an act taking place within the dominant discourse of the state legal system and according to the dictates of a patriarchal law while her journey to London may be read as an assault on these discourses by the alternative voice of the margins as she argues the case for the spirit of the law, feminine compassion and for the special needs of the Scottish nation. Several critics have attempted to read the novel in this way. Their conclusions, however, are revealing, for they suggest that a critique of it that tries to reorganise these discourses into a kind of hierarchy cannot be sustained. James Kerr's attempt to read the novel as 'a romance of national regeneration' for example – an assault by Scottish identity on the English episteme – is problematic, since there is ultimately a retreat 'out of history' towards what he sees as a regressive pastoral construction of Scotland.[9] Judith Wilt's attempt to read the novel in feminist terms, as a female assault on male constructions of power, also runs into difficulties since Wilt recognises that power is only temporarily located with the feminine before being handed back to patriarchy.[10] The conclusions of these critics should hardly be surprising, however, since we have seen in earlier chapters that any attempt to impose a hierarchy of discourse on Scott's texts is only ever partially adequate. As Caroline McCracken-Flesher notes, an apparently 'tidy package' in which gendered concerns are substituted for political ones breaks down into a 'bulky yet challenging dialogic complex'.[11] In this novel, perhaps his most complex commentary on the relationship between discourse and identity, the voices that are put into play at the start of it are once again introduced not that they might be subjugated one to the other but, rather, to explore the difficulties of locating identity within *any* one episteme, and, indeed, the linguistic complexities upon which this tension rests.

This becomes increasingly apparent if we look more carefully at the exploration of the construction and location of personal identity that is taking place in this text. Earlier in this study the relationship between Scott's ideas of language and Enlightenment commentaries on rhetoric and communication was explored, demonstrating the ways in which his inherent scepticism towards language (and what can be recognised as an emerging resistance to Dogmatism) can be traced to his Enlightenment precursors. However, this is only one side of the Enlightenment coin and Hume's adversaries were at pains to reinstate a philosophy of 'first principles' rather than the free play of mental images and passions that his writing seems to imply. Moreover, as Susan Manning notes even Hume's philosophies could take fiction towards the 'prison house of language'. In

*The Heart of Mid-Lothian* it is this tendency in Enlightenment thought that is examined, most particularly, via two epistemes; the legal system in Scotland, and David Deans's particularly rigorous brand of Protestant faith.

As discussed above it is misleading to speak of Enlightenment thought as a homogenous mass for there were many discords even within the Scottish Enlightenment such as those between David Hume and Thomas Reid. Post-structuralists are often particularly guilty of figuring the Enlightenment in overly simplistic terms, ironing out the debates within in it in order to construct a 'bad other' against which they can formulate their own theories of knowledge and language. Nevertheless, in spite of the pitfalls implicit in referring to the Enlightenment in this way, there are clearly basic tenets of it which can be identified, and which appear to be figured in the ways by which both the legal system and David Deans's religious codes are presented to the reader of *The Heart of Mid-Lothian*, since both proceed by the formulation of logic, reason, and the search for epistemological certainty.

In its most fundamental formulations the Enlightenment can perhaps be summarised in Kant's phrase, 'have courage to use your own reason'.[12] By this formulation the individual is thrown back upon his or her own powers of logic and understanding in order to evaluate the primary concerns of the Enlightenment: the nature of the rational individual, and the location of the self within society. In Scotland those central tenets were both inscribed within its institutions – the Law and the Church – and had arisen from their philosophical assumptions. The law was codified early in Scotland by the work of Stair and Mackenzie, two writers to whom Scott frequently refers, and the founding principles of this system, in which Scott himself had been educated, lay in the rational observation of human nature and in a scrutiny of the law as it was codified in the legal system with almost scientific rigour. Alexander Broadie elaborates:

> By the end of the seventeenth century, students in the Scottish universities were reading Stair and Mackenzie, and were learning from them that, while the tables of the law brought down from Mount Sinai taught us moral principles, those same principles could be learned from an appropriately slanted investigation of nature. Such rational exercises resulted in the body of natural law theory, and that theory, which has great intellectual and moral strength, would in due course play a major role in Scottish Enlightenment legal writings. It should be added that the intellectual and moral strength of Scottish law, as represented especially by the works of Stair and Mackenzie, was no doubt one explanation of the provision for the continued separate identity of Scots law that was written into the 1707 Acts of Union.[13]

Behind this emphasis on rigour and scrutiny lay the assumption that by virtue of sufficient reason and logic the individual might come to an essential understanding of the nature of the workings of the human mind and, by extension, the society within which it is inscribed. It was these principles which were encoded in Scots Law; principles which recognised that the law must rest on an understanding of human nature, but which presupposed that general systems could be extrapolated from such study.

While in the novel David Deans's particular branch of Protestantism (and Scott is careful to avoid defining with which of the multifarious offshoots of the Covenanters he may be aligned) is opposed to the legal system on the basis that it upholds the principles of an 'Erastian Government', the philosophical assumptions which underpin Deans's religious tenets share much in common with the Enlightenment epistemes which shape and codify Scots Law. Berlinische Monatsschrift defines Enlightenment as 'man's release from his self-incurred tutelage'[14] and the principles of the Reformation, with its emphases on the authority of the Bible as the written word of God, on the individual's right to form a personal relationship with God, and on a reasoned freedom from the imposed tutelage of the Roman Catholic Church both enshrined these principles and, with the dissemination of knowledge which followed the Reformation, encouraged such freedom of thought.

In Scotland, these founding principles of Protestantism were taken to the extreme, and much of the nation's history in the seventeenth century – the history which lies behind Deans's tales of his Covenanting boyhood – had been shaped by dissent over the parameters within which the nature of an individual's relationship to God could be defined. The Covenanting Movement had been inspired by the attempt to impose a prayer book modelled on its English counterpart on the Scottish people and by the imposition of a system of patronage within Scottish church government. It is this, of course, which lies behind Deans's scruples in the last volume of the novel and his insistence that the people of Knocktarlitie must choose Butler 'by a real harmonious call'; in other words by the dictates of their own conscience, and without any 'scruples'.

Scott deals more completely with the Covenanting Wars in *The Tale of Old Mortality*, published in 1816, yet while Deans's religion is not the foregrounded subject matter of *The Heart of Mid-Lothian* as the chronicle structure of the text implies it is certainly one of its shaping epistemes, and the extent to which its dictates of reason, logic and personal conscience may offer a valid system in which to locate identity emerges as one of the novel's chief concerns. At the time when Scott was writing the novel he was also building the first phase of his new home at Abbotsford, and while furnishing it he describes among his many other acquisitions 'a pair of thumbikins', the favoured instrument for torturing Covenanters.[15] In a letter to Lady Compton he also states 'I have for my spiritual consolation a Cameronian preacher . . . as mad on the subject of the solemn league and covenant as if one of the Grassmarket martyrs had risen from the dead'.[16] Most significant of all, as already discussed in the introduction to this study, he was simultaneously engaged in reviewing Kirkton's *History of the Church of Scotland*, a task which encouraged him to return to the Covenanting histories which he had read in his youth, so that the text that ensues, is, as the notes to the Edinburgh Edition reveal, a matrix of allusion not only to texts such as Shakespeare's *Measure for Measure* (which acts as a kind of meta-narrative to Effie's and Jeanie's tale) but also to these Covenanting testimonies that represent the strength of religious faith in seventeenth-century Scottish life.[17]

The nature of Covenanting principles, their relationship to Scottish history and society, and their value as a system of moral and ethical codes were therefore profoundly to the forefront of Scott's mind as he wrote this novel. In *The Heart of Mid-Lothian* then, two systems of thought broadly based on Enlightenment premises, Scots Law and David Deans's religion, are offered as possible epistemes within which to locate the individual, and by extension his or her place in society. However, Scott explores the ways in which both these discourses and the philosophical assumptions on which they rest are, ultimately, inadequate as sites in which to locate a construction of the self. Both the legal system in Scotland and the system of Protestant ethics proposed by David have a fundamental contradiction at their centre; as paradigms inherently located in abstraction from the individual's thinking mind they lay an emphasis on a personal construction of conscience and identity, such as David promotes when he urges his daughter to make up her own mind over the thorny question of whether to testify in court. However, as systems designed in order to inscribe power within a nation, their inevitable codifications overrule individual human nature in order to abstract a general principle. Although the Enlightenment principles of reason, rigour and human understanding might have much to offer therefore (and it is clear that Scott held such principles in the deepest respect) codification of such systems into a general principle for society is inherently problematic. It is this contradiction which was at the centre of Scottish church history (and must have been very clear to

Scott as he read Kirkton) for while the Reformation may have had as its founding principle the individual's relationship with God, the organisation of such principles into a national church must lead inevitably, as indeed it did and does in Scotland, to a series of schisms as the general formulation of church rule collides repeatedly with a series of individual consciences. It is this dilemma which is repeatedly dramatised in the details of Covenanting dispute in the novel, and which lies behind Baillie Middleburgh's dry description of David as a '*Deanite*' since his own particular blend of Protestant ethics seems to belong to no-one but himself (p. 176).

This paradox is also at the heart of Scots Law as it is dramatised in the novel and is the underlying principle behind the Porteous riots, which exemplify precisely the tensions between the inscribed legal system, and the rights of individuals to exercise their own moral conscience by taking the law into their own hands. Such questions were of course pertinent in the first quarter of the nineteenth century, for the French revolution had on one level at least been an enactment of the principle of the rights of the individual, while riots and calls for reform within Britain exemplified a similar dichotomy between self and state. They were also at the heart of much Enlightenment writing which, in Scotland at least, was fundamentally concerned with the relationship of the individual to civic society. Whatever Scott as a man may have felt about these political developments – and there is plenty of well documented evidence to suggest that he was opposed to them – as a fiction *The Heart of Mid-Lothian* shows considerable sympathy towards the Porteous mob. Tony Inglis comments that he finds this impulse in the novel disconcerting, suggesting, rightly, that 'the narrative voice of the novel, on some level, *approves*, in a way strangely at odds with Scott's personal humanity, his public position and his known political attitudes'.[18] An explanation for this, however, may be found if we recognise that what is being explored via the Porteous mob is precisely a tension between the needs of individual identity and those of generalised, societal systems. It is this, perhaps, which prompts Scott's deviations from history in his description of the murder of Porteous, for he is anxious to suggest that the mob behave according to an act of principle, if not by the letter of the law. Attempts to murder Porteous as he is dragged from his hiding place in the chimney are quickly halted by Robertson on the basis that to kill Porteous in this way would simply be murder; an act of violence rather than an acting out of the law on the basis of personal conscience:

"Are ye mad?" he said, "or would ye execute an act of justice as if it were a crime and a cruelty?—this sacrifice will lose half its savour if we do not offer it at the very horns of the altar. We will have him die where a murderer should die, on the common gibbet—we will have him die where he spilled the blood of so many innocents!" (p. 58)

It is this emphasis on the tensions between the letter of the law and its spirit, between the individual conscience and the codified principle which links the Porteous riots to the main subject matter of the novel, the trial and condemnation of Effie Deans, thereby implying a critique of Enlightenment epistemic certainty and the discourses that it generates at the very heart of the narrative.

The plight of Effie Deans as it is presented in *The Heart of Mid-Lothian* similarly exemplifies the inadequacy of the legal system to deal with the needs of the individual. It is again his concern with this dichotomy which leads Scott to deviate from his historical sources, for while the real Tibby Walker *did* drown her child in the Cluden, Effie Deans has *not* murdered her child. This portrayal of Effie moves the focus of the novel away from the moral rights and wrongs of the situation, towards a focus on the plight of the individual who cannot prove herself innocent within the terms by which the law is constructed. While the law has been extrapolated from observation of the Scots peasantry – the tendency for Puritan women to murder their bastard bairns as the King's Counsel puts it – as part of a codified system it is inadequate for dealing with Effie's particular case. The judge reminds both the jury and the reader that "'he and the jurors were sworn to judge according to the laws as they stood, not to criticise, or to evade, or even to justify them'". And he states: "'For himself, he sincerely grieved to say, that a shadow of doubt remained not upon his mind concerning the verdict which the inquest had to bring in'" (p. 214). Effie's trial, then, is a dramatisation of the inadequacy of this particular law, but also of the legal system *in general* for dealing with human nature. Within its rigid epistemes of 'guilty' and 'not guilty' Effie's idiosyncratic situation seems to lead inevitably to her condemnation and death; ultimately a negation of her identity.

A similar critique of the inadequacies of epistemic systems for dealing with the complexities of individual experience is also dramatised in David Deans's responses to his daughter's plight. In his review of Kirkton's *Church History* Scott writes of the Covenanting leaders:

But in the imperfect state of humanity, even virtues carried to extremity run into error and indeed into vice. Conscious rectitude of intention hurried these eminent men (for many of them deserved that name) into the extremes of spiritual pride and intolerance; and what they esteemed the indubitable truth of their cause made them too anxious to enforce their tenets to hesitate about the means of accomplishing an event so desirable. Their friends were the friends, their opponents were the enemies of heaven; it was scarcely possible to do too much in behalf of the one or for the suppression of the other.[19]

It is an attitude similar to this which Scott describes in his depiction of David's response to Effie's misdemeanours. David's moral codes may seem at first ludicrous, even faintly humorous, as when, for example overhearing his daughters mention the word 'dance' he responds:

"And now, if I hear ye, quean lassies, sae muckle as name dancing, or think there's sic a thing in this warld as flinging to fiddler's sounds and piper's springs, as sure as my father's spirit is with the just, ye shall be no more either charge or concern of mine!" (p. 88)

David's claim that his daughters will be disowned simply for mentioning the word 'dance' seems faintly absurd to our modern ears, but the full implications of this moral code are enacted when David hears of Effie's pregnancy. His response is that Effie must be denied life:

"Where is she, that has no place among us, but has come foul with her sins, like the Evil One, among the children of God?—Where is she, Jeanie?—Bring her before me, that I may kill her wi' a word and a look." (p. 94)

For David, no matter how much it must cost him in terms of personal pain, the price that Effie must pay for her behaviour can only be (as it is for the law) death; the only categories which can exist within his religious system are the friends of heaven and its enemies (and many Covenanting disputes were grounded in a reasoned scrutiny of how a 'saint' could be defined), and within such an episteme Effie's fall from grace must lead inevitably to her exclusion. As David explains to Mr Middleburgh "'when she became a child of Belial, and a company-keeper, and a traitor in guilt and iniquity, she ceased to be bairn of mine.'" (p. 174) This response reinforces the fact that the price Effie must pay for her misdemeanours, if judged within Deans's religious system is, just as when she is judged by the law, denial of identity; negation.

If read in this way *The Heart of Mid-Lothian* and the portrayal of Effie's plight within it emerges as an enactment of the inadequacy of generalised epistemes as models within which to posit individual experience, for within them, the novel suggests, individuals such as Effie must be excluded, condemned to death. This dilemma between the needs of the individual and those of society is one which the twentieth century inherited from the Enlightenment and it is a problem upon which Scott elaborates in *The Heart of Mid-Lothian*, suggesting that it rests not only on the clash between personal identity and society, but on far more fundamental concerns within Enlightenment thought. In *The Post-Modern Condition* Jean-François Lyotard famously explores the paradoxes of our Enlightenment inheritance. 'The nineteenth and twentieth centuries have given us as much terror as we can take' he argues. 'We have paid a high enough price for the nostalgia of the whole and the one, for the reconciliation of the concept and the sensible, for the transparent and the communicable experience'.[20] Lyotard's comments are of course made in the context of a wider postmodern debate and in the light of the apparent collapse of what he calls the 'grand-narratives' of Enlightenment thought in post-war western society. Nevertheless, his discussion posits dilemmas inherent in all totalising systems, and is part of a broader critique by which postmodern, post-structural and post-colonial theories have called into question the philosophical assumptions of Enlightenment thought.

Post-structuralism's argument with Enlightenment discourse obviously runs far deeper than the conflict between individual and society enacted in the circumstances of Effie's trial. Its critiques reveal deconstructing flaws not only in general principles of Enlightenment models as structures of societal organisation, but suggest that they are flawed in their very conception, in the very models of knowledge, of the knowable, which they formulate. Post-structuralism suggests that the Enlightenment project is intrinsically teleological, having, in other words, at its centre a search for the ultimate referent, an epistemological end-point as it seeks to locate by reason, rigour and scrutiny the limits of knowledge concerning the human mind, the natural world and society. Thinkers such as Derrida, however, propose that such a project is inherently mis-founded since all discourse (including that of Enlightenment thought, and of course, that of post-structuralism) is located within the closed system of language. While Thomas Reid may have argued, as Broadie puts it, 'that nothing more clearly demonstrates our belief system than the structure of our language', post-structuralism proposes (as several Enlightenment commentators on language already discussed, including Hume, foresaw) that all the structures of our language can tell us are the parameters of themselves.[21] While epistemes such as Law, Religion, Enlightenment and even Society may behave as if they move increasingly towards a point of ultimate knowledge this is futile, since all 'knowledge' is figured only within language itself; a 'language' which does not reflect an external referent – the end point of enquiry – but is in fact inescapably reflexive. In their desire for ultimate knowledge, however, all grand narratives have inscribed within them an essentially teleological impulse, an impulse towards closure; what Lyotard defines as 'terror', and what Heidegger recognises as 'the essential relation between language and death'.[22]

All this may seem somewhat removed from *The Heart of Mid-Lothian*. Yet if we accept it as a model of post-structuralism's argument with the Enlightenment project it may serve as a useful paradigm in which to discuss Scott's broader critique of language systems in this novel, and offer a way to approach the increasing preoccupation with language which we have identified in Jeanie's letters and which becomes ever more apparent in his fiction. Jeanie's letters aside, linguistic preoccupations are featured early in this novel. The Introductory Chapter is shaped around a word-game, the puns which can be played upon the name 'heart of Mid-Lothian'. Here too, the whole novel is figured as a linguistic trope as a 'Last Confessions and Dying Words' for the Tolbooth. A reflexive awareness of language also haunts the novel's early conversations; Mr Saddletree for example has 'a considerable gift of words which he mistook for eloquence' while he and Butler are described walking down the High Street 'each talking as he could get a word thrust in, the one on the laws of Scotland, the other on those of syntax, and neither listening to a word which his companion uttered' (p. 41). What is significant about these repeated references to language and communication, however, is that they alert the reader to the fact that the novel is concerned not only with the inadequacies of Enlightenment epistemes as organisational principles, but also with a critique of the models of language on which they apparently rest.

This claim may be supported if we return to Effie's plight, to the nature of her trial, her father's responses to it, and the models of language which are explored within these situations. James Kerr recognises the significance of models of language within this novel and argues:

> Jeanie refuses to use language to conceal the truth as she knows it . . . Jeanie's adherence to truth is grounded in a radically representational notion of how language ought to be used, based on the assumption that there can be a

genuine correspondence between word and world, language and reality. In the courtroom, Jeanie will not declare that an event occurred that did not, in simple fact, take place. From her perspective, Staunton's desperate pleas that she dissemble in order to save her sister bespeak a moral degeneracy. But Staunton's entreaties, along with the advice of Effie's lawyers at the trial, imply that language is the vehicle of moral and political intentions, and not simply a medium for stating things as they are.[23]

Kerr's interpretation of the significance of language in the novel is revealing, but it is only partly appropriate as a way of exploring Jeanie's motives. The Adamic model of language that he outlines, however, tells us much more about the models of discourse on which David Deans has founded his moral and religious epistemes. A fundamental principle of Protestant (and in particular of Covenanting) faith lay in the importance of the word, in the significance of a metonymic model of Biblical language within which the word of God is taken in its literal sense as it is given to us in the Scriptures. It is this concept of Biblical language which lies behind the Covenanting outrage at the Book of Common Prayer, at Jeanie's suspicion of the elder Mr Staunton when he reads his sermon, and which underlines David's frequent sarcasms when Butler uses Latin versions of the Scriptures. This literal, representational model of language, a model which seeks to reconcile, as Lyotard puts it, 'the whole and the one' is demonstrated when Mr Saddletree suggests a list of advocates whom David might employ:

> "Weel, weel, but somebody ye maun hae—Kittlepunt?"
> "He's an Arminian."
> "Woodsetter?"
> "He's, I doubt, a Cocceian."
> "Auld Whulliewhaw?"
> "He's ony thing ye like."
> "Young Næmmo?"
> "He's naething at a'."
> "Ye're ill to please, neighbour," said Saddletree; "I hae run ower the pick o' them for you, ye maun e'en choose for yersell; but bethink ye that in the multitude of counsellors there's safety.—What say ye to try young Mackenyie? he has a' his uncle's practices at the tongue's end."
> "What, sir, wad ye speak to me," exclaimed the sturdy presbyterian in excessive wrath, "about a man that has the blood o' the saints at his fingers' end? Didna his eme die and gang to his place wi' the name of the Bluidy Mackenyie? and winna he be kenned by that name sae lang as there's a Scots tongue to speak the word?" (p. 113)

This conversation is a mark of David's stubbornness, but it also enacts a process of Nominalist naming and categorisation, the 'radically representational' model of language which Kerr identifies, a precise correlation between 'word' and 'thing', advocate and heresy. It is a model of language which, in post-structuralist terms, allows no room for the spaces between language, the slippages, elisions and deferrals by which discourse operates, but which, on the contrary suggests that by language the world may be definitively categorised. What it neatly exemplifies is the essentially teleological impulse in David's discourse as it attempts to close the world down into epistemic certainty. It is not surprising that Saddletree should reply in exasperation, '"Hout tout, neighbour, ye maunna take the warld at its word, . . . the very de'il is no sae ill as he's ca'd."' (p. 112). His words are revealing, for they suggest that such a model of language as that which David employs offers no means to proceed. In terms of Effie's situation this is literally the case, for if her father will not employ what Middleburgh calls 'human means' she will, by default, be condemned to death. Earlier, David has stated that he will kill her with a *word*, and here it is implied that it is precisely his model of language, and the view of the world built upon it, which leaves no room for Effie's salvation.

This understanding of Effie's situation is also one implied by her relationship to the legal system, her trial, and the nature of her condemnation. David's interpretation of the relationship between word and world is of course extreme but there is an extent to which it simply dramatises a teleological impulse within all epistemes. The connections between language and the parameters of Effie's crime are outlined from the outset, for as Mrs Saddletree explains the nature of Effie's situation to Butler she adds, '"But we a' think her sister maun be able to speak something to clear her"' (p. 45) and as if to reinforce the ability of language to cause either physical harm or good she almost immediately turns to her orphan shop-boy and states '"and what are ye maundering and greeting for, as if a word was breaking your banes"' (p. 46). Language is thus positioned as both a force for salvation, and a tool of destruction.

Such throwaway comments on the connections between Effie's situation and language become more pertinent when we recall that the crime for which Effie stands committed is itself one which has been created out of language; out of the very logic and rhetoric which lies behind Scots Law. '"The case of Effie (or Euphemia) Deans,"' Saddletree explains, '"is one of those cases of murder presumptive, that is, a murder of the law's construing or construction . . . the crime is rather a favourite of the law"' he elaborates, "'this species of murther being one of its ain creation"' (pp. 46–7). The crime for which Effie must stand trial, consequently, is one constructed out of language itself, one from which the law *construes* a dead child from the nature of its mother's circumstances. Such a crime is surely one of the law gone mad, for as Mrs Saddletree argues "'so that . . . she'll be hanged by the neck, if the bairn was still-born, or if it be alive at this moment?"' (p. 47). This is reason taken to its terrible, logical extreme, but it is also an illustration of the end-game of all teleological discourse; death as a quite literal construction of language.[24]

Effie's condemnation, however, rests not only on the nature of the law itself but also on the fact of her own refusal to communicate something of her situation, to speak, in other words, in her own defence. It also rests, more famously, on the refusal of Jeanie to perjure herself by testifying in her sister's favour, and any critical framework for reading *The Heart of Mid-Lothian* must find a way to account for these circumstances. Post-structuralism suggests that all grand narratives, all teleological discourses, seek to silence those forces which serve to deconstruct their own totality, to disrupt their impulse towards closure. Thus, argues Derrida, discourse seeks to paper over the ruptures, slippages and deferrals, the traces with which it is haunted, in order to shore up its homogeneity; seeks, in other words, to silence the voices at play within it which deconstruct the myth of its own totality. It is tempting to read the silence of Effie and Jeanie Deans in these terms, for Hélène Cixous argues that it is precisely voices such as theirs – the feminine, the emotional, the marginal – which are silenced by the teleological impulses of white Enlightenment male epistemes. This argument can only be taken so far as a reading of *The Heart of Mid-Lothian*, however, for it is only partly true that Effie and Jeanie are silenced *by* the patriarchal system – both in fact are encouraged to speak. A more apt description of their situation is that finding themselves locked within a totalising episteme, both *choose* not to speak and their decision to remain silent demonstrates a more fundamental problem in the relationship between discourse and articulation at work in this novel.

This philosophical impasse can be exemplified by looking in more detail at the nature of both Effie's and Jeanie's silence. Effie has failed to communicate her situation to both her employers and her family – the fact on which the prosecution rests – and refuses to name those individuals who have been told of her pregnancy:

"Interrogated, why she does not now communicate these particulars, which might, perhaps, enable the magistrate to ascertain whether the child is living or dead . . . declares, in general, that she is wearied, and will answer no more questions at this time." (pp. 206–7)

The reasons for Effie's silence, of course, lie in the fact that by naming the father of her child she will condemn her lover George Robertson, who must then be apprehended in order to prove her innocence. Effie consequently is powerless, for she must condemn either her lover by articulation, or herself by her silence. Effie's double bind is one re-enacted in Jeanie's situation. Many modern critics have questioned Jeanie's decision not to testify in her sister's favour stating that it is hard for our modern sensibilities to empathise with her dilemma. This is a tension inscribed within the novel itself, for both Staunton and Ratcliffe urge Jeanie to speak out stating "'it's d—d hard, that when three words of your mouth would give the girl the chance to nick Moll Blood, that you mak such scrupling about rapping to them'" (p. 189). Critics such as James Kerr justify Jeanie's decision by seeing it as part of a wider adherence to literal truth, to what Scott himself describes as a 'Quaker-like' honesty. Yet again, however, this reading of Jeanie can only take us so far, since Jeanie is not always as rigorously honest as she may claim; she is, after all, selective in what she chooses to tell Reuben and her father, and is not afraid of a white lie to get out of an awkward situation – to shake off the laird's attentions, for example. This is significant, for it reminds us that it is the semiotics of a lie under oath which is the issue here, the fact that as Jeanie recognises "'I shall be man-sworn in the very thing in which my testimony is wanted'" (p. 141).

The importance of this of course is that a lie under oath is, unlike other lies which inhabit a more quotidian reality, one before God, a fact reiterated as Jeanie steps into the witness box. The implications of such a lie, especially within Jeanie's religious framework, would be the death of her eternal soul. "'But that word is a grievous sin, and it's a deeper offence when it's a sin wilfully and presumptuously committed,'" she tells Effie, outlining the parameters in which her dilemma is framed (p. 189). "'O father'", she tells David, "'we are cruelly sted between God's laws and man's laws—What will we do?—What will we do?'" (p. 180). Jeanie's dilemma, like Effie's, is a mortal one, for however she speaks the result must be death, the death of Effie, or the death of her own immortal soul. Like Effie, the only response available to her is to say nothing, to repeat Effie's lack of communication, "'Alack! alack! she never breathed word to me'" (p. 211).

Both Jeanie's and Effie's lack of language, their silence, rests on an awareness that however they speak, the consequence remains the same: the death, one way or another, of an individual. Their dilemma re-enacts a philosophical problem recognised by post-structuralist theories, for as Julia Kristeva has argued, if all language, all articulation is located within what she calls the 'symbolic order', the domain of the dominant episteme, no act of utterance can take place which does not collude with it. For many feminist theorists this impasse has been a matter of debate, raising the question of how feminism may use the language of patriarchy to attack its systems. The dilemma for Effie and Jeanie is not dissimilar, for both recognise that once locked into the legal system, 'man-sworn' within it, any act of utterance will lead inevitably to death. This dynamic at the centre of *The Heart of Mid-Lothian* reveals surprisingly contemporary concerns and signals an increasing concern with the nature of language and the problems inherent in it in Scott's fiction. The novel enacts not only the inadequacies of Enlightenment models as discourses by which to organise society and locate the individual, but also the paradoxes within the philosophical and linguistic assumptions upon which these epistemes rest. Within the narrative such epistemes emerge as sites where there is no room for identity to be located, for life to flourish, since the teleological impulses within them seemingly lead inevitably towards closure, to an end-point of death.

However, as already stated there are many forms of discourse at play within *The Heart of Mid-Lothian* and the novel also offers an exploration of whether any of these may offer an alternative to the prison-house of language figured within patriarchal, Enlightenment epistemes. Romanticism is frequently posited as the natural counterpoint to the discourses apparently endorsed by the Enlightenment since its privileging of imagination, organic creation and emotion offers an alternative to the Enlightenment's emphasis on reason, logic, and the drive towards teleological closure. Scott's relationship with Romanticism is, however, problematic, for while J. R. Watson may argue that the 'Romantic movement began with the French Revolution and ended in 1832 with the death of Sir Walter Scott',[25] many see in his work a renunciation of emotion, imagination, and Romanticism itself in favour of pragmatism, progress and what Lukács has famously called the 'middle way'; a trajectory grounded in the Enlightenment faith in progress and stadial development.[26] However, there is clearly a sense in which in *The Heart of*

*Mid-Lothian* Scott is also exploring the extent to which the Romantic discourse which he favours in a poem such as *Marmion*, for example, may offer a location in which to situate the self and for 'life' to flourish in the discursively vexed world of this text.

In *The Heart of Mid-Lothian* Romantic discourse is figured, as in so much of Scott's fiction, in those characters at the peripheries of the novel, and correspondingly at the periphery of society; those characters, like the gypsies in *Guy Mannnering*, seemingly cast out from the Enlightenment ideal state, excluded from its paradigm of the knowable – or at least only allowed a very tenuous foothold in it. Similarly, the Romantic interludes in his fiction are frequently situated in aspects of narrative outside of the dominant discourse of Enlightenment experience in songs, ballads or broadsheets, within tales embedded within the main structure, or, as here, in Jeanie's disruptive letters. Such narrative modulations offer sites where that which is in *excess* of the totalising impulses within language may gain a hold.

The notion of such Romantic discourses as an alternative to the end-game of teleological rationalist thought is initially appealing. Harold Bloom's claim that 'the whole enterprise of Romanticism . . . was to show the power of the mind over a universe of death'[27] is highly suggestive in the context of the present discussion. As we have seen, several readings of *The Lay of the Last Minstrel* imply such an enterprise in the poem where imagination, and the acts of both creation and recitation (or annunciation) are presented as processes of rejuvenation, apparently saving both the minstrel himself from a fast approaching death and the Buccleuch family from oblivion. Moreover, for many post-structuralist commentators Romantic discourses, with their emphases on imagination, boundaries and liminal aspects of experience offer prime examples of the ways in which epistemic models of discourse begin to unravel and disintegrate, giving a glimpse 'through' to those arenas of experience 'beyond' or 'behind' teleological discourse; arenas which Julia Kristeva has loosely described as the 'semiotic'.

The trappings of Romanticism include, of course, wayward sons, disguises, madwomen, lost children, dangerous lovers and illicit relationships – people and actions at the very boundaries of society, contained within it but peering over its edges towards either an abyss or an illuminating universe beyond. Madge and her mother Meg (the hag and the madwoman) are in many ways archetypal Romantic figures, as is implied by Scott's description of Madge deep in the woodland, weeping over the grave of her own dead child in a clearing 'such as the poet of

Grasmere has described' (p. 273). As such, Madge, as we might expect, seemingly offers access into an alternative form of discourse from that posited by Enlightenment epistemes, offering glimpses into an alternative construction of reality where knowledge and identity potentially may be more meaningfully, or richly, located.

This alternative model of knowledge is suggested by the following scene. Robertson, if we recall, borrows Madge's clothes, and indeed her identity (thus de-stabilised as a commodity) to lead the Porteous Riots. As a result, Madge is called before the magistrates the next day in order that they might ascertain her role in the murder. Sharpitlaw – who as his name implies is a fit representative for the rational legal system – attempts to gain evidence from Madge by speaking to her in 'a coaxing manner' (p. 150). He can, however, make nothing of her, and Ratcliffe, who has of course himself lived life on its margins, intervenes to comment:

> "She is ower far past reasonable folk's motives, sir," said Ratcliffe, "to mind siller, or John Dalgleish, or the cat and nine tails either; but I think I could gar her tell us something." (p. 150)

Ratcliffe's comments are revealing, for they demonstrate the fact that Madge is operating within a different discursive mode from Sharpitlaw, and that it is a discourse which, in spite of the apparent ramblings of her mind, may offer some access to knowledge if one can operate within its systems. Rat, consequently, by entering into Madge's reality, Madge's form of discourse, learns that George Robertson has indeed borrowed her clothes to take part in the riots. It is only when the procurator again intervenes, that the clash of competing discourses reduces Madge to silence:

> "And whare did he change his clothes again, hinnie?" said Sharpitlaw, in his most conciliatory manner.
> "The procurator's spoiled a'," observed Ratcliffe, drily.
> And it was even so; for the question, put in so direct a shape, immediately awakened Madge to the propriety of being reserved upon those very topics on which Ratcliffe had indirectly seduced her to become communicative. (p. 151)

This exchange is interestingly paralleled when Sharpitlaw attempts to interview Effie – temporarily deranged by grief – and later as Jeanie attempts to gain information about Effie's child by letting Madge ramble on in her story.

Such moments suggests that Madge may offer access to an alternative kind of language, an alternative form of discourse which may contain knowledge if only we can gain access to it. This is emphasised by the metaphors which Scott uses to describe the workings of her brain, like 'a quantity of dry leaves . . . put in motion by the first casual breath of air' (p. 151) or 'like a raft upon a lake . . . agitated and driven about at random by each fresh impulse' (p. 280) and by the way in which she enacts an altogether different model of language from that adopted by David Deans. While David argues identity out of existence by his 'naming of names' Madge informs Jeanie "'never ask folk's names, Jeanie – it's no civil'":

> "—I hae seen half a dozen o' folk in my mother's at anes, and ne'er ane o' them ca'd the ither by his name; and Daddie Ratton says, it is the maist uncivil thing may be, because these baillie bodies are aye asking fashious questions, whan ye saw sic a man, or sic a man; and if ye dinna ken their names, ye ken there can be nae mair about it."
>
> In what strange school, thought Jeanie to herself, has this poor creature been bred up, where such remote precautions are taken against the pursuits of justice? (p. 276)

Madge, then, operates within a model of language apparently diametrically opposed to David's, a kind of free play which, like the wanderings of her mind, has cut free all connection between word and object, name and identity; a model which Wittgenstein recognises as intrinsic to all language 'games' where '[l]anguage is a labyrinth of paths. You approach from *one* side and know your way about; you approach the same place from another side and no longer know your way about'.[28] While, moreover, David's linguistic model may leave no room for life to flourish, Madge's seems to contain somewhere within it the information which Jeanie requires in order to save her sister's life. This is enacted in the number of times that Madge comes close to telling Jeanie the fate of Effie's child, almost revealing it at the side of her own child's grave, and again just before her own death:

> "Oh Jeanie Deans—Jeanie Deans!" exclaimed the poor maniac, "save my mother, and I will take ye to the Interpreter's house again—and I will teach ye a' my bonnie sangs,—and I will tell ye what came o' the"— The rest of her entreaties were drowned in the shouts of the rabble. (p. 363)

Moreover, if Madge fails ever to actually communicate her secret to Jeanie, it is nevertheless, via very unusual means that the secrets of identity are revealed in this text. Effie's lost child, after all, is eventually found via a broadside recounting the 'Last Speech . . . of Margaret Murdockson'. This strange text, which again breaks free from the Enlightenment constraints of the main narrative, holds the secret of the fate of Effie's and Staunton's child. It comes to Jeanie, notably, wrapped around a 'muckle cheese', a reminder that the semiotic is always present in the quotidian, ready to erupt through it with alternative forms of discourse, alternative forms of 'knowledge' (p. 431).

There is a degree, then, to which the novel seems to suggest that Romantic discourses may offer aspects of knowledge, insights into the location of identity, which are denied the more dominant Enlightenment epistemes, serving as a model of disruption to their totalising impulses, and giving access to the semiotic, a site where the secrets of identity may be posited outwith or beyond language. However, elsewhere we have seen that the Author of Waverley has reservations about the Romantic episteme as an *ultimate* location for identity, and here too, the degree to which Romantic discourse is finally satisfactory is called into question.

This is, of course, inscribed within Madge's own fate, for while the free play of language within which she operates may provide glimpses of knowledge beyond the teleological and rational, the novel suggests that such a model cannot provide any compellingly consistent site in which to locate identity. The cost for Madge of such free play is, ultimately, a complete loss of self; '"God help me, I forget my very name in this confused waste"' (p. 286) she poignantly tells Jeanie, and this loss of identity, a total failure of language to find any mode of meaning, ultimately leads to her death. The dark side of Madge's 'semiotic' discourse, the novel suggests, lies in the fact that it is always on the brink of slipping into non-communication, into a silence as fraught with death as Effie's and Jeanie's. This is what is re-enacted on Madge's death bed where her songs offer a poignant lament on her own tragedy but 'died away with the last notes' (p. 366), offering Jeanie no information, no key by which her sister might be saved. Like Madge's words 'drowned by the rabble' this is a slippage into the semiotic beyond the site of communication, beyond the point where it can offer any means to proceed.[29]

Judith Wilt recognises that Madge Wildfire is a kind of dark sister to Effie.[30] Madge's slipping into silence and death, consequently, suggests the limitations of Romanticism as a discourse in which Effie might find the means of life, a location for identity. This is a limitation also enacted in Effie's own fate and her relationship with Staunton. Effie's relationship with Staunton, her lost child, and her elopement all seem to follow a Romantic trajectory. Staunton's urging Jeanie to testify for Effie in court is also in keeping with an essentially Romantic impulse, since he urges her to use her imagination, rather than her reason, in order that justice may be served. '"You *must* remember that she told you all this, whether she ever said a syllable of it or no. You must repeat this tale, in which there is no falsehood, except in so far as it was not told to you before these Justices"', he tells Jeanie (p. 141). Jeanie, however, refuses to comply, and saves Effie by other means. Yet Staunton persists in offering Effie his own particularly Romantic form of salvation, offering her, by her elopement, a transformation into the beautiful heroine which Romantic discourse would have her be. While George's rescue of Effie after her pardon may be seen as a triumph of Romantic imagination over and above the draconian Puritanism of her father, and the model of language on which it rests ('"her father had put her in mind of her transgression"', Effie tells Butler) there are clearly limitations to what this can ultimately offer as a site within which to locate the self (p. 392). Effie's transfiguration has, after all, already been mirrored in the grotesque transfiguration of Madge outside Staunton senior's church, where Madge 'began to bedizen and trick herself out with shreds and remnants of beggarly finery' and which 'made her appearance ten times more fantastic and apish than it had been before' (p. 280). Madge's transfiguration, here, however, is a form of madness, and serves as a prelude to her death at the hands of the rabble.

Not surprisingly then, the identity which George Staunton can offer Effie can only ever be a hollow one. '"I am a Lie of fifteen years' standing"' (p. 439) she tells her sister (emended from the much weaker 'liar' by the Edinburgh Edition), and her life with Staunton is spent in fear that her 'real' identity (as daughter of a Cameronian cow-feeder) will be revealed. Staunton, similarly, may have taken the reverse journey towards his 'real' identity as Lord Staunton of Willoughby, but the Romantic excesses of his youth have left him haunted by the traces of those imaginative others which he has figured for himself, and which lurk behind him to destroy any sense of self. The fates of Effie and Staunton suggest that the Romantic 'imagining' of identity via an alternative, 'metaphorical' form of discourse offers only a partly adequate site for its location, for just as the rationality of Enlightenment thought may lead to a form of falsification it is easy for imagination to spill over into 'lie', to re-invent itself to the point of identity's nothingness, its negation.

In *The Heart of Mid-Lothian* Scott suggests, then, that neither Enlightenment nor Romantic epistemes can offer in themselves an adequate location for personal identity, thus re-enacting the tension between radical referentiality (the fixed system) and free-play which lies at the heart of both Enlightenment debates on language and their twentieth-century counterparts. While such conclusions may be prefigured in his earlier work in this novel he moves towards an increasing suggestion that this inadequacy lies not only in finding the 'right' form of words in which to express stories of personal and national identity, but in the philosophical and linguistic assumptions on which all discourse rests. While the teleological impulses within Enlightenment models lead inevitably to a silencing of identity, its negation, the attempt to position the self outside its discourse – beyond the symbolic order – also slips inevitably towards non-communication, silence, a negation of meaningful identity.

Yet in *The Heart of Mid-Lothian* Scott is not quite ready to give up on his quest to find a form of words in which identity might be articulated and the self (and the national story which it may represent) communicated. Still searching for a form of discourse which may circumvent the double bind of language which apparently defeats the novelist, in the second half of *The Heart of Mid-Lothian* Scott explores whether it is possible to proceed in a world where the only models of language available appear to be the Nominalist epistemic certainty which leads to death or a labyrinthian 'confused waste' where communication disintegrates. It is this exploration that is encapsulated in Jeanie's walk to London and her interview with Caroline.

Early in the novel Mr Middleburgh tells David Deans: "'if you would save your daughter's life, you must use human means'" (p. 175). It is unclear, however, what these human means might be, for acting within the parameters of the legal system Jeanie can see no way to help her sister. The suggestion is, of course, that, in spite of its limitations, it must be by language that Effie will be saved, for Mrs Saddletree has pointed out that Jeanie might "'speak something to clear her'" and Effie herself, condemned by Jeanie's silence in court, laments, "'What signifies coming to greet ower me . . . when you have killed me?—killed me, when a word of your mouth would have saved me'" (p. 224). This is clearly problematic, however, since it is by language that Effie has been in the first place condemned, and it is, similarly, a realisation that language can do nothing but harm that has reduced both sisters to silence in court. The problem inherent in this novel then, is one of how Jeanie may use language to save her sister, while avoiding it own destructive, teleological impulses. Caught in this prison-house of language, can Jeanie yet find a way to release Effie?

This dilemma is precisely what is explored in *The Heart of Mid-Lothian*, for Effie's trial may be read as the moment when for Jeanie 'language invades the universal problematic'; the moment when she recognises that her father's Adamic model of discourse is insufficient as a way of saving her sister. Her journey to London, consequently, may be read as a quest for a means of employing language that moves beyond referentiality and that allows, somehow, for negotiations and re-negotiations of identity to exist within its systems. This reading of the novel may be supported if we recognise that while the novel is no straightforward developmental fiction a degree of self-discovery is encapsulated within it but that it is one that takes the form of a recognition of the irreducible complexities of locating the self within discourse and of the ways in which language operates. In these terms James Kerr's assessment of Jeanie's 'radically representational notion of how language may be used' is mistaken because it implies that Jeanie's character is static; while it may describe Jeanie at the outset of the novel a recognition of the inadequacy of such a model of discourse is precisely what is encapsulated in Jeanie's journey. Simple though it may be, this is what is implied by Jeanie's change of dress. Setting out in her plaid and bare footed, Jeanie soon learns that this is not an appropriate way to behave south of the border:

> Hitherto she had been either among her own country-folks, or those to whom her bare feet and tartan screen were objects too familiar to attract much attention. But as she advanced, she perceived that both circumstances exposed her to sarcasms and taunts, which she might otherwise have escaped; and, although in her heart she thought it unkind, and unhospitable, to sneer at a passing stranger on account of the fashion of her attire, yet she had the good sense to alter those parts of her dress which attracted ill-natured observation. Her checked screen was deposited carefully in her bundle, and she conformed to the national extravagance of wearing shoes and stockings for the whole day. (p. 249)

Jeanie recognises that it is wise not to be 'kenspeckle' (p. 249). Her good sense also tells her that Argyle will 'warm to the tartan' and she resumes her plaid to visit him (p. 324). This is a political act, just as his own desire that she should visit the Queen wearing her plaid is one of diplomacy. Though this may seem insignificant, it reminds us that Jeanie, in spite of her apparent 'authenticity' of identity, has learnt that identity need not stay fixed, but can be changed to meet the parameters of the given situation.

This minor act of fashion consciousness underlines a greater willingness on Jeanie's part to adapt in order to meet circumstances, and also reflects a linguistic dexterity which Jeanie has learnt along the way. While in the opening scenes of the novel she may claim an absolute adherence to the truth, telling the laird, "'I hae but ae word to bestow on ony ane, and that's aye a true ane'" (p. 238), she learns that 'truth' may be a variable commodity, learns indeed the virtue of the 'white lie', of the nuances and evasions in language by which her journey, and her saving of Effie, might proceed. The greatest marker of the linguistic dexterity that Jeanie has gained, however, comes in her interview with the Queen.

The appearance of Queen Caroline in the novel is an entirely fictional addition to the story of Helen Walker. The Queen was not Regent in April 1737 and Tibby Walker's pardon was orchestrated entirely by the Duke of Argyle without her intervention. Some have read Scott's decision to place Caroline at the centre of the fictional story as a sop to her grandson to gain court favour. 'The queen was fat and dropsical', suggests John Sutherland, and the scene acts as a form of flattery to 'her grandson, Scott's fat and dropsical friend'.[31] However true this may be from a biographical point of view, there are clearly reasons consistent with the impulses of the fiction for including the Queen within it. For one thing, it moves the site of Effie's pardon into the hands of women, keeping alive the play of feminine discourse in the text; significantly, it also allows the Queen the opportunity of alluding to the Porteous Riots, thus also referring to the Scottish questions at work here, as Jeanie pleads the unique circumstances of religion and morality within Scotland which give rise to her sister's situation. The Queen's presence, then, acts as a device by which to reiterate the various discourses which arise early in the novel, reminding us, nearly three volumes later, that these voices are all still at play. The interview, however, also allows the opportunity for Jeanie to plead her sister's case for herself, thus offering a mirror image of Effie's trial, and her refusal to testify there in her favour.

As she sets out for London Jeanie tells Reuben that she must plead in person, "'A letter's like the music that the leddies have for their spinets— naething but black scores, compared to the same tune played or sung. It's word of mouth maun do't, or naething, Rueben'" (p. 246). As if to reiterate this distinction, Jeanie suggests to Argyle that it might be better if he write down her cause, in order that she might memorise it, and the Duke, an expert diplomat responds, "'that would be like reading a sermon you know, which we good presbyterians think has less unction than when spoken without book'" (p. 329). Such interludes remind us that Jeanie's plea acts as a counterpart to her earlier silence, a marker of the ways in which she has learnt to operate within language, but without entering into its totalising epistemes. The interview consequently is curiously figured as a kind of linguistic game, a play on truth, evasion and meaning that reflects the linguistic punning with which the novel opens. The whole scene is a playing out of linguistic elision, slippage and deferral, from Lady Suffolk's deafness, the advance and retreat of each lady at the unexpected insults, to Jeanie's evasion of questions which might lose her the Queen's favour, and development of those which will have most influence. Jeanie, for example, is happy that the question concerning Porteous is 'so framed that she could . . . answer it in the negative' (p. 340) yet to do so requires a degree of linguistic sophistication which is surely beyond Jeanie at the start of the novel. Jeanie's impassioned plea, "'O, madam, if ever ye kenn'd what it was to sorrow for and with a sinning and a suffering creature'" (p. 340) is far removed from the bleak response in court "'Alack! alack! she never breathed word to me'" (p. 211). The difference is a mark of how far Jeanie has travelled, a mark of her move away from a concept of language which equates word precisely with world, to a recognition of the subtle forces within which it operates, and the fluidity and flexibility with which it must be negotiated. "'This is eloquence'" the Queen responds as she awards Effie's pardon (p. 341).

George Campbell, encapsulating the scepticism towards a merely referential or epistemic view of language we have seen in other of his Enlightenment contemporaries, suggests that 'eloquence' may be defined as 'that art or talent by which the discourse is adapted to its end',[32] recognising it as the ability to use language pragmatically, to adapt it to meet the needs of a given situation; or, as Wittgenstein describes it in *Philosophical Investigations*, the ability to proceed by 'grammar'. It is indeed the skill of eloquence which Jeanie has learnt on her way to London, the discovery that to save her sister there must be times when she is prepared to use language as 'game'. It is after all in such 'eloquence', such flexibility and re-negotiation that life has been seen to flourish in this novel, and while her silence in Edinburgh has caused her sister's condemnation, it is her eloquence in London that wins her pardon.

It is a Jeanie schooled in these lessons that inhabits the last volume of this novel. To the disputes between her father and her husband, we are told, 'Mrs Butler was a mediating spirit, who endeavoured, by the alkaline smoothness of her own disposition, to neutralize the acidity of theological controversy' (p. 414). Jeanie, in other words, has learnt the virtue of diplomacy, knowing that it is thus that life may proceed. It is this same Jeanie who chooses not to tell her husband about the correspondence with her sister, or, for that matter, about her own part in the Whistler's escape. Jeanie may have begun the novel with a 'radically representational' notion of language, but she ends it with a much more sophisticated sense of how it must be negotiated, an instinctive understanding that it is only in the spaces within and between representation – in grammar, syntax or 'eloquence' – that life might flourish.

If Jeanie's interview with the Queen is a mark of how far she has travelled, however, it also offers a suitable metaphor for how far Scott has journeyed in his exploration of the relationship between discourse and meaning by this point in his writing career. While his early work may offer an exploration of the relationship between the form of words and their meanings *The Heart of Mid-Lothian* suggests a darker vision, offering an increasingly complex critique of discourse itself, and a growing realisation that, trapped within language, no form of words can achieve the certainty that he may have strived for in his earlier fiction. It is, surely, this impulse which lies behind the polyphonic nature of the novel, in its modulations of genres, modes and narrative forms; the impulse behind those troublesome letters with which this discussion began. For as a narrative *The Heart of Mid-Lothian* is an enactment of the fact that it is only by keeping voices at play that we may avoid silence, only by maintaining a word game – keeping it up, as Hardie puts it – that identity might survive. Only thus can death – the closure of the system – be avoided. It is this impulse too which surely lies behind the repeated deferral of the novel's closure, moving the reader beyond Effie's pardon, beyond Jeanie's marriage and into the unexpected fourth volume.

However, while this reading of *The Heart of Mid-Lothian* may suggest that in it Scott has found some solution to the problematics inherent in language that his early work identifies it is clear that a tension remains for the description of the novel given above suggests a far more 'easy' conclusion to this fraught text than most readers experience. While some critics have read the closing chapters of the novel as Scott's attempt to provide a comic 'romance' of the Scottish nation the last volume in fact offers a much darker vision, problematising any 'happy ending' for it. While Jeanie's journey may have saved Effie's life it is, as we have already seen, only that she might become 'a Lie of fifteen years standing'. Moreover, the additional volume suggests that Scott, confronted by the implications of his own contemplation on language, is (as he is so often in his work) at a loss as to how to bring this text to any satisfactory conclusion; closure when it comes is, of course, simply a pastiche, a formula which nobody believes in. Similarly, while Jeanie's ability to play the 'language game' in the last volume may allow her to liberate her nephew it is only that he might be sent to yet another kind of wilderness in America; the Whistler's uncertain future is in a labyrinth that may have worrying parallels with the world that Madge inhabits. Consequently, in the novels that were soon to follow The Author of Waverley offers a far darker exploration of the ways in which the nature of language itself operates to preclude telling the story of either personal or national identity, moving into terrain where the unsettling understanding of the limits of language suggested in *The Heart of Mid-Lothian* is played out as the very fabric of his texts.

## Notes

1 Jane Millgate, *Walter Scott: The Making of the Novelist* (Toronto: University of Toronto Press, 1984), p. 153.

2 David Hewitt and Alison Lumsden, 'Historical Note', *The Heart of Mid-Lothian*, p. 596.

3 Jane Millgate, *Walter Scott: The Making of the Novelist*, p. 153.

4 Gifford, Dunnigan and MacGillivray argue that the generic complexity signals Scott's attempt to create 'his most potent symbol for Scottish regeneration'. See *Scottish Literature in English and Scots*, ed. by Douglas Gifford, Sarah Dunnigan and Alan MacGillivray (Edinburgh: Edinburgh University Press, 2002), p. 217.

5 This is signalled by Caroline McCracken-Flesher's comment that the last volume is a kind of fairytale. See 'Narrating the (gendered) Nation in Walter Scott's *The Heart of Midlothian*', *Nineteenth-Century Contexts* 24.3 (2002), pp. 291–316 (p. 306).

6 Jane Millgate, *Walter Scott the Making of the Novelist*, p. 160.

7 Hugh Blair, *Lectures on Rhetoric and Belles Lettres*, pp. 1.7–8.

8 The manuscript of *The Heart of Mid-Lothian* is in the National Library of Scotland, MS 1548. A full account of the changes made to the letters may be found in the emendation list to the Edinburgh Edition.

9  James Kerr, *Fiction against History: Scott as Storyteller* (Cambridge: Cambridge University Press, 1989), p. 64.

10  See Judith Wilt, *Secret Leaves*, pp. 123–6.

11  Caroline McCracken-Flesher, 'A Wo/man for a' that? Subverted Sex and Perverted Politics in *The Heart of Midlothian*' in *Scott in Carnival*, pp. 232–44 (pp. 232 and 233).

12  See Alexander Broadie, 'Introduction: What was the Scottish Enlightenment?' in *The Scottish Enlightenment: An Anthology*, pp. 3–31 (p. 3).

13  Ibid. p. 12.

14  Ibid. p. 3.

15  To William Laidlaw, February 1818, *Letters*, p. 5.73.

16  To Lady Compton, February 1818, *Letters*, p. 5.92.

17  James Kirkton's *The Secret and True History of the Church of Scotland, from the Restoration to 1678*, ed. by C. K. Sharpe (Edinburgh, 1818). For a full account of the ways in which Scott draws on Walker see the notes to the Edinburgh Edition of *The Heart of Mid-Lothian*. As well as *Measure for Measure* several other intertexts operate to generate meaning in this novel. See for example, Alison Lumsden, 'Burns, Scott and Intertextuality' in *The Edinburgh Companion to Robert Burns*, ed. by Gerard Carruthers (Edinburgh: Edinburgh University Press, 2009), pp. 125–36.

18  Tony Inglis, 'Introduction' in Walter Scott, *The Heart of Mid-Lothian*, ed. by Tony Inglis (London: Penguin, 1994), pp. ix–l ( p. xxx).

19  'Kirkton's Church History', *Prose Works*, pp. 19.213–82 (pp. 232–3). This review was first published in the *Quarterly Review* of January 1818.

20  Jean-François Lyotard, *The Postmodern Condition: A Report on Knowledge*, translated by Geoff Bennington and Brian Massumi (Manchester: Manchester University Press, 1984), pp. 81–2.

21  Alexander Broadie, 'Introduction: What was the Scottish Enlightenment?', p. 22.

22  See Jean-François Lyotard, *The Postmodern Condition*, p. 15 and Martin Heidegger, *Being and Time* (1927).

23  James Kerr, *Fiction against History: Scott as Storyteller*, p. 74.

24  The significance of language in the text is noted by Carol Anderson. See 'The Power of Naming: Language, Identity and Betrayal in *The Heart of Midlothian*' in *Scott in Carnival,* pp. 189–201. Reading the novel in feminist terms she notes that 'At the heart of the novel is an association between language and power' (p. 189). More recently it has been commented on by David Hewitt in 'Teaching *The Heart of Mid-Lothian*' in *Approaches to Teaching Scott's Waverley Novels*, pp. 150–6 (p. 155).

25  J. R. Watson, *English Poetry of the Romantic Period 1789–1830* (London: Longman, 1985), p. 1.

26  Georg Lukács, *The Historical Novel*, p. 32.

27  Harold Bloom, *The Ringers in the Tower: Studies in Romantic Tradition* (Chicago and London: University of Chicago Press, 1971), p. 335.

28  Ludwig Wittgenstein, *Philosophical Investigations*, p. 82.

29  Robert P. Irvine draws attention to the fact that ultimately Madge represents a lack of agency. See *Enlightenment and Romance*, p. 195.

30  Judith Wilt, *Secret Leaves*, p. 133.

31  John Sutherland, *The Life of Walter Scott: A Critical Biography* (Oxford and Cambridge, MA: Blackwell, 1995), p. 209.

32  George Campbell, 'The Philosophy of Rhetoric' in *The Scottish Enlightenment: An Anthology*, pp. 685–94 (p. 686).

# Chapter 4

## Lost in Translation:

### *Ivanhoe*, *The Fortunes of Nigel* and *Peveril of the Peak*

*The Heart of Mid-Lothian* emerges as a kind of crisis in Scott's writing. In Graham McMaster's schema, it is the point where his optimism ends and his disillusionment begins.[1] More pertinent to this discussion, however, it can be seen as the moment where the question of language assumes a new urgency for the Author of Waverley, his focus moving from the question of how to capture the 'ultimate referent' of the past to one of how the novelist may escape the prison house of language wrought by it. As a result the novels of the 1820s see a significant shift both in terms of the subject matter of Scott's fiction and the complexity with which he approaches the topic of the relationships between meaning and discourse and the implications of these for the novelist.[2] As Scott's fiction moves towards a more distant past he grapples with new questions concerning how, or if, that past might best be articulated. Most significantly in terms of the present study, however, the novels of this period see an increasing interest in the question that was becoming increasingly vexed in his work; the ways in which language operates (or fails to operate) and the limits of its communicative possibilities.

By 1820 Scott was clearly weary of subjects dealing with Scotland's relatively recent history. By the early 1820s, consequently, he was to embark on a series of texts which pushed the subject matter of his novels back into Scotland's middle past – *The Monastery* and *The Abbot*, for example – or, as with the texts we will explore here, re-located his subject matter, like Effie Deans, 'firth of Scotland', incorporating settings in twelfth century, seventeenth century and Restoration England. While these texts of the early 1820s involve a temporal and geographical movement, however, more significant is the corresponding philosophical shift in Scott's approach to the act of writing fiction. Characterised as what is often called the period of 'great preface writing', novels such as *Ivanhoe*, *The Fortunes of Nigel* and *Peveril of the Peak* demonstrate an increased self-reflexivity in Scott's work and offer us meditations on fiction and its relationship to history which have led several critics to recognise an overtly postmodern impulse at play in his work, as noted in the introduction to this study. Patricia Gaston, for example, has suggested that the prefaces exhibit a Quixotic impulse that disrupts the essentially realist mode of Scott's fiction and leads to 'an almost inevitable confrontation with the text at hand as text'.[3] Similarly, Jerome McGann suggests that the prefaces 'establish the basic narrative terms of Scott's fiction' as essentially postmodern making 'the subject of tale-telling an explicit and governing preoccupation of the fiction'.[4] While we should perhaps be cautious about simply applying the term 'postmodern' to Scott's work it is clear, as Judith Wilt recognises, that *Ivanhoe* marks something of a watershed – a sudden quickening of Scott's thinking – and the 'Introductory Epistle' to *The Fortunes of Nigel* and the 'Prefatory Letter' of *Peveril of the Peak* also offer heightened levels of debate on the relationship of virtue to fiction and fiction to truth. However, while in some ways these texts do offer a break from the past it is also evident that the self-reflexive turn which Scott's fiction takes in the 1820s both arises from, and owes much to, an interrogation of the potentialities in language and an awareness of its communicative limitations which has taken place in his earlier work. So what kinds of questions does Scott actually raise in the prefaces to these novels, and more importantly, how do they map onto the understanding of the exploration of language which we have seen operating within his writing generally and in the texts which these prefaces frame?

As has been well documented the prefaces demonstrate Scott expressing some anxiety concerning the relationship of the historical novel to history, as though dealing with a much earlier historical period prompts the Author of Waverley to confront new questions about how it may be captured and articulated. For example, in *Ivanhoe* the ostensible author of the text Laurence Templeton explains to Dryasdust that he is aware that his work is potentially 'slight, unsatisfactory and trivial' when viewed in relation to the antiquarian researches that have informed it, and that it is perhaps best classed with the 'idle novels and romances of the day' (p. 5). However, while he also admits that 'the severer antiquary may think that, by thus intermingling fiction with truth, I am polluting the well of history with modern inventions' (p. 8) he defends the work that he has produced by arguing that 'I neither can, nor do pretend, to the observation of complete accuracy, even in matters of outward costume, much less in the more important points of language and manners' (p. 9). In essence, what Scott is arguing here is that the historical novel, in spite of its close connection with historiography, does not operate by mimetic impulses but, on the contrary, is essentially imaginative and metaphoric in its dynamics. While this is, of course, apparent from *Waverley* onwards, it is clear that Scott's decision to move the subject of *Ivanhoe* to a much earlier period in history demands that this question be revisited in new ways. The writer who deals with Scotland's relatively recent past, argues Templeton, has all his materials at hand, and has only to select those most appropriate for his purposes. Commenting on the successes of Mr Oldbuck of Monkbarns (the protagonist of *The Antiquary*) in writing about Scottish history, Templeton continues:

> It seemed then to be your opinion, that the charm lay entirely in the art with which the unknown author had availed himself, like a second M<sup>c</sup>Pherson, of the stores of antiquity which lay scattered around him, supplying his own indolence or poverty of invention, by the incidents which had actually taken place in his country at no distant period, introducing real characters, and scarcely suppressing real names. It was not above sixty or seventy years, you observed, that the whole north of Scotland was under a state of government nearly as simple and as patriarchal as those of our good allies the Mohawks and Iroquois. Admitting that the author cannot himself be supposed to have witnessed these times, he must have lived, you observed, among persons who had acted and suffered in them; . . .
>
> . . . Many men alive, you remarked, well remembered persons who had not only seen the celebrated Roy McGregor, but had feasted, and even fought with him. All those minute circumstances belonging to private life and domestic character, all that gives verisimilitude to a narrative and individuality to the persons introduced, is still known and remembered in Scotland. (pp. 5–6)

Verisimilitude, this seems to imply, is more complex when one deals with the remote past. 'In England', Templeton continues, 'civilization has been so long complete, that our ideas of our ancestors are only to be gleaned from musty records and chronicles' (pp. 6–7). An idea of the past, therefore, has to be constructed imaginatively, or conjectured, to borrow an Enlightenment phrase. In this context the fact that the historical novel is operating by impulses other than mimesis (or straightforward referentiality) is thus thrown into relief.

While the 'Introductory Epistle' to *The Fortunes of Nigel* concerns itself more with matters of artistic style and composition than with the relationship of novel to history, questions concerning the ways in which it 'refers' to the past are not entirely absent. Commenting on Scott's earlier novel, *The Monastery*, Clutterbuck points out that 'the White Lady is no favourite' (p. 6). The critics, it seems, do not welcome the 'mystic, and the magical, and the whole systems of signs, wonders, and omens' with which Scott has imbued his earlier text (p. 6). In their place, gesturing back towards eighteenth-century concerns, Clutterbuck demands the 'natural and the probable' (p. 6), that category of fiction promoted by *Tom Jones*.[5] The Author of Waverley, however, reminding us that this essentially imitative impulse may not be his primary concern, dismisses the possibility that he will write in this way.

The much-quoted 'Introductory Epistle' to *Nigel* tends to overshadow *Peveril*'s 'Prefatory Letter' but this Introductory Chapter also has much to tell us about how Scott perceives the relationship between history and fiction. In *Peveril*, as Dryasdust peruses the manuscript which has ostensibly been sent to him by the Author of Waverley, he observes 'Here are figments enough . . . to confuse the march of a whole history – anachronisms enough to overset all Chronology' signalling that the specific anxieties which are to haunt *Peveril* concern the role and function of the historical novelist (p. 4). When the Author appears Dryasdust informs him that he makes 'aberrations . . . from the path of true history' (p. 8) creating narratives which are 'seductively dangerous' (p. 9). 'Real' history, he argues, is neglected as readers become 'contented with such frothy and superficial knowledge as they acquire from [his] works, to the effect of inducing them to neglect the severer and more accurate sources of information' (p. 10). In his defence the Author of Waverley responds that he is in fact constructing an altogether more complex relationship between fact and fiction than that based on referentiality; he is not attempting to offer 'true history' but rather 'ransacks' its narratives, lights on striking circumstances and 'bedizens' them with imagination to provide 'lively fictitious pictures' (p. 9). If by doing so he refers readers to more serious researches, he comments, well and good; if not 'must one' he asks 'swear to the truth of a song' (p. 10) thus implying that it is an altogether different kind of 'truth' that he is trying to convey to his reader; 'a degree of knowledge' as he puts it 'not perhaps of the most accurate kind, but such as he might not otherwise have acquired' (p. 11).

What has been less frequently discussed in relation to these prefaces, however, is that the Author of Waverley is drawing our attention to the fact that the alternative to a referential 'truth' that he is offering here is essentially textual, and as such, it is by necessity constructed, fabricated from the problematic structures of language. This issue is foregrounded by Templeton's assertion that England's past can only be accessed by 'musty records and chronicles' and 'amidst the dust of antiquity, where nothing was to be found but dry, sapless, mouldering and disjointed bones' (*Ivanhoe*, p. 7). With such 'scantiness of materials' to work from (p. 8), the author who hopes to write about this period can only rely upon 'hints concerning the private life of our ancestors [which] lie scattered through our various historians' (p. 8). Templeton elaborates in a passage that it is worth quoting at some length:

> It is true, that I neither can, nor do pretend, to the observation of complete accuracy, even in matters of outward costume, much less in the more important points of language and manners. But the same motive which prevents my writing the dialogue of the piece in Anglo-Saxon or in Norman-French, and which prohibits my sending forth to the public this essay printed with the types of Caxton or Wynken de Worde, prevents my attempting to confine myself within the limits of the period in which my story is laid. It is necessary, for exciting interest of any kind, that the subject assumed should be, as it were, translated into the manners as well as the language of the age we live in . . .
>
> . . . In point of justice, therefore, to the multitudes who will, I trust, devour this book with avidity, I have so far explained our ancient manners in modern language, and so far detailed the characters and sentiments of my persons, that the modern reader will not find himself, I should hope, much trammelled by the repulsive dryness of mere antiquity . . .
>
> . . . He who would imitate the ancient language with success, will attend rather to its grammatical character, turn of expression, and mode of arrangement, than labour to collect extraordinary and antiquated terms, which, as I have already averred, do not in ancient authors approach the number of words still in use, though perhaps somewhat altered in sense and spelling, in the proportion of one to ten. (pp. 9–10)

To write using the language of the past, Templeton avers, is like Joseph Strutt or Chatterton, to render oneself unintelligible; the past cannot be presented to the modern reader without mediation, but must be interpreted for him by the author. As Graham Tulloch recognises, the language of *Ivanhoe* is, as a result, 'a mixed, artificially created language' incorporating French, Latin, and a host of technical and specialist terms.[6]

The past, then, can only be constructed from text and via fictions which are themselves overtly, and explicitly, textual in their nature, implied by the fact that there are repeated references to 'dry scrolls' and textual fragments within these three prefaces. The author of *Ivanhoe*, for example, has little to say about his materials, except that he has gained access to 'The Wardour Manuscript' a document in the keeping of the fictional Sir Arthur Wardour who appears in *The Antiquary*. In *Nigel*, the author has just as little to work from, describing how he has rescued the 'few greasy and blackened fragments of the elder Drama' from a 'coal-hole' (p. 12). Captain Clutterbuck encounters the Author of Waverley in the back shop of his own publishing house, 'employed in reading a blotted *revise*' (*Nigel*, p. 4) and Dryasdust's visit by the Great Unknown is prefaced by his receiving the novel which we are about to read, in the form of 'a large roll of papers' written in 'a hand . . . so small and so crabbed' that he is obliged to use 'strong magnifiers' (*Peveril*, pp. 3–4). Such references signal that, within the new terrain that these novels inhabit, the very materials with which the Author of Waverley has to work, and not simply the novels which necessarily ensue, are essentially fragmentary, if not avowedly fictional, and above all, textual in their nature.

Moving the focus of his historical lens towards England and into the more distant past, then, prompts the Author of Waverley to revisit and refine questions about how that past can be retrieved, understood, and communicated. The message of the prefaces seems clear; mimesis is not an option when describing a past that can only be known via dry fragments and which cannot be communicated in the language of its own time. As a consequence, the author must assume, as Templeton argues, what is essentially a process of *translation*; while this has been implied as early as *Waverley*, in these novels it becomes overt, resulting in texts that, as the following discussion will demonstrate, exhibit a near obsession with the problems implicit within communication. The novels of the early 1820s, consequently, are ones about language in crisis; whereas *The Heart of Mid-Lothian* might be seen as a novel which encapsulates 'dying words', these fictions move increasingly towards non-communication and silence.

## The Fortunes of Nigel

In *The Fortunes of Nigel* the protagonist of the novel is caught in the underworld of Alsatia. There Duke Hildebrod tells him that if he is to better his fortunes he '"in plain words . . . must wap and win"' (p. 258). The Edinburgh Edition informs the reader that the expression comes from beggars' cant and can be understood in the context of the phrase 'If she won't wap for a Winne, let her trine for a Make', which is further glossed as 'If she won't Lie with a Man for a Penny, let her Hang for a Half-penny'.[7] Another inhabitant of Alsatia uses an equally unintelligible phrase '"Tour out, tour out . . . tout the bien mort twiring at the gentry cove!"' In this instance Scott provides his own gloss: 'Look sharp. See how the girl is ogling the strange gallants' (p. 191). The Edinburgh Edition note informs us:

as a place apart from the city that surrounds it, Alsatia is distinguished by its own language, the cant or broken language derived from several tongues spoken by beggars, criminals, gypsies, and other such outcasts for purposes of mutual recognition and concealment from regular society. Though not specific borrowings, the phrases used here and below are typical and occur in the plays in the *A[ncien]t B[ritish] D[rama]*. A *gentry cove* is a 'gentleman'. (p. 604)

In answer to the first of these comments Nigel states '"your words must be still plainer before I can understand them"' (p. 258). As readers we sympathise with his response, since these phrases offer examples of the many instances of obscure and incomprehensible language used not only in Alsatia but throughout this text, a 'broken language', to borrow the expression of the Edinburgh Edition editors, that defies direct translation and which can only be glossed or annotated, as above, in the most general of terms or via several layers of interpretation.[8]

Indeed, of all Scott's novels *The Fortunes of Nigel* is perhaps that which offers the greatest linguistic challenge to readers since it draws not only on the cant language described here, but also has embedded within it passages in dense Scots, French, Latin and even Greek. As the Edinburgh Edition editor Frank Jordan puts it this novel is inhabited by 'colourful characters – Scots-speaking, English-speaking, French-speaking, Latin-speaking, mulatto-speaking and these inflected for dialect and social class'.[9] It is hardly surprising, therefore, that this novel should have, at thirty-five pages, the longest glossary of any of the Edinburgh Edition volumes, with the exception of *The Heart of Mid-Lothian*. If we compare this with other novels of the 1820s we find that the glossary for *The Monastery* is twenty pages, *The Abbot* twenty-one, and *Ivanhoe* ten. Even compared to some of the Scottish novels *Nigel* is far ahead. The glossary for *The Antiquary* is nineteen pages and that for *The Tale of Old Mortality* extends to twenty Edinburgh Edition pages. In addition the notes to *Nigel* refer us to twenty-seven instances where phrases are derived from cant language, one hundred and forty-three from Latin, seventeen from Greek and fifty from French. These statistics alone suggest the polyphonic nature of this text, a fact signalled by the language of James I himself who, as he first meets *Nigel*, converses with him in a mixture of English, Scots, Latin and Greek. Moreover, having confronted us with several pages of dialogue in Latin, Scott himself offers his readers – many of whom would not have followed the conversation – only the following consolation:

> Lest any lady or gentleman should suspect there is aught of mystery
> concealed under the sentences printed in Italics, they will be pleased to
> understand that they contain only a few common-place Latin phrases,
> relating to the state of letters in Holland, which neither deserve, nor would
> endure, a literal translation. (p. 111)

Even as he speaks this *lingua franca* James bemoans the decline of a
scholarly *communis lingua*, or common language (pp. 111–12),
suggesting that *The Fortunes of Nigel* may be a novel about failure to
understand as much as it is a novel about understanding; one in which a
crisis in the communicative capacities of language become the very
subject of the fiction.

This, however, may seem at odds with what, ostensibly at least, is the
aim of *The Fortunes of Nigel* which, like so many of Scott's fictions,
announces itself as setting competing discourses in dialogue. Set in the
years following the Union of the Crowns in 1603, it takes as its stated
theme the tensions between the Scots and English:

> The long-continued hostilities which had for centuries divided the south and
> the north divisions of the Island of Britain, had been happily terminated by
> the succession of the pacific James I. to the English crown. But although the
> united crown of England and Scotland was worn by the same individual, it
> required a long lapse of time, and the succession of more than one
> generation, ere the inveterate national prejudices which had so long existed
> betwixt the sister kingdom were removed, and the subjects of either side of
> the Tweed brought to regard those upon the other bank as friends and as
> brethren. (p. 19)

This theme is one that is elaborated upon repeatedly throughout the text
particularly in relation to those Scots who, like Nigel, and indeed James I,
have come to London to better their fortunes. On his first sight of Richie
Moniplies, for example, Frank Tunstall describes him as "'A raw
Scotsman . . . just come up, I suppose, to help the rest of his countrymen
to gnaw old England's bones; a palmer-worm, I reckon, to devour what
the locust has spared"' (p. 27). A familiar dynamic seems to emerge,
whereby Scott is setting his 'raw Scotsmen' in a context where he will
excuse their 'foibles' (to borrow his own term) in relation to their English
neighbours. The dynamic is further refined via Lord Huntinglen and his
son Lord Dalgarno whom George Heriot describes as "'the old and the
new fashion"', suggesting that one represents the values of pre-Union
Scotland, the other the Anglified Scot of the new times: "'The father"', he

states, "'is like a noble old broad-sword, but harmed with rust, from neglect and inactivity – the son is your modern rapier, well mounted, fairly gilt, and fashioned to the taste of the time'" (pp. 129–30). A traditional reading of Scott would suggest that he places these binaries in dialogue and by doing so tentatively demonstrates the ways in which common ground can be found between them; within such a paradigm the death of Lord Dalgarno could be read as a symbolic exclusion of the worst aspects of Union and the marriage trope with which the novel closes figured as a successful dialogue between two nations.

Offering a more complex reading of the dynamic operating in this text Caroline McCracken-Flesher has expressed it in terms of circulation and value:

> Circulation is inevitable, and wayward circulation may even prove rewarding—yet at the end of *Nigel* the hero has recovered his estate and seems likely to withdraw there with his wife. By the intervention of the King, romance overcomes money and delimits play. Circulation has ceased because value is achieved.[10]

While recognising that the dialogue that Scott creates in his fiction, and particularly in *Nigel*, is a problematic and to some extent a fabricated one, McCracken-Flesher's thesis acknowledges that it is also a dialogue which is crucial in keeping Scotland and Scottish identity in an economy of exchange so that it may be renegotiated by future generations.

However, any reading of *The Fortunes of Nigel* which constructs it as opening a form of dialogue or exchange between Scottish and English identities is surely rendered problematic if we recognise that it is also a text that both frequently and overtly draws attention to the linguistic constraints on dialogue and indeed upon conversation of any sort at all. *The Fortunes of Nigel* in fact is a novel that is obsessed with the ways in which language operates and the potential limits of such communication. For example, it is worth noting that it contains within it a discussion of the ways in which both similes and metaphors operate. In *Of the Origin and Progress of Language* Lord Monboddo voices an anxiety about metaphors and the way in which they function commenting 'we cannot understand perfectly a metaphorical expression, unless we know the proper meaning of the word; for we cannot tell whether two things be like or not, if we do not know them both'.[11] After meeting Dalgarno's gay companions Nigel similarly comments on the obfuscating potential of metaphor, complaining about the extravagant (and for him inadequate) nature of their language where "'Every man's invention seemed on the stretch, and each extravagant simile seemed to set one half of your men of wit into a brown study to produce something which should out-herod it'" (p. 151). Similes are also maligned by Jin Vin (p. 235) and metaphor is called into question when the Lady Hermione informs Margaret Ramsay that "'Metaphors are no arguments'" and she responds "'I am sorry for that, madam . . . for they are such a pretty indirect way of telling one's mind when it differs from one's betters'" (pp. 208–9). Such discussion is particularly interesting when we note that this is a novel where characters frequently speak in metaphor, with the notes drawing our attention to the fact that there are one hundred and five proverbial sayings (themselves a kind of metaphor) embedded within the text.

Such observations alert us to a concern with the ways in which language operates. A more complex discussion of this question is also embedded in the repeated instances of unintelligible language which appear throughout this text, where both the characters in the novel, and indeed readers of it, are confused by the language by which it is functioning. For example, as George Heriot tries to explain to Lord Huntinglen the nature of Nigel's difficulties he states "'in order to secure the lender, he must come in the shoes of the creditor to whom he advances payment'". Not surprisingly, Huntinglen responds with the question "'Come in his shoes! . . . Why, what have boots or shoes to do with this matter?'" "'It is a law phrase'" responds Heriot, and proceeds to give an explanation in terms scarce more intelligible than his first exposition of the situation. While the reader may follow the gist of what is going on concerning 'wadsett' and 'conveyance', it is clear that the technical language of law employed by Heriot is designed (as so often in Scott's fiction) to conceal as much as to communicate (p. 119).

A similar process is also at work in the language of the underworld which permeates this novel, both in Alsatia and outside of it. Dame Ursula, who frequently flatters to deceive and who, as Jin Vin comments, speaks through the dubious mode of similes also communicates via a strange patois 'derived from several languages' but which, of course, succeeds in being intelligible in none:

"And here is this fantastic ape, pretty Mistress Marget forsooth—such a beauty as I could make of a Dutch doll, and as fantastic, and humorous, and conceited, as if she were a duchess. I have seen her in the same day as changeful as a marmozet, and as stubborn as a mule. I should like to know whether her little conceited noddle, or her father's old crazy, calculating jolter-pate, breeds most whimsies. But then there's that two hundred pounds a-year in dirty land, and the father is held a close chuff, though a fanciful—he is our landlord beside, and she has begged a late day from him for our rent; so God help me, I must be conformable—besides, the little capricious devil is my only key to get at Master George Heriot's secret, and it concerns my character to find that out; and so, *andiamos*, as the lingua franca hath it." (p. 97)

Such *lingua franca* renders the novel almost unintelligible in places and this linguistic confusion also extends to the subject of names. Having already adopted several pseudonyms, it is hardly surprising that Nigel should have to adopt yet another when he enters Alsatia, and this the most bizarre corruption of his name of all. After being called 'Grime', 'Graam' and 'Greene' in place of his mother's name of 'Grahame' we are informed that Hildebrod 'spelled Nigel with two g's instead of one' (p. 195) a fact that allows Scott to add the joke that 'rigorous as Ritson' Dr Dryasdust has demanded that the novel should therefore be called 'The Fortunes of Niggle'.[12]

Such incidents of linguistic confusion and non-comprehension are part of the texture of this novel and at times afford the opportunity for both local colour and humour. They also, however, make a far more serious point about the ways in which language may fail to communicate once cut free from referentiality, and the potential implications of this. In particular, where cultures or competing discourses clash in this text, the resulting confusion is often manifested in linguistic incomprehensibility. The episodes in Alsatia offer the extreme example, but similar disjunctions occur elsewhere. In the gaming-house, for instance, Beaujeu speaks in a mixture of English and French (some of which is restored by the Edinburgh Edition) which is amusing but which also, as Scott highlights, causes misunderstanding:

> "Saar," said the Chevalier, "Monsieur le Capitaine, I vas not at the siege of the Petit Leyth, and I know not what you say about de cock-loft; but I will say for Monseigneur de Strozzi, that he understood the grande guerre, and was grand captain—plus grand—that is more great it may be, than some of the capitaines of Angleterre, who do speak very loud—tenez, Monsieur, car c'est à vous!"
>
> "O Monsieur," answered the swordsman, "we know the Frenchman will fight well behind his barrier of stone, or when he is armed with back, breast, and pot."
>
> "Pot!" exclaimed the Chevalier, "what do you mean by pot—do you mean to insult me among my noble guests? Saar, I have done my duty as a pauvre gentilhomme under the Grand Henri Quatre, both at Courtrai and Yvry, and, Ventre saint gris! we had neither pot nor marmite, but did always charge in our shirt." (p. 145)

As the Edinburgh Edition note informs us, 'Beaujea mimics a nonsense oath the monarch is reputed to have used . . . but takes the soldier's word *pot* literally, associating it with the earthenware cooking pot or stock-pot known as "marmite"' (p. 589).

The most significant meeting of discourses in this text, however, is that between Scot and Englishman, and between pre- and post-Union Scots. It is this binary which is posited, as we have seen, via Lord Dalgarno and his father, and it is one which is to some extent expressed in linguistic terms. While, as the above exchange concerning the law with Heriot suggests, Lord Huntinglen is plain speaking, his son has adopted the Anglified speech of the new court and the new times. This is evident in his first exchange with Nigel, when the latter fails to understand what Dalgarno is communicating. On first seeing Moniplies Dalgarno whispers into Lord Glenvarloch's ear a quotation from Macbeth: '"the devil damn thee black, thou cream-faced loun, / Where got'st thou that goose look?"' Nigel, however, we are told, 'was too little acquainted with the English stage, to understand a quotation which had already grown matter of common allusion in London' (p. 123). Recognising that Nigel does not understand him, Dalgarno offers an explanation, '"That fellow, by his visage, should either be a saint, or a most hypocritical rogue"' (p. 123). This exchange highlights a fundamental lack of understanding between Dalgarno and Nigel – representative as they are of two different discourses of Scottish identity. It also illustrates that while Dalgarano may attempt to 'translate' for Nigel, such translation will bring Nigel no nearer to understanding.

It is, after all, in essence a failure to understand Lord Dalgarno, a failure to learn his new language, which leads ultimately to Nigel's misfortunes. A similar but more sinister moment of misunderstanding occurs as Dalgarno leads Nigel to the gambling den that is to be the source of his downfall. Nigel asks his friend if they are to dine at a tavern, and when he hears Dalgarno's description of what occurs there asks if it is a gaming-house. Dalgarno, however, does not give a straight reply but instead beguiles Nigel with the specialist vocabulary of gambling and concludes: '"it is but, in plain terms, an eating-house, arranged on civiller terms, and frequented by better company, than others in this town; and if some of them do amuse themselves with cards and hazard, they are men of honour, and who play as such, and for no more than they can well afford to lose"' (p. 139). Dalgarno's 'plain language' however, is no translation for what he has just stated in the fashionable vocabulary of the times, for his purpose is to trick Nigel into debauchery.

Nigel's failure to fully understand the import of Dalgarno's jest at his landlady's reputation also contributes to his troubles (p. 131) leading Mungo Malagrowther to comment that "'naething but lies are current in the circle'" (p. 169). The consequence of such linguistic confusion is that by the end of the novel words are thoroughly devalued in this text. When they meet in the Tower Nigel tells Heriot that he "'could not prevent other idle tongues and idle brains from making false inferences'" but Heriot retorts that he could have silenced them: "'You would have known well enough how to stop their mouths'" (p. 326). In response to Nigel's attempts to defend his reputation Heriot states:

> "It is well mouthed, my lord . . . but a cunning clerk can read the Apocrypha as loud as the Scripture—frankly, my lord, you are come to that pass, where your words will not pass without a warrant." (p. 331)

In *Philosophical Investigations* Wittgenstein, having acknowledged that language does not operate by the kind of radical referentiality described in *The Heart of Mid-Lothian* but by a kind of 'free play', notes that 'we are so much accustomed to communication through language, in conversation, that it looks to us as if the whole point of communication lay in this: someone else grasps the sense of my words – which is something mental: he as it were takes it into his own mind. If he then does something further with it as well, that is no part of the immediate purpose of language'.[13] The misfortunes of Nigel point towards a similar conclusion, suggesting that when language is cut free from a *communis lingua*, as James puts it, what results when cultures meet is not conversation, but confusion. Such conclusions clearly create considerable tensions for a novelist like Scott who, on the face of it at least, has sought to translate one culture for another and to recover the past through words. It is, consequently, no surprise that his next novel, *Peveril of the Peak*, confronts moments of radical non-communication and has at the very heart of its plot a discussion of the right to remain silent.

## Peveril of the Peak

*Peveril of the Peak* is by far Scott's longest novel and many consider it to be among his least successful, sharing with its fictional editor Revd Dr Dryasdust a sense of being 'a little exhausted towards the close of the second volume' (p. 4). While some critics maintain that it is good in parts few argue that it is worth a second read. D. W. Jefferson, for example, describes *Peveril* as a 'long cumbersome work' with a 'shapeless plot' and concludes that the one scene that is 'superb' – that of Alice at Chiffinch's and her rescue by Julian – is 'virtually wasted' since 'few people read the book'.[14] Only Graham McMaster and Fiona Robertson have tried to redeem the novel critically; McMaster by reading it as offering a kind of symbolic parallel with the political situation in 1821 and Robertson by recognising that there is a 'positive aesthetic fashioning' of Gothic elements within it.[15] Current opinion of *Peveril of the Peak* is pretty much in step with contemporary responses to the novel. Sydney Smith of the *Edinburgh Review*, for example, writes to Archibald Constable thanking him for his complimentary copy: 'A good novel', he writes, 'but not so good as either of the two last, and not good enough for such a writer. The next must be better or it will be the last'.[16] Even Scott's greatest apologist, J. G. Lockhart, is forced to conclude that:

> Its reception was somewhat colder than that of its three immediate predecessors . . . Fenella was an unfortunate conception; what is good in it is not original, and the rest extravagantly absurd and incredible . . . The story is clumsy and perplexed; the catastrophe . . . foreseen from the beginning, and yet most inartificially brought about.[17]

It is common to account for the perceived failure of *Peveril of the Peak* by seeing it as a symptom of the over-production and money-spinning which many see as characteristic of Scott's literary production in the 1820s. It was published in 1822, a year in which three novels by the Great Unknown ostensibly appeared; *The Pirate*, *The Fortunes of Nigel*, and *Peveril* itself. In spite of the date given on their title-pages *The Pirate* was in fact published at the end of 1821 and *Peveril* at the beginning of 1823, yet nevertheless this year was one of phenomenal output by the author. Scott's publishers Constable and Co. had a contract with Scott for five novels beginning with *The Pirate*[18] and were anxious that their golden goose, as they called him, should continue to lay golden eggs – preferably as swiftly as possible.

Their enthusiasm is not surprising; 10,000 copies was now the standard print run for a new Scott novel and this had been increased to 12,000 with *The Pirate* in response to advance orders. Some 7,000 copies of *The Fortunes of Nigel* had been sold by 10.30am on the day of its publication,[19] and while Scott's publisher Constable advises that they should be cautious about printing too many copies of *Peveril* he still reckons that they should print 10,500.[20] There are ways then in which the perceived inadequacies of *Peveril* may be justifiably seen as a consequence of the pressures placed upon Scott to feed a market hungry for his novels and a publisher equally hungry to maximise his profits. Certainly, there are signs that Scott experienced some difficulty in writing *Peveril*, for while it is completed at the end of a year when Scott had been at his most productive it in fact took him some time to write. As the 'Essay on the Text' for the Edinburgh Edition outlines the idea for the novel was clearly beginning to form in Scott's mind early in 1822. In a letter to Archibald Constable of 25 February Scott responds to a suggestion that he write the story of Pocahontas by stating that he does not have the knowledge to do this, but that it might be married to that of Whalley the Regicide, a story which is told by the character Bridgenorth in *Peveril*.[21] Later in the same letter he first mentions that he is considering writing a novel about the Popish Plot, commenting 'I am turning my thought to that . . . period of Charles 2ds reign which was disturbd by the popish plot. Let me know what you think about it'.[22] It is not until 8 May, however, when *The Fortunes of Nigel* was complete, that Scott begins to write and by the 15th of that month he already has the title of the book and ten manuscript pages written.

Yet Scott made little headway with his tale of the Popish Plot over the summer and the novel was not completed until the end of December.[23] Scott's apparent difficulty in writing *Peveril of the Peak*, however, was not due only to artistic difficulties but also to personal circumstances. During July and August Scott was engaged with arranging the visit of George IV to Edinburgh. The early autumn also proved difficult. On 14 August during the King's visit Scott was to lose what Lockhart calls his dearest friend, William Erskine, Lord Kinneder. Erskine was Sheriff-depute for Orkney and had, only the year before, supplied Scott with information about the islands as he was writing *The Pirate*. Erskine's death and the circumstances of it was a severe blow to Scott and in a letter in October, just as a fourth volume of *Peveril* was first being mooted, he describes himself as 'damnably out of spirits'.[24] Certainly, it is the depression caused by Erskine's death that, for Scott, accounts for *Peveril*'s weaknesses. 'The depression of my own spirits arising from poor Lord Kinneder's death & a sort of thickness of the blood has infested this same Peveril', he writes to James Ballantyne.[25] There are, then, reasons enough to justify why *Peveril of the Peak* may not be among the finest of Scott's literary creations; over production on the one hand and personal circumstances on the other were both taking their toll on Scott as the novel was being written and it would be easy to dismiss it simply as a bad novel written under bad circumstances.

However, this is to dismiss *Peveril* too lightly and if we revisit it with an increased alertness to its concern with language new dynamics, and new ways to account for the 'exhaustion' it exhibits, begin to emerge within it. It is clear that Scott was inspired by the ideas and subject matter behind the novel even if for a variety of reasons he found it difficult to write. Scott was, indeed, fascinated by the Restoration and by its literature. His own work on Dryden and on the *Ancient British Drama* meant that his knowledge of the period was immense and he quotes from Buckingham's *The Rehearsal* (a text which features in *Peveril*) over ten times in his letters. Given this context, therefore, it is worth considering if the 'clumsiness and perplexities' which Lockhart identifies in this text may be symptomatic not of a kind of emerging redundancy in Scott's writing in the 1820s but rather, as Graham McMaster has suggested,[26] of an altogether more intellectually interesting anxiety or perplexity about the novel form itself which evolves as Scott addresses a crisis concerning the potential of historical fiction and the limits of communicating the past via language.

Certainly, as has been signalled in the earlier discussion of the 'Prefatory Letter', *Peveril of the Peak*, like so many of Scott's texts, engages in a debate on the nature and purpose of the historical novel. Elsewhere Scott approaches the problem of historical process by offering a series of novels on the same topic – the Jacobite Risings for example – thus seeking via the 'sequel' to demonstrate the ways in which history shapes itself into a pattern over a number of years. An alternative approach is explored in *The Heart of Mid-Lothian* where Scott uses David Deans and the time span which his memory provides to extend the period of the novel back into the Covenanting Wars, thus allowing him a chronology where he can depict the political turmoil of the seventeenth century evolving into the more benign circumstances of post-Union Scotland. In many ways *Peveril* follows the pattern of *The Heart of Mid-Lothian* and has far more in common with that favourite of Scott novels than is initially apparent. It too is a four volume novel, these being the only two Scott wrote, and there are direct references to *The Heart of Mid-Lothian* in the 'Prefatory Letter' as if the author is suggesting, subliminally or otherwise, a link between these two texts; as Dryasdust sits musing after dinner he tells us that he gazes for a certain time on a portrait of '[his] uncle . . . who is mentioned in *The Heart of Mid-Lothian*' (p. 4) and later one of the censures he makes to the Author is that 'Your

Puritan [Bridgenorth in *Peveril*] is faintly traced, in comparison to your Cameronian [David Deans of *The Heart of Mid-Lothian*]' (p. 11). Similarly, in *Peveril*, as in *The Heart of Mid-Lothian*, Scott is exploring the possibilities of the chronicle as a device to demonstrate historical progress. The necessary 'oversetting of chronology' which ensues is one of the main complaints offered by Dryasdust who laments that the author offers 'a Countess of Derby, fetched out of her cold grave, and saddled with a set of adventures dated twenty years after her death' (p. 11). This stretching out of the natural time scheme of the novel is also in evidence in the leaps of first four or five years, and then around ten, which take place towards the end of the first volume. 'The progress of the history hath hitherto been slow' comments the narrator, 'but after this period . . . we must hurry over hastily the transactions of several years' (p. 98). While this hasty leap might be construed as an example of the clumsiness identified by Lockhart it is a Shakespearean device (used in *Henry V* and *The Winter's Tale*, for example) which in fact enables Scott, within a chapter, to depict his hero Julian and heroine Alice as young adults and to shift the focus of his plot from the Restoration with which the novel opens to the later point of conflict embodied in the Popish Plot and the potential political upheaval surrounding it. Consequently this rupture in the narrative condenses the process of history and allows the patterns within it to emerge; the chronicle form permitting him, in both these long novels, to depict the children achieving some kind of resolution to the conflicts which have vexed their parents' generation.

Further similarities emerge if we note that, in spite of their length, these two novels share a tension in their conclusions. The fourth volume of *The Heart of Mid-Lothian* is problematic, and the troubled closure that it allows suggests that not even the time scheme offered by the chronicle truly allows reconciliation and harmony to emerge from the vicissitudes of history. The conclusion to *Peveril* is similarly dissatisfying; Lockhart complains that 'the catastrophe is seen from the beginning and yet most inartificially brought about' seemingly voicing what has become a recurrent criticism of this long text, that its ending is contrived and disappointing. But this response is inadequate, for it suggests a failure to understand the dynamics by which Scott's texts operate; the endings of Waverley novels are nearly *always* contrived, denouement being self-consciously deferred to postscripts and afterwords. The ending of *Peveril* is only another example of such contrivance writ large, and in its overtness may tell us something about what troubles its author both in this text and elsewhere.

Indeed, if Scott is in the habit of drawing attention to the contrived nature of conclusions he does so in pantomime in *Peveril* as he has King Charles observe: "'Here is a plot without a drop of blood; and all the elements of a romance, without its conclusion . . . all ends without either hanging or marriage'" (p. 494). A marriage is in fact brought about and reconciliation ostensibly achieved in the wedding of Julian and Alice. Yet as in *The Heart of Mid-Lothian* there are too many loose ends to make marriage a convincing trope for, as Ann Schlossman-Robb puts it, in this text 'violent acts become signifiers of a tearing away of the appearance of reconciliation'.[27] Dark undercurrents haunt the conclusion of the novel – the fate of poor Fenella, for example, the banishment of her father Christian and King Charles's acknowledgment that he knows the depth of the Duke of Buckingham's treachery against him. "'I would . . . that all our political intrigues and feverish alarms could terminate as harmlessly as now'" states the King (p. 494), but in fact his words serve only to alert the reader that even this long novel cannot truly show history working towards such satisfactory ends. Here, Scott seems to give space to an anxiety which, as Graham McMaster has hinted, exists in all the novels of the middle period; the fear that the supposed Enlightenment model of history as pattern and progress cannot be adequately expressed within the novel any more than it is in reality.

However, if the 'Prefatory Letter' and the working out of the plot in *Peveril of the Peak* suggest an anxiety on the part of its author concerning the relationship of fictional narrative to Enlightenment models of progress, it also shares with both *The Heart of Mid-Lothian* and *The Fortunes of Nigel* deeper anxieties concerning language itself. Earlier in this chapter the use of cant language in *The Fortunes of Nigel* was discussed. Scott loves vocabulary of this sort and uses it whenever the opportunity presents itself. The language of gypsies, for example, is used in *Guy Mannering*; thieves' cant also appears in *The Heart of Mid-Lothian* where Jeanie falls in with Madge Wildfire and her mother's rogues on the way to London, and in *The Pirate* Scott employs the sailors' slang which he had picked up on his voyage with the Lighthouse yacht in 1814. This 'broken language' also features in *Peveril*. Like Nigel, Julian Peveril falls in with a parcel of rogues, and as he tries to make his escape via the Thames we are told that he is met with 'A volley of water language'; this time the language of the ferry men (p. 340). As in *Nigel*, it is insufficient to dismiss this exchange as local colour, since the watermen's cant is set within a text where our attention is constantly being drawn to the fissures within signification.

*Peveril of the Peak* like *Nigel*, is a novel which foregrounds the slippery and ambiguous nature of language; it is full of puns and linguistic misunderstandings, some witty, but others clearly treacherous. The Duke of Buckingham, for example, is a source of much word play in the text. The following passage gives one example, which is worth quoting at some length:

> "come help me to laugh—I have bit Sir Charles Sedley—flung him for a thousand, by the gods."
>
> "I am glad at your luck, my Lord Duke," replied Christian; "but I am come on serious business."
>
> "Serious?—why, I shall hardly be serious in my life again—ha, ha, ha!—and for luck, it was no such thing—sheer wit, and exquisite contrivance; and but that I don't care to affront Fortune, like the old Greek general, I might tell her to her face—in this thou had'st no share. You have heard, Ned Christian, that Mother Cresswell's dead? . . . and that she might not sleep in an unblest grave, I betted—do you mark me—with Sedley, that I would write her funeral-sermon; that it should be every word in praise of her life and conversation; that it should be all true, and yet that the diocesan should be unable to lay his thumb on Quodling, my little chaplain, who should preach it."
>
> "I perfectly see the difficulty, my lord," said Christian, who well knew that if he wished to secure attention from this volatile nobleman, he must first suffer, nay, encourage him, to exhaust the topic, whatever it might be, that had got temporary possession of his pineal gland.
>
> "Why," said the Duke, "I caused my little Quodling to go through his oration thus—'That whatever evil reports had passed current during the lifetime of the worthy matron whom they had restored to dust that day, malice itself could not deny that she was born well, married well, lived well, and died well; since she was born in Shadwell, married Cresswell, lived in Camberwell, and died in Bridewell.' Here ended the oration, and with it Sedley's ambitious hopes of over-reaching Buckingham—Ha, ha, ha!—And now, Master Christian, what are your commands for me to-day." (pp. 443–4)

While such passages in the novel can quickly become tedious they do indicate a more serious dynamic at work here. This form of punning and witty conversation is, as Scott points out, typical of the Restoration period, and in some ways part of its attraction for him. Restoration drama was underpinned by a use of language that seems divorced from meaning; wit, by definition self-reflexive artifice, rather than communication was an integral feature of it. As Cedric Gale outlines in his preface to *The Rehearsal*, the heroic tragedies of the day (written by William D'Avenant and John Dryden, for example) involve characters who 'caught up in extravagant situations and torn by conflicts of love and honor, alternately coo and roar their passions in language heightened far above nature and far beyond sense'.[28] Buckingham's attack in *The Rehearsal* was against this 'rant and bombast', seemingly demanding a theatre of 'sense' rather than 'nonsense':

> But this new way of wit does so surprise,
> Men lose their wits in wond'ring where it lies.
> If it be true, that monstrous births presage
> The following mischiefs that afflict the age,
> And sad disasters to the state proclaim,
> Plays without head or tail may do the same.
> Wherefore for ours, and for the kingdom's peace,
> May this prodigious way of writing cease.
> Let's have at least once in our lives a time,
> When we may hear some reason, not all rhyme.
> We have these ten years felt its influence;
> Pray let this prove a year of prose and sense.[29]

However, while his own witty style serves to satirise the hyperbole of his dramatic contemporaries, and in spite of what appears to be an appeal to clarity, the political intrigues of the Restoration period meant that Buckingham's own language often operates via a process which Rose Zimbardo refers to as the 'unspoken understood'; in other words by a kind of double coding since explicit reference to the subjects of its satire would have been impolitic, if not at times dangerous.[30] In order to fully comprehend the subtleties of *The Rehearsal*, consequently, it was necessary for later generations to provide 'keys' to the text in order, to borrow phrases from its Epilogue, to make head or tail, or rhyme and reason of its veiled attacks.[31] The language of Restoration plays, consequently, is deliberately set adrift from referentiality, its purpose being to obfuscate rather than to communicate, thus setting a precedent for Scott's own interest in ambiguous or double coded language in *Peveril of the Peak*.

Zimbardo also draws attention to the fact that Restoration drama is not mimetic in its impulses but primarily performative, arguing that while the period from 1660 to 1700 is one in which a shift takes places towards a process of 'approximat[ing] life' in the 1660s '*all* drama . . . imitates abstract, ideal reality'.[32] Much of it, she demonstrates, is concerned with self-artifice, a fact supported by the number of plays within plays in the drama of the period, and with the subject of 'man the image maker'.[33] Taking as an example Etherege's *The Man of Mode* she argues that within it 'characters stage deliberate scenes for one another' to explore 'the difference between self-fashioning artifice that serves, imitates, or embellishes nature, and the artifice that inhibits, distorts, or substitutes for nature'.[34] Within this drama, she argues, 'self-dramatization and artificing are inescapable human tendencies' and the only question being explored is 'how successful and pleasing a correspondence one makes between the image one creates of oneself and the underlying nature it imitates and decorates'. Surface realism is, consequently, only a 'satiric device' for to be 'a human being – is to be a player and a shaper of scenes'.[35]

Scott takes his cue from these unnervingly modern concerns in *Peveril of the Peak* for it is a novel which is similarly full of such acts of performance (by Ganlesse and Fenella, for example, who play roles in order to deceive) but also by the world weary Count of Derby and the Duke of Buckingham both of whom seek to enliven the degeneracy of the age by creating for themselves alternative roles on the social and political stage. It also contains its own 'play within a play' in the staged charade of its ending and much of the criticism of the novel arises from a recognition that some of its plot seems little more than a series of set pieces.

However, while Scott's Restoration novel may be imbued with the puns, word play and charade that is typical of writing of the period his reference to it in *Peveril of the Peak* seems to be generated by more than the desire to reflect the times of the Popish Plot (although, it does, of course, also serve this function). Rather, he employs such discourses in *Peveril* to explore a far deeper anxiety about the implications of a language which can operate in this 'double-coded' way where meaning becomes lost in a kind of linguistic maze that is 'all rhyme and no reason'. In one notable passage the King pays a visit to the Tower of London where his party comes across a veteran of the Civil War. To Buckingham, this old and broken down man is simply another foil for his wit and we are told that the excursion is punctuated by 'many gallant jests, good or bad . . . which, spoken with a fashionable congee and listened to with a smile from a fair lady, formed the fine conversation of the day' (p. 409). However, as the visit continues the King's neglect of his royal responsibilities with regard to those who have supported him in difficult times becomes evident and it is clear that Buckingham's linguistic glibness is evidence of a failure in his (and the age's) ability to engage with deeper moral resonances and levels of experience. The evasion of meaning by which his conversation operates demonstrates that language can in fact distance us from meaningful or value-bearing signification, creating rupture rather than communication. Lack of linguistic connection also has more direct and serious narrative implications in the text; as Julian is taken to prison for example he asks to share a cell with his father, already there for alleged treason (p. 349). He fails, however, to specify which Sir Geoffrey he wishes to be lodged alongside and finds himself, ludicrously, in a cell with Sir Geoffrey Hudson, the famed dwarf of Henrietta Maria, leading to much confusion before the plot is finally brought to its conclusion.[36]

While linguistic delinquency and the dislocation which ensues are thus built into the *plot* of this novel they also lie at the very heart of the political issues upon which it is based; the tensions which it explores, Scott suggests, rest in part at least upon the failure of words to communicate in any 'fixed' or meaningful way. *Peveril* opens just at the point of the Restoration and as so often in Scott's fiction the political dynamics being explored are figured in terms of opposing families; one Royalist – Peveril of the Peak and his son Julian – and the other Presbyterian – Major Bridgenorth and his daughter Alice. And their disagreement is, as we might now expect, figured in linguistic terms. As Bridgenorth puts it "'he [Peveril senior] uses the Church Service, and I the Catechism of the Assembly of Divines at Westminster'" and he dismisses the 'mangled mass in English' which Peveril observes (p. 26). Later, as Bridgenorth decides to move away from the area following the Restoration the disagreements between the two men are again delineated by linguistic disjunction; he writes to Sir Geoffrey attempting to explain his motives but as the letter is written in the language of 'religious fanaticism' Sir Geoffrey fails to comprehend:

> The Knight of the Peak began to peruse the letter accordingly, but was much embarrassed by the peculiar language in which it was couched. "What he means by moving of candlesticks, and breaking down of carved work in the church, I cannot guess; unless he means to bring back the large silver candlesticks which my grandsire gave to be placed on the altar at Martindale-Moultrassie; and which his crop-eared friends, like sacrilegious villains as they are, stole and melted down." (p. 86)

Such 'embarrassment' delineates not only a failure to communicate in the most basic terms but also marks a dangerous inability to comprehend what is essentially the alternative discourse by which Bridgenorth is motivated; here as elsewhere in the text, verbal confusion signals the inability of opposing factions to find common linguistic (and hence any other) ground.

However, if episodes such as these in the novel hint at a concern with both the dislocating powers of language and its consequent limitations, in the second half of *Peveril* these anxieties concerning a discourse grounded in linguistic free-play become explicit. As noted earlier the time scheme moves suddenly forward, and while the novel opens with the Restoration, its main action focuses upon the Popish Plot of 1678–9 (and we might note, its location moves to a Restoration London characterised by buildings, such a Buckingham's home, which are themselves described as physical 'mazes', designed to confuse and cover corruption). Perhaps of all the historical periods Scott chooses to write about in his fiction the Popish Plot is the event which most overtly foregrounds the capacity of language to distort and deceive. Historically the Popish Plot was no more than what its chronicler Roger North, one of Scott's main sources for *Peveril*, calls a 'sham' plot. As North elaborates, the very concept of a 'sham plot' has at its base something created out of a perversion of language, the word 'sham' itself reflecting this distortion. 'It may be expected' writes North, 'that before we enter upon the Subject Matter, this Term of Art, sham-plot, should be decyphered':

> The word *Sham*, is true cant of the Newmarket Breed. It is contracted of ashamed. The native signification is a Town Lady of Diversion, in Country Maid's Cloaths, who, to make good her disguise, pretends to be so *Sham'd*! Thence it became proverbial, when a maimed Lover was laid up, or looked meagre, to say that he had met with a *Sham*. But what is this to Plots? The noble Captain Dangerfield, being an Artist in all sorts of Land Piracy, translated this Word, out of the Language of his Society, to a new Employment he had taken up of false Plotting. And as, with them, it ordinarily signifies any false or counterfeit Thing, so annexed to a Plot, it means one that is fictitious and untrue; and, being so, applied in his various writings, and sworn Depositions, of which we shall have much to observe, it is adopted into the English language.[37]

North's point is that the Popish Plot was one created out of nothing; its intention was simply to generate panic in England and stir up bad feeling against British Catholics and Charles's brother James. Historically the Popish Plot was something of a pamphlet war, its power resting on rumour and counter-rumour and on the power of the word (both written and spoken) to distort and to be distorted. McMaster comments that this national corruption is echoed in the novel when Julian is imprisoned; 'the jail' he suggests, 'is like the whole of the nation vis-à-vis the lies, rumours and deceits broadcast by the authors of the plot'.[38] But the significance of the Plot resonates throughout the novel and the linguistic foundations on which it rests are foregrounded when Edward Christian, Bridgenorth's brother-in-law and a hypocrite and fanatic of the deepest dye, warns Julian how easily he could construct and publish a narrative to prove the part the Peveril family have played in the conspiracy:

> "You have travelled in my company long enough to devise a handsome branch of the Popish Plot. How will you look, when you see come forth, in comely folio form, The Narrative of Simon Canter, otherwise called Richard Ganlesse, concerning the horrid Popish Conspiracy for the Murther of the King, and Massacre of all Protestants." (p. 221)

The type of narrative which Christian (or Ganlesse as he is called here) is referring to is the very stuff of which the Popish Plot itself was made. Scott's library at Abbotsford contains over sixty pamphlets relating to the Popish Plot with such titles as *The Narrative of the horrid plot and conspiracy of the Popish party against the life of his sacred majesty, the government and the Protestant Religion* and *Just narrative of the hellish new counter-plots of the Papists, to cast the odium of their horrid treasons upon the Presbyterians*. The power of these narratives – the printed discourses constructed out of the distorted words upon which the Plot rests – is clearly intriguing for the Author of Waverley who draws on them in many instances in *Peveril*, suggesting not only that he had read them, but that the resonant details out of which they constructed their falsities were of significant interest to him.[39]

In *Peveril of the Peak*, then, the main focus of Scott's interest lies with the ways in which words, divorced from any basis in signification, can be employed to distort; the Sham Plot as it is constructed both historically and in the text is based largely on rumour and false evidence, on words, 'garnished' to construct a corrupt version of events. This is evident in an early exchange between Topham and Captain Dangerfield, two agents for the Plot:

> "And you, Captain Dangerfield, and Master Everett, you must put on your Protestant spectacles, and shew me where there is the shadow of a priest, or of a priest's favourer; for I am come down with a broom in my cap to sweep this north country of such like cattle."
>
> One of the persons he thus addressed, who wore the garb of a broken-down citizen, only answered, "Ay, truly, Master Topham, it is time to purge the garner."

The other . . . was more loquacious. "I take it on my damnation," said this zealous Protestant witness, "that I will discover the marks of the beast on every one of them betwixt sixteen and seventy, as plainly as if they had crossed themselves with ink, instead of holy water. Since we have a King willing to do justice, and a House of Commons to uphold prosecutions, why, damn me, the cause must not stand still for lack of evidence."

"Stick to that, noble captain," answered the officer; "but, prithee, reserve thy oaths for the court of justice; it is but sheer waste to throw them away, as you do, in your ordinary conversation."

"Fear you nothing, Master Topham," answered Dangerfield; "it is right to keep a man's gifts in use; and were I altogether to renounce oaths in my private discourse, how should I know how to use one when I needed it? But you hear me use none of your Papist abjurations. I swear not by the Mass, or before George, or by any thing that belongs to idolatry; but such downright oaths as may serve a poor Protestant gentleman, who would fain serve Heaven and the King."

"Bravely spoken, most noble Festus," said his yoke-fellow. "But do not suppose, that although I do not use to garnish my words with oaths out of season, that I will be wanting, when called upon, to declare the height and the depth, the breadth and the length, of this hellish plot against the King and the Protestant faith." (p. 208)

The connection between the distorting potential of language and the Plot is, however, expressed most clearly in Scott's depiction of the key conspirator of the Plot, Titus Oates. In the novel Scott describes Oates's face as 'having the mouth, as the organ by use of which he was to rise to eminence, placed in the very centre of the countenance' (p. 422). Scott's description seems a strange one – where else after all, would someone's mouth be but in the middle of his face – but his meaning became clearer when the original source was sought for the purposes of annotating the Edinburgh Edition. Roger North provides a fuller description of Oates and what he sees as the link between his appearance and his corruption:

> He was a low man, of an ill cut, very short neck; and his visage and his features were most particular. His mouth was in the center of his face; and a compass there would sweep his nose, forehead and chin within the Perimeter . . . In a word, he was a most consummate cheat, Blasphemer, vicious, perjured, impudent and saucy foul-mouth'd wretch.[40]

Contemporary accounts of Oates also delineate him as talking in the most peculiar of ways. North for example, uses a kind of phonetic transcription to render the peculiar vowel sounds by which Oates speaks, and Scott picks up on this in the novel. 'His pronunciation, too,' writes Scott 'was after a conceited fashion of his own, in which he accented the vowels in a manner altogether peculiar to himself' (p. 422). For example, at one point, Scott has Oates stating '"Maay laard . . . aye do not come here to have my evidence questioned as touching the Plaat" (p. 423).[41] Oates's very form of speech, then, is a kind of perversion of language, a twisting of it so that it becomes almost unintelligible, just as the literal meaning of what he actually says is a perversion of the ability of language to communicate any kind of moral truth or authenticity. McMaster comments that there is no other character in Scott whose 'individual speech . . . [is] so described and criticised';[42] he is, indeed, rendered here as 'foul-mouth'd' in every sense. Through Oates and his description of the Popish Plot what Scott is depicting is not justice operating through the power of rhetoric, but rhetoric subverting the very possibility of justice (itself a discourse). As the king recognises, the Plot is like '"men who talk in their sleep"' (p. 329) – an expression, as it were, of language without agency. The consequence of the Plot and the hysteria which surrounds it, writes Roger North, was such that 'the People fell into ambiguous Forms of Common Speech, using words, one for another, as we might imagine at Babel, when all language was confounded'.[43]

    Incidents within the text such as these and the context that lies behind them (recovered by Edinburgh Edition's act of annotation) suggest that in this novel the Author of Waverley is exhibiting a peculiarly modern anxiety concerning the implications that ensue once language is cut free from signification. It is, consequently, hardly surprising that the Popish Plot, both as it was historically constructed and as it is depicted here, should have been of interest to him at this point in his writing career. It is, perhaps, also not surprising given the crisis in language which emerges in the text, that this should be a novel which places a great deal of emphasis on the role of silence.

    This is seen most overtly in the person of the Duchess of Derby's supposed mute Fenella, or Zarah as she later re-names herself. Fenella, a character who is presented to us as deaf and dumb at the outset of the narrative only to emerge as a spy for the Presbyterian party later in the text, has been the source of much unease for readers of this novel – an 'unfortunate conception' to quote Lockhart. However, if we accept that this text is exploring a crisis in the ability of language to communicate with any kind of agency the presence of Fenella and what emerges as her wilful decision to remain silent may also be seen as symptomatic of deeper anxieties about language and communication that are operating within this text, particularly if we consider it alongside the silence of Effie and Jeanie Deans. As Graham McMaster notes, it is Fenella's 'silence and not her size' which is of interest here.[44] While silence, or what might be called 'negative narration', can be found throughout Scott's earlier work the role of such silence becomes extreme in *Peveril* and Fenella's failure to communicate is only the most significant; characters are repeatedly rendered speechless at key moments of crisis and conflict. Silence, like linguistic dislocation, often serves to underpin the gulf that exists between characters and the apparent irreconcilability of the positions they assume. The seeming impasse between Alice and Julian, ill-fated lovers from opposing families, as they meet at Black-Fort, for example, is punctuated by moments of silence; Julian, we are told, 'took in silence a seat removed at some distance from hers' and Alice expresses the apparent hopelessness of their position by telling Julian that he has '"spoken enough"' and spoken '"in vain"' (p. 124). Later, confronted by Alice's father about his proposal to her, Julian once again can only retreat into silence 'mute for a moment, in the vain attempt to shape his answer so as at once to be an acquiescence in what Bridgenorth stated, and a vindication of his own regard for his parents, and for the honour of his house' (pp. 176–7). Sir Geoffrey, similarly, recognising that he shares no common ground – linguistic or otherwise – with the Plot conspirators '"will not open [his] mouth to utter a single word while [he] is in the company of such knaves"' (p. 246). These moments of silence, or perhaps suppression of speech, are only a few of many such incidents in this novel as though for its author a recognition of the fissuring and distorting nature of language goes hand in hand in this text with a realisation that, at times of crisis, the only option available may, indeed, be silence; as Wittgenstein states, '[w]hat we cannot speak about we must pass over in silence'.[45]

In spite of the silence at the heart of it (and it is of course both ironic and fitting that it contains more words than any other Scott novel) *Peveril*, does, eventually, move towards a conventional narrative closure – the revelation of Christian's treachery and the marriage of Alice and Julian. As we have already seen, however, in this text the conventions of closure are only a gloss to a far darker and more disruptive conclusion; a conclusion that is peculiarly marked by further acts of silence. Julian, for example, when requested to give information on Bridgenorth's conspiracy becomes a 'dumb witness' refusing to co-operate (p. 487) and even the loquacious and witty Buckingham is rendered silent when the king acknowledges that he knows of his treachery (p. 491). Most telling of all, however, is the fate of poor Fenella. Tricked by the king into revealing her true identity Fenella gives one 'loud scream of agony' (p. 492), revealing that she is not the deaf and dumb mute we have believed her to be, but her talkative alter-ego Zarah. Having betrayed both herself and her father by her one act of utterance, however, the traumatised Fenella can only retreat once more into a stammer never to speak in the novel again. Ann Schlossman-Robb recognises that in personal terms Fenella's retreat back into silence 'can only be read as defeat, [relinquishing] her claims to self-identification and self-determination';[46] but these other moments of silence are also markers of a wider defeat or disempowerment. While Scott's earlier work may be shaped by a search for the ideal form of words by which to articulate the past by the time he comes to write *Peveril* his exploration of the limits of language has brought him to the point where he must acknowledge that at key moments of historical conflict and crisis there may, indeed, be nothing to be said. Just as its contrived ending might suggest that *Peveril* is an historical fiction which foregrounds an anxiety concerning the ability of the novel, or perhaps *any discourse*, to delineate the passage of time moving towards a pattern of progress and reconciliation, so too it may be one which offers a narrative which evokes a crisis located in the very substance of narrative itself – linguistic communication.

If, as has been suggested here, these are questions which haunt *Peveril of the Peak* it is hardly surprising that, to use Lockhart's phrase, it is a perplexed text. An awareness of these perplexities may not make *Peveril* any more popular with readers, but it does, perhaps, make it a more intellectually interesting novel, encouraging us to read beyond our exhaustion at the end of the second volume. If we are alert to this foregrounding of questions of language in the novels of the early 1820s it becomes evident that the period of self-reflexive preface writing coincides with a period where the Author of Waverley reaches a crisis in relation to the limits of language; haunted by questions concerning how language actually conveys meaning and allows dialogue to take place these troubled novels are marked by moments of non-communication where language becomes, in every sense, broken. In these texts what Scott describes elsewhere as a 'poverty' of words[47] ceases to function, both for the novelist and as a tool by which he may, to borrow Templeton's phrase, 'translate' one culture for another. Reading Scott in these terms it becomes apparent that at the core of these, the most self-reflexive of his texts, lies an awareness of a far more modern type of linguistic 'exhaustion', a sense of the very limits of language, so that the strange 'cant or broken language derived from several tongues spoken by beggars, criminals, gypsies, and other such outcasts for purposes of mutual recognition and concealment from regular society' identified by the Edinburgh Edition as a function of Alsatia in *The Fortunes of Nigel* can be recognised not only as a feature of that 'place apart', but as a common thread in all of Scott's work. While language may at times facilitate 'mutual recognition' in these troubled texts of the 1820s, haunted as it is by the tensions between radical representations and free play that has been explored in his earlier work, it just as often conceals or fails to communicate leading, indeed, to exhaustion and to an awareness not only of what can be said via language but, more perplexingly for the novelist, of what *cannot* be said.

## Notes

1 Graham McMaster, *Scott and Society* (Cambridge: Cambridge University Press, 1981), p. 149.

2 Fiona Robertson states that 'He changed the nature (not just the subject) of his fiction not in 1826, but with his first novel set outside Scotland, *Ivanhoe*, in 1819. See 'Walter Scott' in *The Edinburgh History of Scottish Literature*, ed. by Ian Brown, Thomas Owen Clancy, Susan Manning and Murray Pittock, 3 vols (Edinburgh: Edinburgh University Press, 2007), pp. 183–90 (p. 2.189).

3 Patricia S. Gaston, *Prefacing the Waverley Novels*, p. 16.

4 Jerome McGann, 'Walter Scott's Romantic Postmodernity', p. 119.

5 It is interesting to note that Scott's introductions for *Ballantyne's Novelist's Library* are written at around the same time as the Prefaces and it is no surprise that they share similar concerns.

6 Graham Tulloch, *The Language of Walter Scott*, p. 14.

7 See the Explanatory Notes to *The Fortunes of Nigel*, p. 617.

8 For a full discussion of the use of cant language and foreign terms in both *The Fortunes of Nigel* and *Peveril of the Peak* see Graham Tulloch, *The Language of Walter Scott*, pp. 75–81.

9 Frank Jordan, 'Essay on the Text', *The Fortunes of Nigel*, p. 444.

10 Caroline McCracken-Flesher, *Possible Scotlands*, p. 72.

11 James Burnet, Lord Monboddo, *Of the Origin and Progress of Language*, p. 3.41.

12 By the nineteenth century the term 'niggle' also had connotations of

cramped handwriting, reminding us of the manuscript received by Dryasdust. This offers another example of the essentially textual way in which these novels are being constructed.

13  Ludwig Wittgenstein, *Philosophical Investigations*, p. 114.

14  D. W. Jefferson, *Walter Scott: An Introductory Essay* (Edinburgh: Dunedin Academic Press, 2002), p. 94.

15  See Graham McMaster, *Scott and Society*, pp. 129–47 and Fiona Robertson, *Legitimate Histories*, p. 195.

16  Smith states this in a letter of 21 January 1823. See *Scott: the Critical Heritage*, p. 175.

17  Lockhart also notes that Senior in the *London Review* was to give the novel its harshest criticism but that it was 'just as well as severe'. See *Life*, pp. 5.245–46.

18  MS 323, f. 204r; f. 222r–v.

19  *Life*, p. 5.170.

20  Constable to James Ballantyne, 22 July 1822, MS 791, f.311.v.

21  *Letters,* p. 7.81, Feb 1822.

22  *Letters*, p. 7.82, Feb 1822.

23  For a full outline of the genesis of *Peveril of the Peak* see Alison Lumsden, 'Essay on the Text', *Peveril of the Peak*.

24  MS 21059, f.133.

25  MS 21059, f.141.

26  Graham McMaster, *Scott and Society*.

27  Ann Schlossman-Robb, *'The Honour of Men and the Truth of Women': Disguise and its Cultural Implications in the Waverley Novels* (Unpublished PhD thesis, University of Aberdeen, 1997), p. 147.

28  George, Duke of Buckingham, *The Rehearsal* and Richard Brinsley Sheridan, *The Critic*, ed. and with a preface by Cedric Gale (New York: Barron's Educational Series, 1960), 'Preface', p. 5.

29  'Epilogue', George, Duke of Buckingham, *The Rehearsal*.

30  Rose A. Zimbardo, *A Mirror to Nature: Transformations in Drama and Aesthetics 1660–1732* (Lexington: University Press of Kentucky, 1986), p. 19.

31  Cedric Gale reproduces one such key written in 1704 by S. Briscoe.

32  Rose A. Zimbardo, *A Mirror to Nature: Transformations in Drama and Aesthetics 1660–1732*, p. 17.

33  Ibid. p. 115.

34  Ibid. p. 115.

35  Ibid. pp. 116–18.

36  Graham McMaster comments that 'In prison . . . language is something that

deceives' (p. 144) and that there is evidence in the novel of a 'disregard for propriety and likelihood so great that it amounts to an abuse of language' (p. 133).

37 Roger North, *Examen: Or, An Enquiry into the Credit and Veracity of a Pretended Complete History* (London, 1740), p. 231. See also the note to 483.13 in the Explanatory Notes in *Peveril of the Peak*.

38 Graham McMaster, *Scott and Society*, p. 144.

39 For a full illustration of the extent to which Scott draws on these pamphlets for material see the Explanatory Notes in *Peveril of the Peak*.

40 North, p. 225.

41 As readers might expect this peculiar form of depicting Oates's speech is more marked in the manuscript than in the first edition. Most of these oddities have been restored in the Edinburgh Edition.

42 Graham McMaster, *Scott and Society*, p. 144.

43 North, p. 125.

44 Graham McMaster, *Scott and Society*, p. 144.

45 Ludwig Wittgenstein, *Tractatus Logico-Philosophicus*, p. 74.

46 Ann Schlossman-Robb, *'The Honour of Men and the Truth of Women': Disguise and its Cultural Implications in the Waverley Novels*, p. 164.

47 See Walter Scott, 'Henry Fielding', pp. 82–3.

# Chapter 5
## 'Narrative Continued':
## *Redgauntlet* and *Chronicles of the Canongate*

In his influential essay 'The Literature of Exhaustion' John Barth argues that, confronted by a post-Saussurean crisis in language and a realisation of the limitations of its communicative capacities, the novel reaches a 'dead end', signalling 'the used-upness of certain forms or the felt exhaustion of certain possibilities'.[1] For many critics Scott's novels of the 1820s represent a similar dead-end, the beginnings of a slow demise for the Author of Waverley. However, Barth was later to redress his own conclusions in an essay called 'The Literature of Replenishment' where he acknowledges that, against all odds, the 'postmodern' turn that had been taken by fiction since his earlier essay has served to reinvigorate the form:

> What my essay 'The Literature of Exhaustion' was really about, so it seems to me now, was the effective 'exhaustion' not of language or of literature, but of the aesthetic of high modernism: that admirable, not-to-be repudiated, but essentially complete 'program' of what Hugh Kenner has dubbed 'the Pound era.' In 1966/67 we scarcely had the term *postmodernism* in its current literary-critical usage—at least I hadn't heard it yet—but a number of us, in quite different ways and with varying combinations of intuitive response and conscious deliberation, were already well into the working out, not of the next-best thing after modernism, but of the *best next* thing: what is gropingly now called postmodernist fiction; what I hope might also be thought of one day as a literature of replenishment.[2]

The feature of 'what is gropingly . . . called postmodernist fiction' which Barth chooses to concentrate upon is 'authorial self-consciousness, often manifested as narrative self-reflexiveness'[3] and borne out of 'the problematics, not only of language, but of the medium and processes of literature'.[4] Rather than a dead-end, consequently, a recognition of the perplexed nature of language and the processes by which literature inevitably operates becomes a gateway into a new and radically self-reflexive form of fiction that seeks to 'short circuit' the limits of language. Similarly, for Scott, the exhaustion with both plot and language which marks his novels of the early 1820s does not signal the 'beginning of the end' for the Author of Waverley but, rather, leads to what is perhaps his greatest period of narrative experimentation. This chapter will explore the extent to which in texts such as *Redgauntlet* and *Chronicles of the Canongate* Scott moves beyond the aesthetic 'exhaustion' of the early 1820s to offer fictions which create new relationships with language and explore the necessity of proceeding in the face of the fractured and problematic nature of all human communication.

Published in 1824 *Redgauntlet* has remained one of the most popular of Scott's fictions and is arguably his most overtly autobiographical.[5] While modern criticism has discussed this text in relation to the ways in which it brings Scott's Jacobite sequence to a form of uneasy closure what has only been incidentally noted is that, as we might expect from a text which follows on from Scott's writing of the early part of the decade, it demonstrates a near obsession with the relationship between signifier and sign, posing questions concerning the relationships between words and meaning and the implications of this relationship for both personal and national identity.[6] *Redgauntlet* lends itself to a discussion of this sort for, taking as its subject matter a semi-fictional and abortive Jacobite Rising of 1765, it is set in a covert world of spies and smugglers and the oblique language via which they communicate, suitable terrain for the kind of 'double coding' of language we have seen operating in *Peveril of the Peak*. The 'broken' language of slang appears again here too, described as, 'conversation . . . disguised so completely by the use of cant words and the thieves-Latin called slang, that even when [Alan] caught the words, he found himself as far as ever from the sense of their conversation' and Scott's own professional idiolect, the language of the law, is mangled to incomprehensibility in the case of Poor Peter Peebles (p. 245). As such, it is not surprising that in this text Scott is concerned with the ways in which the novelist might proceed given the 'broken' nature of the medium in which he is operating.

The novel's overt concern with linguistic fracture is demonstrated in the closing pages of the novel where Prince Charles Edward Stuart finally makes an appearance, circumstances which require a particular use of language as well as a particular code of etiquette:

> Redgauntlet laughed scornfully, and was about to follow the fiery young man, when Sir Richard again interposed. "Are we to exhibit," he said, "the last symptoms of the dissolution of our party, by turning our swords against each other?—Be patient, Lord—; on such conferences as this, much must pass unquestioned which might brook challenge elsewhere. There is a privilege of party as of parliament—men cannot, in emergency, stand upon picking phrases.—Gentlemen, if you will extend

your confidence in me so far, I will wait upon his Majesty, and I hope my Lord—and Mr Redgauntlet will accompany me. I trust the explanation of this unpleasant matter will prove entirely satisfactory, and that we will find ourselves at liberty to render our homage to our Sovereign without reserve, when I for one will be the first to peril all in his just quarrel." (pp. 352–3)

This passage is interesting for it demonstrates several features that are true of the novel as a whole, and in particular of its closing pages. Here, for example, in the space of a few short lines, Charles Edward is referred to as both 'his Majesty' and 'our Sovereign', while other names are left unsaid. Elsewhere in these closing pages, he is also called the 'Royal Wanderer' (p. 353), a 'Prince' (p. 354), 'Father Buonadventure', 'Charles Edward', 'his Majesty', the 'Unfortunate Prince', 'Charles Stuart' (pp. 354–6) and 'the Wanderer' (p. 358). He is also referred to as the 'King' twice (p. 356 and p. 371) and finally as an 'unhappy Adventurer' (p. 374), 'the last heir of the Stuarts' (p. 375) and 'the Chevalier' (p. 377). This problem with nomenclature also extends to other characters in the novel; Redgauntlet himself is called, among other things, Mr Ingoldsby, and Herries of Birrenswork. The editors of *Redgauntlet* for the Edinburgh Edition note that Scott had particular difficulties with names in this text, offering many variants on 'Birrenswork' in the manuscript before being prompted to standardisation by James Ballantyne. 'On other occasions' they comment, 'Scott does not appear to have remembered what he called minor characters nor how he has spelt their names' with a consequent confusion within the text.[7] While much of this muddle was resolved as usual in the first edition and finally removed in the Edinburgh Edition it is symptomatic of the fact that the relationship of names to identity could almost be taken as the theme of this novel, which concerns itself with the dual quest for the identity of the true king and of its protagonist Darsie Latimer. The first of these is, moreover, articulated via a rhyme that plays on the ambiguous nature of language:

God bless the King!—God bless the Faith's defender!—
God bless—No harm in blessing the Pretender.
Who that Pretender is, and who that King,—
God bless us all,—is quite another thing. (p. 186)

The second theme is woven into the very fabric of the text and is encapsulated in the title of the novel itself, which simultaneously refers to the character of the name 'Redgauntlet' who appears throughout the text, and to the character Darsie Latimer who discovers himself to be 'Sir Arthur Darsie Redgauntlet of that Ilk' (p. 312).[8]

Language in *Redgauntlet*, consequently, is demonstrably 'broken', as much about concealment as it is about revelation; concerned as much with what is not said via the power of naming, as with what is communicated by it. As Jina Politi puts it this text is, above all, one about 'the arbitrariness of the signifier'.[9] However, while this anxiety about language may be an increasingly prominent feature of Scott's texts throughout the 1820s what is interesting about *Redgauntlet* is the extent to which it appears to impact upon the very fabric of the novel itself both in terms of its overall narrative structure, and at local levels. As a consequence, *Redgauntlet* is far more radically self-reflexive than any of Scott's earlier texts. We will turn to the larger scale manifestations of this later, but at a local level what is evident is the highly 'textual' nature of the novel.

The 'authorial self-consciousness' that Barth identifies as a feature of the 'literature of replenishment' is manifested in *Redgauntlet* in the extent to which it is a text shaped out of highly wrought and constructed discourses. As we have seen, proverbs are a feature of the broken communication in *The Fortunes of Nigel* and *Redgauntlet* is also marked by the number of proverbs or proverbial-sounding phrases that occur within its pages. The Edinburgh Edition identifies nearly eighty such phrases and while this may be comparable to other texts what is interesting here is that these proverbs occur in clusters so that there seem to be points where characters resort to this metaphorical and highly rhetorical form as their main means of communication. This is particularly noticeable in chapter 11 of volume 2, for example, when Alan enters the rather dubious world of Provost Crosbie, Maxwell and Summertrees where Jacobite undercurrents are being papered over by the use of language. There are sixteen proverbial phrases in this chapter alone (all annotated and sourced by the Edinburgh Edition), drawing attention to a form of language that has a particular relationship to meaning. While phrases such as 'Scornful dogs will eat dirty puddings' (p. 224) or 'The sooth bourd is nae bourd' (p. 218) are in straightforward syntactical terms meaningless (or so far removed from their original meaning that it is essentially lost), they do, of course, carry a meaning of a sort, themselves drawing attention to a kind of rupture between the signifier itself and what is being signified.

A second instance of a highly textual form of language also occurs in the frequent references to song. The presence of Wandering Willie facilitates this and song (both in its verbal and non-verbal forms) is used as a means of communication in the novel. For example, when Willie comes to Darsie's aid during the period of his captivity, Darsie recognises him by the fact that he 'played twice over the beautiful Scottish air called Wandering Willie' (p. 200). To express his state of captivity Darsie sings three lines of the 137th psalm (the first of which is printed in the text). To raise his spirits Willie then plays a 'lively Scotch air' and as the words 'instantly occurred' to Darsie four lines are reproduced. Darsie then whistles to Willie, although in order to help with the meaning implied by the tune the words are given for the reader: 'Come back again and lo'e me / When a' the lave are gane' (p. 201). In response Willie changes his air to 'There's my thumb, I'll ne'er beguile thee' (p. 201) although while the Edinburgh Edition note informs us that this is 'the choric line in a love-song, found in varying degrees of outspokenness', these remain unspoken here.[10] In the chapter we have just been discussing in relation to proverbs, allusions to Jacobite song are also used to show political allegiances and to test out Alan's own loyalties. Referring to the dismissal of Peter MacAlpine, Provost Crosbie comments: "'I understand that he lost the music-bells in Edinburgh, for playing 'Ower the Water to Charlie,' upon the tenth of June. He is a black sheep, and deserves no encouragement.'" (p. 216). The novel continues:

> "Not a bad tune though, after all," said Summertrees; and, turning to the window, he half hummed, half whistled, the air in question, then sang the last verse aloud:

> "Oh, I lo'e weel my Charlie's name,
>     Though some there be that abhor him;
> But oh to see the deil gang hame,
>     Wi' a' the Whigs before him!
> Over the water, and over the sea,
>     And over the water to Charlie;
> Come weal, come woe, we'll gather and go,
>     And live or die with Charlie." (p. 217)

These instances offer a particularly interesting kind of textual self-consciousness for in some cases the words themselves (in the last example all but the final verse) are completely absent. Consequently, communication must take place here not via what is *said*, but by what is *inferred*. Meaning here resides not in acts of utterance, but in the tunes that have become a particular form of signification for them. As readers, consequently, we are forced to construct the text (and therefore the meaning) for ourselves, or are reliant on a narrator to fill in the gaps and supply the meaning for us. These highly stylised aspects of the novel have the effect of drawing our attention to its nature as text and to the problematics surrounding communication in which it is grounded; when such imprecise forms of communication are at play (proverbs operate upon metaphoric principles, while songs rely on the reader to interpret) it is impossible not to be aware of the arbitrary nature of discourse and its imprecise relationship to any kind of finite meaning; after all, not all readers can be relied upon to 'fill in the gaps' in the same way.

It is clear that this growing self-reflexivity also has implications for the larger narrative structure of *Redgauntlet*. While Scott plays with layers of narration in texts like *The Tale of Old Mortality* and *The Heart of Mid-Lothian*, and offers para-textual frames in *Ivanhoe* and *The Fortunes of Nigel, Redgauntlet* demonstrates a new level of self-reflexivity in its increasing restlessness concerning the nature of narrative form. *Redgauntlet* is, consequently, as several commentators have recognised, a deeply 'metafictional' text,[11] acutely aware of the relationship between forms of discourse and meaning, so that 'shifts in literary mode and discourse emphasise the shifts in perspective, and at the same time keep the reader aware that the perception of "truth" is at least in part determined by narrative mode'.[12] What critics are recognising in such descriptions of the novel is the extent to which it plays with forms of narrative. As a text it consists of what David Hewitt has called a 'formal *melange*',[13] merging together a host of different discursive modes such as the epistle, the journal, straightforward (although highly and overtly focalised) narrative, and the famous interpolated episode 'Wandering Willie's Tale'. As Hewitt points out none of these forms is in itself new, and all are, indeed, 'in some way characteristic of the 1760s, and appropriate to a novel much of which was purportedly written in 1765'.[14] Nevertheless by putting them together in a highly stylised way Scott is drawing attention to the very nature of narrative form and the meanings contained within different forms of discourse.

While this 'melange' may be recognised as a continuation of the generic experimentation and indeterminacy found elsewhere in Scott's work it is particularly foregrounded in the very narrative texture of *Redgauntlet* for it draws attention to its own highly eclectic nature by offering chapter headings such as 'Letter One: Darsie Latimer to Alan Fairford' and 'Letter Seven The Same to the Same'. The whole of the first volume of the novel takes the form of letters between Alan and Darsie. The epistolary form is, of course, a gesture towards the eighteenth-century setting of the text but it also lends itself to a novel which is concerned with the shifting and arbitrary relationship between events and the point of view from which they are perceived since, as David Lodge has suggested, the form allows the writer to 'have more than one correspondent, and thus show the same event from different points of view'.[15] Writing a novel in this form as late as 1824 in itself suggests a certain self-reflexivity but this is exacerbated by the fact that Scott does not stick with the epistolary mode throughout the text but opens his second volume with a chapter deliberately termed 'Narrative' and with a highly self-conscious (and tongue-in-cheek) commentary on the disadvantages and advantages of a novel transmitted via letters:

> The advantage of laying before the reader, in the words of the actors themselves, the adventures which we must otherwise have narrated in our own, has given great popularity to the publication of epistolary correspondence, as practised by various great authors, and by ourselves in the preceding volume. Nevertheless, a genuine correspondence of this kind, (and Heaven forbid it should be in any respect sophisticated by interpolations of our own!) can seldom be found to contain all in which it is necessary to instruct the reader for his full comprehension of the story. (p. 125)

The second volume also contains chapters headed 'Narrative Continued', 'Journal of Darsie Latimer' (which allows Scott to employ first person narration), 'Narrative of Alan Fairford' (a section of the novel focalised via Alan but told in the third person) and 'Narrative of Alan Fairford Continued'. The final volume continues in a similar vein with further chapters headed 'Narrative of Alan Fairford' and 'Narrative of Darsie Latimer', before concluding, when all characters are once more gathered together, with a section once again headed simply 'Narrative Continued'. These headings may draw attention to the formal dexterity of the novel but by embedding them within the structure of his fiction Scott is also offering us something highly self-conscious which foregrounds its very nature as constructed text; while the headings 'Letter' or 'Journal' for example, may not strike a reader as particularly odd, the heading 'Narrative' only describes, after all, what we have come to expect of any novel. The presence of the word in the text (in small capitals and at the head of a chapter) serves to reinforce the artifice of the story being told and draws attention to the text's metafictional status.

The metafictional status of the text is also reinforced by the many other forms of narrative which exist within this novel besides those formally foregrounded by chapter headings. The most famous of these is, of course, 'Wandering Willie's Tale', which appears within one of Darsie's letters to Alan. Set off from the text of the letter and with a title in Gothic script 'Wandering Willie's Tale', like the larger chapter divisions, is announced as occupying a different form of narrative space; the word 'tale' reinforces this since the word suggests a form of narrative that occupies the liminal space between formal narrative prose and oral 'story'. It is worth noting, for example, that many of James Hogg's shorter pieces are designated as 'Tales', while the 'Fortunes of Martin Waldeck' in Scott's own *The Antiquary* is also so designated (p. 137) and occupies a similar kind of narrative terrain to the material presented here in *Redgauntlet*. What all these fictions have in common is that they contain material of a supernatural, or potentially supernatural, nature with the term 'tale' seemingly marking their status as material that sits alongside, but not entirely within, the post-Enlightenment space of the novel.

While material such as this may overtly announce itself as a 'tale within a narrative' or a 'tale within a historical novel', there are, however, other examples of stories within the more formal divisions of the text. One such example is the way in which Darsie finally uncovers the details of his identity. Having had this hinted to him by 'Wandering Willie's Tale', the full details are also given to him via story, in the form of the revelations by his sister 'Greenmantle', contained within a chapter headed 'Narrative of Darsie Latimer, Continued'. While this section of the novel is ostensibly narrated in the third person, the details of Darsie's past are, like Willie's tale, offered to the reader in the form of what is essentially an interpolated 'story'. While Darsie does at times interrupt his sister, the chapter opens in a way that seems to announce that Lilias is adopting the role of story-teller, and Darsie's interruptions act only as prompts to facilitate her narration. This is evident in the opening lines of Lilias's narrative:

> "The House of Redgauntlet," said the young lady, "has for centuries been supposed to lie under a doom, which has rendered vain their courage, their talents, their ambition, and their wisdom. Often making a figure in history, they have been ever in the situation of men rowing against both wind and tide, who distinguish themselves by their desperate exertions of strength, and their persevering endurance of toil, but without being able to advance themselves upon their course, by either vigour or resolution. They pretend to trace this fatality to a legendary history, which I may tell you at a less busy moment." (p. 299)

It is interesting to note that Lilias's speech is constructed here not as conventional dialogue, but as narrative or story. The fact that her words constitute the opening of a chapter (with the consequent small capitals marking the opening words) contributes to this, but so too does the fact that she begins her revelations about Darsie's identity with context, or 'back story'. Her language is also highly constructed (the reference to wind and tide being proverbial) and finally, the story she is telling here is also connected to other tales or stories in the text, the 'legend' already recounted via 'Wandering Willie's Tale'. In short, Lilias's account operates much like Willie's narrative, and occupies a similar kind of space within this text.

These set pieces within the already highly self-reflexive format of *Redgauntlet* serve to de-stabilise the nature of narrative, reminding the reader of the formalised nature of novel writing and novel reading. As John Barth puts it, 'stories within stories . . . always to some degree imply stories *about* stories and even stories about story*telling*'.[16] While Scott may have spent the earlier part of his career struggling to find the correct form to communicate meaning it seems that by 1824 his interest lies elsewhere. As Barth himself may have put it, faced with the exhaustion of linguistic redundancy Scott turns to self-consciousness, the 'self-transcendent parody' of self-reflexivity, for replenishment.[17]

## Chronicles of the Canongate

*Redgauntlet*, then, demonstrates Scott at what is perhaps his most experimental up to that date, 'rapid cycling' through a series of narrative forms in order to foreground the relationship of discourse to identity as a response to a recognition of the arbitrary nature of the relationship between signifier and signified. It would not have been unreasonable to expect such self-reflexive experimentation to continue in the novels of the later 1820s.

However, in 1825 an event was to occur that was to change Scott's life and his relationship to his writing. That event was, of course, the well-documented financial crash of late 1825 that was to render Scott insolvent, and was to result, in part, in the death of Lady Scott. The details of this event do not need to be reiterated here.[18] However, Scott's account of what he sees as the literary implications of his financial hardship are worth noting, for they have direct relevance for the texts which Scott was to write after this point:

For myself the magic wand of the Unknown is shiverd in his grasp. He must henceforth be termd the Too well Known. The feast of fancy is over with the feeling of independence. I can no longer have the delight of waking in the morning with bright ideas in my mind, haste to commit them to paper, and count them monthly as the means of planting such groves and purchasing such wastes, replacing my dreams' fiction by other prospective visions of walks by

> Fountain-heads and pathless groves
> Places which pale passion loves—

This cannot be—But I may make substantial husbandry—write history and such substantial concerns. They will not be received with the same enthusiasm—at least I much doubt the general knowledge that an author must write for his bread, at least for improving his pittance, degrades him and his productions in the public eye. He falls into the secondrate rank of estimation.

> While the harness sore galls and the spurs his side goad
> The high mettled racer's a hack on the road.

It is a bitter thought, but if tears start at it let them flow.[19]

Scott was right to recognise that his own financial problems would result in his unmasking as the Author of Waverley. Scott's authorship was acknowledged at a meeting of his creditors in January, 1826 and made more widely known at a Theatrical Fund Dinner in February of 1827.[20] As a consequence, therefore, *Chronicles of the Canongate* was the first work of fiction to be published where Scott's authorship was transparent. These circumstances were to generate a text that both prompts Scott to revisit and recast his ideas about the ways in which the past can be re-negotiated and understood for present times and galvanises a self-reflexivity that was to become increasingly present in his later works.

This relationship between Scott's 'unveiling' and the text that follows may not be immediately apparent for in the 'Introduction' to *Chronicles of the Canongate* Scott comments: 'As for the work which follows, it was meditated, and in part printed, long before the avowal of novels took place, and originally commenced with a declaration that it was neither to have introduction nor preface of any kind' (pp. 10–11). However, Claire Lamont's 'Essay on the Text' for the Edinburgh Edition demonstrates that this is not quite true. While writing may have begun significantly before the Theatrical Fund Dinner of 23 February 1827, which Scott pinpoints as the moment of his public unveiling in the 'Introduction', it clearly had commenced by May 1826,[21] after the creditors' meeting where Scott had been forced to reveal his authorship for reasons of copyright, and, crucially, after that moment in December

1825 when Scott wrote in his *Journal* that his 'magic wand' was 'shiverd'. While we may quibble about the precise moment of public revelation, therefore, it is clear that psychologically Scott felt himself unveiled before *Chronicles* was begun.

This act of 'unmasking' is, consequently, intrinsic to *Chronicles of the Canongate*. Scott alludes to it directly in the 'Introduction' to the text for there, writing for the first time in his own character, he lays 'aside his incognito' (p. 3). Likening the event to the decision by an actor on the Italian stage who 'played Harlequin barefaced' he demonstrates some trepidation in revealing his identity; for the actor this unmasking meant that 'he had lost all the audacity which a sense of incognito bestowed' and Scott fears that he will suffer the same fate:

> Perhaps the Author of Waverley is now about to incur a risk of the same kind, and endanger his popularity by having laid aside his incognito. It is certainly not a voluntary experiment, like that of Harlequin; for it was my original intention never to have avowed these works during my lifetime, and the original manuscripts were carefully preserved, (though by the care of others rather than mine,) with the purpose of supplying the necessary evidence of the truth when the period of announcing it should arrive. But the affairs of my publishers having unfortunately passed into a management different from their own, I had no right any longer to rely upon secrecy in that quarter; and thus my mask, like my Aunt Dinah's in Tristram Shandy, having begun to wax a little threadbare about the chin, it became time to lay it aside with a good grace, unless I desired it should fall in pieces from my face. (pp. 3–4)

Writing for the first time with his 'magic wand . . . shiverd in his grasp', Scott fears that the text that follows will lose some of the 'reckless play of raillery which gave vivacity to his original acting' (p. 3) and that without the 'caprice' of his incognito he will '[degrade] the character of the children of [his] imagination' (p. 9). It is not surprising, therefore, that writing in his own character as 'the sole and unassisted author of all the Novels published as the composition of the "Author of Waverley"' (p. 10), Scott should write an altogether new kind of text, and one which is more experimental and self-reflexive than any of his previous fictions, incorporating within it a discussion of the status of the writer and his relationship to a broken and fractured world.[22]

As with *Redgauntlet* this self-reflexivity is manifested in the structural and generic complexity of the collection for one of the first problems that confronts us when we speak about *Chronicles of the Canongate* is that which has vexed all of Scott's work, how we may categorise it generically. Clearly *Chronicles* is not a novel in any conventional sense and the individual tales of which it is constituted can clearly stand on their own, a feature confirmed by the fact that many have argued that 'The Two Drovers' may be the first British short story. Yet in spite of the disparate nature of the texts W. J. Overton's view that *Chronicles* as a collection is 'an expedient of limited success' and that the 'links in the *Chronicles* are so weak [that] "The Two Drovers" loses nothing by being read independently'[23] seems an inadequate response. This account sees only the surface superficiality of the immediate subject matter of the tales and must leave aside Croftangry's narrative – the connective tissue which binds these three tales together. *Chronicles*, therefore, may not be a novel, but nor is it *simply* a conventional collection of short stories.

This generic complexity has, however, been obscured by the publication history of *Chronicles*. Following their initial publication in the format in which they appear in the Edinburgh Edition the separate parts of *Chronicles* were, largely for commercial reasons, frequently split up. In the Magnum Opus edition of Scott's work, for example, part of Croftangry's narrative is printed in Volume 41, along with 'The Highland Widow', 'The Two Drovers', and several other short stories that originally appeared in Christmas annuals. 'The Surgeon's Daughter' and the remainder of Croftangry's text appear in volume 48, far removed from the earlier material with which it first appeared. This separation of the parts of *Chronicles* is reinforced by the way in which it has been treated by criticism; while many critics have written on 'The Highland Widow' or 'The Two Drovers' and a few on 'The Surgeon's Daughter', very few critics have considered the collection as a whole and in the context of their original circumstances of publication alongside Croftangry's narrative. This serves to reinforce the generic enigma posed by what Scott famously calls 'an *olla podrida* into which any species of narrative or discussion may be thrown'.[24]

The generic complexity of this text, and the ways in which it evolved towards increasing self-reflexivity, are, moreover, apparent if we consider its composition. Claire Lamont points out that in early June 1826 Scott 'does not have a title for the work',[25] and it goes through several interesting variations before the final one was settled upon. Moreover, it was still undecided how the author's name was to appear on the title page, Scott contemplating whether to 'escape under the disguize of one of [his] own imitators' or to 'just avow it'.[26] This indecision about the extent to which he was to reveal himself coincides with the way in which the narrative itself evolved. Claire Lamont suggests that Scott actually began writing not with Croftangry's narrative, but with 'The Highland Widow', 'at the passage now found at 55.28, the opening of Chapter 6 of the first volume'; in other words, with the doubly framed narrators of Croftangry and Mrs Bethune Baliol already in place, and, crucially, with the conceit of Croftangry already established in his head. By mid June, however, Scott had written much more of the narrative but, rather than continuing with the story of 'The Highland Widow' with which he had begun, Scott expanded the conceit of his framing narrative, fleshing out the idea of Chrystal Croftangry:

> He had started to write *Chronicles* with a description of Mrs Martha Bethune Baliol, told by an ageing narrator who wishes to turn author and who had just received a 'packet' from her executors. The second batch of leaves was to precede what he had first written. They fill out the life and character of the proposed author in five chapters. It is clear from the second batch also that the Canongate, where Baliol's Lodgings was situated, was now to be a linking idea. In placing the account of Croftangry before what he had written about Mrs Bethune Baliol, however, Scott had introduced two characters who are fertile of material before starting his first tale, and so tantalises with delay any reader who is more interested in the tale than the teller.[27]

As Lamont's comments imply, as it evolved Scott shifted the focus of this text; while the opening of 'The Highland Widow' as it was originally conceived occupies the space of an eighteenth-century concern with 'provenance' (where the tale has come from and what is the source of its authority), by the time it was published *Chronicles of the Canongate* with its extended framed narration inhabits the altogether more modern terrain of the self-reflexive novel moving its interest to 'teller' rather than 'tale'.

It is this aspect of *Chronicles* that was lost when it was reprinted in later formats. With the publication of Claire Lamont's edition, however, we share a luxury with Scott's first readers; the ability to read *Chronicles* in its complete form. And this is crucial, for it allows us to see that this is not just three short stories squeezed together but that all three tales, and Croftangry's narrative, are intrinsically linked. One early title for the collection that was considered was *Conversations of the Canongate*, a title that captures the essentially dialogic nature of the relationship between its constituent parts.[28] Reading the collection as a whole facilitates a new understanding of the self-reflexivity of this position and of the ways in which the separate sections of *Chronicles* and Croftangry's narrative operate together to generate new kinds of meaning beyond that contained within each individual tale.

One major preoccupation in all three of the tales is, of course, one that resonates in all of Scott's fiction and it is hardly surprising that he should revisit it at this point in his career; the passing away of old ways of life and the way in which this might be negotiated to facilitate the new. This is certainly true of 'The Highland Widow' for it is a tale in which the clashing of old values and the new is all too evident and its tragic denouement is built around a historical moment when Highland society is on the cusp of change. While less overtly stated similar dynamics are also at work in the second of the tales 'The Two Drovers'. This story opens with its protagonist Robin Oig beginning to negotiate that change into modernity that Hamish attempts in the earlier tale. While Elspat's husband had lived the life of a cateran, or Highland cattle raider, Robin has made the transition to drover; a respectable and well paid position which reflects a growing trade with England and an increasing integration of Highland skills into the new commercial economy of a Greater Britain. This cultural shift is also apparent in that Robin has an English friend, Wakefield, an arrangement clearly congenial to them both; while the life of a drover suits the Highlander's 'natural curiosity and love of motion' (p. 125) the two can act as guides within each other's countries helping to negotiate that transition between Scotland and England which marks a new commercial relationship between two previously feuding nations.[29] However, as Robin sets out we are reminded that, in spite of his apparent movement towards a more modern way of life, the moralities and ethical codes of an older Highland society still impinge upon him. The appearance of Janet of Tomahourich pulls both reader, and Robin, back towards an older cultural framework – a life steeped in superstition, and cast here as embodying the Highland gift of second sight. Melodramatic, and perhaps even irrelevant, as this device might seem at the beginning of this story it is, we come to realise, the dynamics of the relationship between this past way of life and the new which are in fact at the heart of the tale. In 'The Two Drovers', just as in 'The Highland Widow', Scott suggests that a dynamic towards modernity and progress will inevitably be vexed by the forces of the past. No matter how much Robin may appear to have affected a transition towards a new commercialism between Scotland and England he is pulled back by his Highland heritage and led inescapably towards his death. 'The Surgeon's Daughter' is, of course, very different from the first two tales in *Chronicles*. But that surface difference belies the fact that it too deals with similar themes, exploring the possibilities of leaving an old world for a new; here too this negotiation has tragic consequences.

In this negotiation of moments of change the three tales of which *Chronicles* is comprised share a common pattern with much of Scott's fiction. However, while elsewhere in his work such moments frequently follow at least a surface Lukácsian paradigm of moving towards reconciliation the tales of *Chronicles of the Canongate* overtly subvert any such trajectory, thus undermining any residual faith in the Enlightenment narrative of stadial development that may have appeared to linger in Scott's work. As we read 'The Highland Widow', 'The Two Drovers' and 'The Surgeon's Daughter' it becomes apparent that Scott's interest here is not with how progress may be facilitated but with the tensions that result from the transition from past to future and with the clash of cultural value systems that inevitably ensues. While Scott's earlier work concerns itself with the compromises that can be worked out at such historical moments here his interest lies with the disjunctions and dislocations between these frameworks. Such dislocations embody the complexities involved in reconciliation or compromise and are expressed here in terms of linguistic failure as the protagonists struggle to comprehend the language spoken by the other and consequently cannot negotiate or 'translate' the terrain encapsulated within competing discourses.

This is apparent if we return again to 'The Highland Widow'. While Elspat's ideas are governed by the moral codes of an older society, Hamish views the world with the eyes of the young. However, this contrast between past and future embodies only part of the tragedy; Elspat's manipulation of her son is affected by the fact that in order to negotiate this transition from old to new Hamish is confronted by a series of disjunctions between conflicting cultural values which, in spite of all his efforts to escape, he cannot finally overcome. As A. O. J. Cockshut elaborates:

> The great interest of the story here is that it shows the point of breaking between two generations. The mother, having had her character formed before the break came, cannot understand her son's dilemma. It is possible to live by traditional assumptions entirely, and it is possible to form standards by personal choice. For Hamish it is too late in history to do the first, and impossible through temperament and early training to do the second. He is trying to live the old instinctive life with *two* sets of assumptions which at some points are irreconcilable.[30]

What is of most interest to us here, however, is that this 'breaking point' is expressed in linguistic terms. While Scott's poetry involves a play on recurring semantic fields so too *Chronicles* operates via a negotiation – or non-negotiation – of key terms such as 'honour', 'courage' and 'heroism' which are revisited, and reinterpreted, throughout the volume. This is apparent, for example, in Elspat's frustration with her son and the terms in which it is expressed. Unaware of the 'substitution of civil order for military violence' (p. 78) the only concept of honour she has available to her is that which she recognised in his father: 'She thought of the death of MacTavish Mhor as that of a hero who had fallen in his proper trade of war', we are told, 'and who had not fallen unavenged' (p. 83). Hamish however, is equally aware that such a path towards honour is no longer available and that a new interpretation of the term must be found: 'Hamish yet perceived that the trade of cateran was now alike dangerous and discreditable, and that if he were to emulate his father's prowess, it must be in some other line of warfare, more consonant to the opinions of the present day' (p. 79). Hamish and Elspat, then, are operating with different concepts of 'honour' and similar disjunctions also cluster around the term 'courage'. It is on this score that Elspat finds the way of giving her son pain for by challenging his 'courage' she recognises a weak spot by which she might manipulate him:

> "Hamish," said his mother, "are you again about to leave me?" But Hamish only replied by looking at, and rubbing the lock of his gun.
> "Ay, rub the lock of your gun," said his parent, bitterly; "I am glad you have courage enough to fire it, though it be but at a roe-deer." Hamish started at this undeserved taunt, and cast a look of anger at her in reply. She saw that she had found the means of giving him pain.
> "Yes," she said, "look fierce as you will at an old woman, and your mother; it would be long ere you bent your brow on the angry countenance of a bearded man."
> "Be silent, mother, or speak of what you understand," said Hamish, much irritated, "and that is of the distaff and the spindle." (p. 80)

Ironically, it is this taunt which sends Hamish off to join the government regiment. Paradoxically, for Hamish this is the only route by which courage and honour might be restored: '"Mother," said Hamish, proudly, "lay not faint heart to my charge. I go where men are wanted who have strong arms and bold hearts too. I leave a desert, for a land where I may gather fame."' (p. 89)

In 'The Highland Widow' then, Hamish to some extent attempts to renegotiate or redefine those concepts of honour, courage and heroism that have shaped an earlier Highland society of his father's time; to 'translate' these concepts into the only cultural framework that is apparently available to him in the modern world. The tragedy of the tale, however, lies in the fact that ultimately this is a redefinition which he cannot achieve for he is at last caught out not only by his mother, but by the fact that the values of these two societies are, in the end, incapable of such renegotiation. This is implied by the punishment of the scourge that Hamish so fears. Punishment for desertion has, we are told, been introduced as a measure precisely because of the different cultural parameters in which Highland and Lowland operate. The 'privilege of going and coming' at will was common to the Highland soldier: 'the new-levied Highland recruits could scarce be made to comprehend the nature of a military engagement, which compelled a man to serve in the army longer than he pleased' (pp. 98–9) and as a consequence the punishment of the scourge (or lash) has been introduced. For Hamish, it is this punishment which proves a stumbling block to integrating new and old concepts of honour, for he sees this as a punishment fit for dogs, not for free-born men. To be forced to undergo it will be for him what is 'dishonourable'. '"I cannot be subjected to such infamy"' he tells his mother, '"were I threatened with it, I should know how to die before I was so dishonoured"' (p. 92). It is this statement that suggests to Elspat the strategy of drugging Hamish for she realises that if he does not meet his regiment at the appointed time he will not meet it at all. In the tale's denouement it is, too, a reminder of the lash – '"The scourge—the scourge—my son, beware the scourge"' Elspat whispers to him (p. 109) – that causes Hamish to shoot at the fatal moment, thus ensuring his downfall. For both Hamish and his mother, this punishment is a reminder that, however Hamish might attempt to renegotiate terms such as 'honour' and 'courage' within a military, modern framework, this is a framework which is, as Elspat figures it, based upon slavery rather than freedom. Consequently, it is a negotiation that Hamish cannot ultimately make. While, as the case of Allan Break Cameron shows, it may be possible to successfully make the transition from old world to new the disjunctions between cultural frameworks which Scott explores in the tale suggest that the price to be paid may be too great; cultural tensions cannot be reconciled, but remain, on the contrary, inextricably at odds and incapable of translation from one period into another.

Similar dynamics are at work within 'The Two Drovers'. Earlier it was suggested that Robin Oig had to some extent made progress towards the modern world, embracing the new commercial union between Scotland and England, a fact epitomised in his friendship with Harry Wakefield. However, a closer examination of the tale suggests that this cultural reconciliation is not so simple as may at first appear. This is signalled by an early description of Robin who has inherited his name from Rob Roy, and 'was proud accordingly':

> But his frequent visits to England and to the Lowlands had given him tact enough to know that pretensions, which still gave him a little right to distinction in his own lonely glen, might be obnoxious and ridiculous if preferred elsewhere. The pride of birth, therefore, was like the miser's treasure, the secret subject of his contemplation, but never exhibited to strangers as a subject of boasting. (p. 126)

In one sense, this can be read as illustrative of the fact that Robin has made a necessary adjustment in order to inhabit the new British state. However, if we are mindful of the connections being made to the earlier tale we will recognise that such redefinition of a Highlander's honour comes at a great price and that such suppression of pride may, ultimately, prove futile. Similarly, while Robin's and Wakefield's friendship may seem to offer a happy reconciliation between Englishman and Highlander warnings concerning this relationship are also given. Harry, we are told, 'was the model of old England's merry yeomen' (p. 129) while Robin is the epitome of Highland life. The narrator acknowledges:

> It is difficult to say how Henry Wakefield and Robin Oig first became intimates; but it is certain a close acquaintance had taken place betwixt them, although they had apparently few common topics of conversation or of interest, so soon as their talk ceased to be of bullocks. Robin Oig, indeed, spoke the English language rather imperfectly upon any other topics but stots and kyloes, and Harry Wakefield could never bring his broad Yorkshire tongue to utter a single word of Gaelic. It was in vain Robin spent a whole morning, during a walk over Minch-Moor, in attempting to teach his companion to utter, with true precision, the shibboleth *Llhu*, which is the Gaelic for a calf. From Traquair to Murder-cairn, the hill rung with the discordant attempts of the Saxon upon the unmanageable monosyllable, and the heartfelt laugh which followed every failure. (pp. 129–30)

Robin's and Harry's relationship, it appears, is founded less on the harmonious reconciliation of the different cultural parameters within which each operates but rather on an acceptance of difference or perhaps even a failure to realise the full extent of it. Certainly, it is grounded in very limited linguistic understanding if, indeed, any real exchange is possible between the two men.[31]

As the tale unfolds it becomes apparent that it is a 'linguistic failure' of a more complex kind that is, in fact, at the heart of the tragedy which ensues. The quarrel which divides Robin and Wakefield – the mistake over the hiring of the land – is one which we imagine might be easily resolved. The fact that it is not resolved, however, but on the contrary escalates towards murder, lies deep in the disjunction between Highland and English ethical and moral codes.[32] This has been hinted at earlier in the tale and again centres upon varying, and perhaps irreconcilable, interpretations of those crucial terms 'honour' and 'courage':

> "Hold your peace all of you, and be —," said Wakefield; and then addressing his comrade, he took him by the extended hand, with something alike of respect and defiance. "Robin," he said, "thou hast used me ill enough this day; but if you mean, like a frank fellow, to shake hands, and take a tussle for love on the sod, why I'll forgie thee, man, and we shall be better friends than ever."
>
> "And would it not pe petter to pe cood friends without more of the matter?" said Robin; "we will be much petter friendships with our panes hale than proken."
>
> Harry Wakefield dropped the hand of his friend, or rather threw it from him.
>
> "I did not think I had been keeping company for three years with a coward."
>
> "Coward pelongs to none of my name," said Robin, whose eyes began to kindle, but keeping the command of his temper. (pp. 135–6)

Both Robin and Harry, then, fight to defend themselves against the charge of cowardice. However, what quickly becomes apparent is that they can find no means of fighting that will satisfy both men's sense of honour. To fight with fists is, for Robin, "'to pe peaten like a dog'" just as the scourge was, for Hamish, a punishment fit only for animals. And while his claim that he will fight "'with proadswords, and sink point on the first plood drawn—like a gentlemans'" (p. 136) may seem absurd in English ears, Robin is, of course, offering only that he fight as a Highlander sees honourable, and to defend the honour of what is to him, a suppressed and noble Highland lineage. Once Wakefield has defeated Robin in a fist-fight the outcome of the tale is, then, almost as inevitable as that of 'The Highland Widow'. For while Robin has sought to suppress his Highland notions of honour, pride and lineage, his defeat leaves him no alternative but to avenge those very concepts. Robin, like Hamish, is eventually trapped by an inability to escape the values which have shaped his own societal parameters and which are bound up with the extent to which these are shaped by the discourse in which he operates, a discourse which is, ultimately, untranslatable to English ears.

And it is, too, a failure of one discourse to be renegotiated in terms of another that is encapsulated in the Judge's summing up at the end of Robin's trial. 'The facts of the case were proved in the manner I have related them' the narrator tells us:

> and whatever might be at first the prejudice of the audience against a crime so un-English as that of assassination for revenge, yet when the rooted national prejudices of the prisoner had been explained, which made him consider himself as stained with indelible dishonour, when subjected to personal violence; when his previous patience, moderation, and endurance were considered, the generosity of the English audience was inclined to regard his crime as the wayward aberration of a false idea of honour rather than as flowing from a heart naturally savage, or perverted by habitual vice. (p. 142)

On the face of it, this seems sympathetic, for the crime is recognised as 'un-English', and perpetrated on an alternative idea of honour. However, if we unpick the language of the Judge's comments we can see that in spite of his compassion he, like the young lawyer (Croftangry, or perhaps even Scott) who 'never forget[s] the charge of the venerable Judge to the jury', in fact encapsulates a fundamental failure to accommodate an alternative language or to truly empathise with it. To him, the Highlander's notions of honour are deemed false, not *Highland* – that is recognised as of themselves – but *un-English* – departing from a supposed norm. Robin's notion of what is right is, similarly, 'unhappily perverted', not recognised on its own terms, but as an aberration. And the reason given as to why Robin must, in the end, be punished, lies in his statement that '"should this man's action remain unpunished, you may unsheath, under various pretences, a thousand daggers betwixt the Land's-end and the Orkneys"' (p. 146). While the Judge may appreciate the alternative framework in which Robin is operating, and might even comprehend that it has a value and nobility of its own, ultimately he upholds that the British Isles must come under the same law; what he describes as '"the general principles of justice and equity which pervade every civilized country"' (p. 145). In spite of his pity for Robin, the Judge's agenda remains essentially one of progress via assimilation and, as Seamus Cooney recognises, intrinsically Imperialistic: 'firmly confident' in the 'falsity of any code of conduct other than that of the English judge and jury' and in the fact that they should be imposed upon other cultures even if the results are, as they are for Hamish, inevitably tragic.[33] Such linguistic failure, Scott implies, suggests that it may not be possible to 'translate' another culture as he has suggested in his Introduction to *Ivanhoe*, since key terms will remain 'non-negotiable'.

These issues become even more pertinent in the last of the tales in *Chronicles*, 'The Surgeon's Daughter', where the action of the story takes us into a site that as modern readers at least, we recognise as immediately 'other', India under the East India Company. Certainly, if we wish to consider the tales of *Chronicles* as sharing themes of dislocation there are plenty of examples of cultural disjunction to be found in 'The Surgeon's Daughter'. There is a sense of dislocation through the passing of time in the story, for the reader is left with a sense that the peaceful life of Gideon Gray which is described at the outset belongs to a Scotland that is passing away; young men, it is clear, look elsewhere to seek their fortunes and new opportunities are available to them. There are also dislocations of class. The fate of Richard Middlemas, as he is called throughout the story, hinges upon his own awareness that he has been raised 'dislocated' or out of place from his own social status, and that his pride and honour, consequently, have been thwarted, a pain which he feels as keenly as the men in the earlier two tales. The tales that his nurse has told him of his heritage from an early age are, in fact, not dissimilar to those told by the Highland Widow to her son. Like Hamish, Richard is disinherited from the traditional routes of fulfilling the pride which is thus awakened – his own family, for example, will have nothing to do with him. Shut out from a recognisable social group he must find alternative routes to fulfil his sense of honour: 'Richard was meditating upon nothing else than the time and means by which he was to be extricated from the obscurity of his present condition, and enabled to assume the rank to which, in his own opinion, he was entitled by birth' (p. 181). Defeated in every other attempt to gain a sense of honour, however, it is finally by his journey to India that Richard seeks to regain some sense of worth: '"The game has been played and lost—I must hedge my bets; India must be my back-play"' he states (p. 243), and it is the dislocations and the cultural disjunctions which we meet in India which are the most interesting to be found in this tale.

Yet the ways in which Scott describes India in 'The Surgeon's Daughter' alert us to the fact that it may offer a form of cultural negotiation that will be impossible for Richard – or any other character in the novel – to make. It is, as the description of Tippoo's retinue implies, exotic, colourful, and other. Peppered with specialist vocabulary, this passage delineates the essential difference of Indian custom and society and (just as Scotland had to be translated for an English audience in *Waverley*) figures it as a site that requires narratorial interpretation for the English-speaking reader:

> Tippoo himself next appeared, richly apparelled, and seated on an elephant, which, carrying its head above all the others in the procession, seemed proudly conscious of superior dignity. The howdaw, or seat, which the Prince occupied, was of silver, embossed and gilt, having behind a place for a confidential servant, who waved the great chowry, or cow-tail, to keep off the flies; but who could also occasionally perform the task of spokesman, being well versed in all terms of flattery and compliment. The caparisons of the royal elephant were of scarlet cloth, richly embroidered with gold. Behind Tippoo came the various courtiers and officers of the household, mounted chiefly on elephants, all arrayed in their most splendid attire, and exhibiting the greatest pomp. (p. 279)

India, this suggests, is a discourse that necessitates an act of translation. But, reading this in the context of the earlier tales, we are alert to the difficulties this implies. India thus offers Scott the opportunity to explore the full implications of markers of cultural difference and to explore the extent to which they cannot ultimately be reconciled. While all three of the major characters in the text – Menie Gray, Adam Hartley, and Richard Middlemas – may attempt this re-negotiation all three are ultimately destroyed by it.

If we first consider Richard Middlemas it would not be unreasonable to suspect that his name might imply a character who will follow the traditional Scott route to cultural reconciliation. Middlemas is a name, after all, which implies mediation and compromise, a kind of Lukácsian middle way. It is not, however, his real name, and before the tale ever moves to India it is quite apparent that his is not a conciliatory but a turbulent personality. He is given to selfish extremes in his desire to reinstate his honour, and thus it is unlikely that it will be he who will effect cultural reconciliation. It is, consequently, no surprise that we first encounter Middlemas in India not in the service of the Company which he has joined, but in disgrace – commanding troops for the Nawaub's service, 'employed', we are told 'in whatever could render him odious to his countrymen'. Moreover, we encounter him in disguise – not as an Englishman within Indian culture, but as an Englishman who has attempted to immerse himself within Indian society. Never one with a strong sense of his own cultural identity[34] he has seemingly sought to replace it with another, and like Madge Wildfire, has tipped over into a site where identity is dangerously eroded:

> Richard Middlemas, as the Begum's general or Buckshee, walked nearest to her litter, in a dress as magnificent in itself as it was remote from all European costume, being that of a Banka, or Indian courtier. His turban was of rich silk and gold, twisted very hard, and placed on one side of his head, its ends hanging down on the shoulder. His mustachoes were turned and curled, and his eyelids stained with antimony. The vest was of gold brocade, with a cummerband, or sash, around his waist, corresponding to his turban. He carried in his hand a large sword, sheathed in a scabbard of crimson velvet, and wore around his middle a broad embroidered sword-belt. What thoughts he had under this gay attire, and the bold bearing which corresponded to it, it would be fearful to unfold. (p. 280)

The dangers of such cultural assimilation, or apparent dissolving of the boundaries between cultural difference, have to some extent been prefigured in 'The Two Drovers' and are of course to loom much larger in later texts such as Joseph Conrad's *Heart of Darkness*. They are, however, also pre-empted earlier in this tale through the character of Madame Montreville whom the far more conservative Adam Hartley encounters with a mixture of awe and horror. Madame Montreville has, in some senses, similarly given up her European heritage, aligning herself with Tippoo, and is encountered by Hartley in a 'large and sumptuous residence in the Black Town of Madras, as that district of the city is called which the natives occupy' (p. 255). '"I doubt the propriety of your being under the charge of this unsexed woman"', Hartley tells Menie, '"who can no longer be termed a European"' (p. 259). What is suggested is that the price which might have to be paid for attempting to immerse oneself completely in another culture is not the rediscovery of one's birthright, but rather the complete loss of it. And of course, the loss of identity marks the tragic fate of Richard Middlemas, for his attempts to save his honour by switching first from one culture to another – betraying first his commanding officer and then Tippoo – inevitably have tragic consequences. While Richard might believe that he can restore honour within one cultural framework by temporarily assuming the values of another the grim irony of his crushing to death under the foot of an elephant seems to imply that by giving himself up to a culture that his not his own he will, in fact, be cut morally adrift, and inevitably be 'broken' by the experience.

While, then, in spite of his name, Richard Middlemas does not succeed in negotiating his way through the alternative cultural frameworks which he encounters in India this path is far more successfully followed by his much more level headed counterpart Adam Hartley. While Middlemas appears to have used his knowledge of India to manipulate its culture for his own ends it is clear that Hartley attempts to marry the qualities he has learnt from his old master Gideon Gray onto the skills he has acquired in a new locale, thus reconciling what is good in one culture with what is valuable in another. When we first encounter him in India, he is respected by Europeans and Indians alike, and has learnt much of the language and cultural life of the local people. Alert to cultural difference Adam Hartley is sympathetic to the otherness of Indian society without seeking to immerse himself in it. Yet, somewhat surprisingly, this position is not entirely endorsed, for Hartley's fate is also a tragic one. He too is caught out by the ways in which he chooses to negotiate the Indian experience: 'the gallant and disinterested Hartley' we learn 'fell a victim to his professional courage, in withstanding the progress of a contagious distemper, which he at length caught, and under which he sunk' (p. 285). Hartley's death also denies us the perhaps expected conclusion of the tale in his marriage to Menie Gray and thus ensures that 'The Surgeon's Daughter', like the other tales in the collection, will end in tragedy. Marriage, which so often signals at least the possibility of reconciliation of cultural difference in Scott's fictional world, is defeated. Instead, Menie becomes a shadowy and troubled figure; 'poor Menie Gray'. 'It is consistent with Scott's underlying serious intent', writes J. M. Rignall, 'that the exotic romance turns sour at the end, refusing that return to the original idyllic state that is characteristic of the genre . . . nothing positive results from this experience of empire. Nothing redeems this waste of spirit'.[35]

In 'The Surgeon's Daughter', as in 'The Highland Widow' and 'The Two Drovers', Scott seems to suggest that the negotiation of conflicting and perhaps competing cultural frameworks is a fraught and troubling experience. No matter how the participants in these tales attempt to reconcile the different value systems in which they find themselves, none emerge unscathed. While Scott's earlier fiction, in its movement towards reconciliation of cultural values, may have suggested a faith in the progress of history these late tales seem to suggest that the ruptures and gaps between cultural discourses may in fact, be too large to bridge; the only relationship between them is perhaps, an essentially Imperialist agenda, one that leaves one culture at least with too great a price to pay for its assimilation into the onward movement of history. As Caroline McCracken-Flesher suggests, here Scott offers 'no comfortable, coherent picture of Scottishness, but a harshly truthful image of Scottish culture's increasing disintegration under pressure from English capitalism and colonialism'.[36]

The three tales of which *Chronicles* is comprised could not be more bleak. It is tempting to account for this by considering the personal circumstances of Scott's life when they were being written. Belonging to the darkest period of his own career when his life was apparently tumbling around him these stories can be interpreted as a metaphor for his own plight, suggesting that Scott's faith in the movement of society towards progress and betterment was rocked by the chaos he was experiencing himself. But such a reading is, ultimately, inadequate. Scott is obviously not simply writing about his own position and to interpret the tales in this way is only to read the related themes that make up the separate stories constituting *Chronicles of the Canongate*. It is not a reading of *Chronicles of the Canongate* as a whole. For *Chronicles* is, of course, as was demonstrated at the outset, more than a collection of short stories; it is a series of connected narratives bound together by Chrystal Croftangry's own narratives, which, as Frank Jordan recognises, 'constitute a short fiction in their own right'. This offers a kind of parallel text to the tales themselves, and the insertion of this most self-reflexive of devices into the collection generates an altogether different kind of work.[37]

It is clear that many of the themes that are explored in 'The Highland Widow', 'The Two Drovers' and 'The Surgeon's Daughter' are mirrored in the account we are given of Croftangry's own experiences. Marilyn Orr comments:

> Self-styled prodigal son, Croftangry enacts the classic romantic return, employing terms reminiscent of Wordsworth and Coleridge to confess the failure of vision that caused him to squander his patrimony . . . Thus though he is part of the frame of these tales, he is not outside them; his perspective is the double one of someone outside and inside the scene he describes.[38]

His tale is also one of the passing of old times for new; the fortunes of his own estate, for example, shows the decline of a once ancient and noble family and the transition from landed property ownership to commercialism. Mrs Bethune Baliol, who bequeaths us the tale of the Highland Widow, also provides a bridge back into an older Scotland and her death, and the later destruction of her house, marks the passing away of the age that she represents. Janet too provides a link with the Highland tales, the fate of her own family offering a bitter sub-text for the tragedies of 'The Highland Widow' and 'The Two Drovers'. Most significantly, Croftangry, like Mrs Baliol, is at the end of his life and the last of his race, inhabiting the Canongate like the ghost of an Edinburgh that is almost gone, living next to a palace that no longer has a monarch to occupy it, and deserted by his neighbours for the flourishing New Town which marks Edinburgh's own transition into modernity. Croftangry's narrative is also coloured by the cultural dislocations and disjunctions that haunt the three tales which it encloses. Croftangry returns to Scotland to find himself a stranger in his own country and one far from certain how he is to negotiate its changed cultural parameters. Uncertain even of the derivation of his own family name (p. 23) Croftangry, like Darsie Latimer, is searching for a social structure in which to locate his identity but is unrecognised by his mother's servant and barely recognised by his old friend and benefactor. He too as Christie Steele makes all too clear, is, like the other characters who people *Chronicles*, in some ways disinherited of his honour, cut adrift from any recognisable group of peers: 'I wanted something more than mere companionship would give me', he tells us, 'and where was I to look for it?' Of his old friends 'all community of ties had ceased to exist, and such of my former friends as were still in the world', he laments, 'held their life in a different tenor from what I did' (p. 21). On the death of Mrs Bethune Baliol, Croftangry comments that 'my acquaintance . . . are of that distant and accidental kind' (p. 148).

However, while the characters within his tales can find no point at which cultural understanding can be achieved Croftangry's tale is one of a successful renegotiation of the self within a culture that initially seems to offer no familiar ground. What is most interesting about this text, however, is the ways in which this renegotiation is achieved, for it is shaped in highly self-conscious terms. Croftangry's initial position as he describes it himself is one of loneliness and boredom:

> When the cloth is removed, and I light my cigar, and begin to husband a pint of port, or a glass of old whisky and water, it is the rule of the house that Janet takes a chair at some distance, and nods or works her stocking, as she may be disposed; ready to speak, if I am in the talking humour, and sitting quiet as a mouse if I am rather inclined to study a book or the newspaper. At six precisely she makes my tea, and leaves me to drink it; and then occurs an interval of time which most old bachelors find heavy on their hands. The theatre is a good occasional resource, but it is distant, and so are one or two public societies to which I belong; besides, these are all incompatible with the elbow-chair feeling, which desires some employment that may divert the mind without fatiguing the body. (p. 50)

By the end of *Chronicles*, however, we find Croftangry in an altogether different situation, facing a tea-party of young ladies with his manuscript in his pocket (p. 286). He is reintegrated into a social group.

So how is this act of cultural renegotiation achieved? On the face of it Croftangry's reintegration is achieved by the act of becoming an author; the act of writing itself becomes a means of building relationships with the outside world and of restoring his pride and identity. As Caroline McCracken-Flesher notes, 'In *Chronicles of the Canongate*, like Walter Scott, Chrystal searches for an audience. He struggles to re-establish relationships within which he, as author, can find meaning'.[39] The potential for this is signalled early in the text when Croftangry describes his childhood home; in a quintessentially Romantic moment he notes that memory and imagination act together 'to collect and to complete' an image of his native land (p. 27). Later it is similarly Mrs Bethune Baliol's memory and her ability to embellish her stories that serves to make the past come alive, and finally, it is the act of reading aloud, of narration, which brings Croftangry back into a social circle: with a far wider cultural circle, that of his readers (of which we are a part) also implied. It seems then, that it is via the act of story-telling that the bridges between past and future may be built and a common cultural ground negotiated; the past, and the societies of which it is constituted, living on, if nowhere else, at least in the texts.

It is tempting, consequently, to think that in *Chronicles* Scott has come full circle and that Croftangry's rejuvenation mirrors that found in *The Lay of the Last Minstrel*. Both Croftangry and the minstrel, after all, are apparently reintegrated into a social circle via the act of narration. However, their situations are not the same and the differences between their acts of recitation are telling. The minstrel, it should be recalled, holds his (mainly female) audience wrapt in his words creating an act of emotional transference between the past and the present, via a process of 'retrojection' where the boundaries of time dissolve. But what is highlighted in *Chronicles* is, as we have seen, the dislocations between the times recounted and that of narration; a dislocation that does not allow for lost time to be recovered in any meaningful way. Croftangry's relationship to both his audience and the past he narrates, consequently, is altogether different, and is notably more self-reflexive and parodic. His experiments in fiction are met by observations that '"Mr Chrystal Croftangy might have more wit at his time of day"' as his reading of 'The Surgeon's Daughter' is received by Mr Fairscribe who 'only fell asleep twice' and by ladies (who again make up the majority of his audience) who, only 'politely attentive' break into his narrative to give accounts of their own experience (to tell their own stories) and have conversations about fashion (p. 288). Croftangry concludes philosophically that 'things must be as they may' but this account of his first public reading is a marker of the difference between Croftangry and the earlier minstrel; while the minstrel's role is to recover the past and to dissolve the boundaries of space and time via his poetry, Croftangry, Scott suggests, can achieve no such act of transformation. What has intervened between minstrel and modern author is not only Scott's financial crash and what many have seen as a concomitant loss of faith in the progressive model of history, but an interrogation of the limits of language that has revealed that the novel cannot recover the past via language, but holds only a parodic, fragmentary and fluid relationship to it. Croftangry's act of narration is not so much one of communication, but one governed by the self-reflexive imperative of story-telling. While the earlier *Lay* may have exhibited an Enlightenment faith in the onward progress of society, and in a stable ontological reality that can be recovered and reconstituted through language, ultimately *Chronicles* hints at an alternative (and perhaps Humean) vision: that it is *only* through the processes of our memories and imaginations that we build bridges to the past and restore our sense of cultural identity and community, and that it is the act of writing which offers the only method by which this can be constituted, however provisionally. Poetry and the language out of which it is constituted, cannot 'recover' a knowable past as the minstrel seeks to do in the *Lay* but it can tell stories about it – even if, ultimately, such stories remain no more than this and are received by their audience only as an opportunity to generate their own narratives.[40]

The opportunity that the Edinburgh Edition of the Waverley Novels has given us to read 'The Highland Widow', 'The Two Drovers' and 'The Surgeon's Daughter' as one text may not give us any more clue as to what we may call the generic enigma which is *Chronicles of the Canongate*. It does, however, help us to see that there are common themes that run between the tales – themes which suggest the dislocations and ruptures that may exist within cultural frameworks; disjunctions which may in the end undermine an Enlightenment faith in historical progress and any sense that we can know or 'conjecture' another culture by simply learning its language. While this may be the point towards which Scott has been heading throughout his writing career it seems that *Chronicles*, incorporating as it does the act of unveiling of the Great Unknown, brings to these questions a new urgency. As such it offers us one of the bleakest visions to be found anywhere in Scott's fiction and simultaneously suggests an alternative to this tragic interpretation of human society and to the exhaustion implicit in the imprecise medium of words. While, like Harry Wakefield and Robin Oig, we cannot ever be sure that we understand each other's language, or that we are interpreting it correctly, *Chronicles* seems to suggest that we can, nevertheless, continue to tell stories in the hope that they will at least be heard. It is not surprising, therefore, that Scott's last works should be generated not by an attempt to recover the past in words or to find a means to negotiate between cultures but, rather, by the highly self-reflexive imperative of story-telling.

*Notes*

1  John Barth, 'The Literature of Exhaustion', p. 64.
2  John Barth, 'The Literature of Replenishment', p. 206.
3  Ibid. p. 207.
4  Ibid. p. 209.
5  David Hewitt argues that 'Darsie and Alan together are . . . Scott's self-portrait': 'Introduction' in Walter Scott, *Redgauntlet*, ed. by G. A. M. Wood with David Hewitt (London: Penguin, 1997), pp. xiii–xxxi (p. xxix). This argument has also been put forward by, for example, Arthur Melville Clark, *Sir Walter Scott: The Formative Years* (Edinburgh and London: Blackwood, 1969).
6  Robert P. Irvine comments that in this novel 'Politics itself has now become a matter of creating in words a convenient reality'. *Enlightenment and Romance*, p. 215.
7  See 'Essay on the Text', pp. 404–5.
8  The title of the novel was decided upon relatively late in the process of its composition and was suggested by Ballantyne rather than Scott. As its editors note, the novel originally had the working title 'Herries' which gives a far more definite identification with Darsie's uncle. See 'Essay on the Text', p. 386.
9  Jina Politi, 'The Ideological Uses of Intertextuality' in *Scott in Carnival*, pp. 345–57 (p. 351).
10  See the Explanatory Notes to *Redgauntlet*, note to 201.38, p. 497.
11  See, for example, David Hewitt, 'Introduction', p. xvii, Jina Politi, 'The Ideological Uses of Intertextuality', p. 349, James Chandler, *England in 1819: The Politics of Literary Culture and the Case of Romantic*

*Historicism* (Chicago: University of Chicago Press, 1998), p. 223 and Fiona Robertson, *Legitimate Histories*, p. 254.

12 David Hewitt, 'Introduction', p. xvii.

13 Ibid. p. xv.

14 Ibid. p. xv.

15 David Lodge, *The Art of Fiction Illustrated from Classic and Modern Texts* (London: Penguin, 1992), p. 23.

16 John Barth, 'Tales Within Tales Within Tales' in *The Friday Book*, pp. 218–38 (p. 221).

17 John Barth, 'The Literature of Replenishment', p. 205.

18 See *Life*, volume 6 and John Sutherland, *The Life of Walter Scott: A Critical Biography*, pp. 272–98.

19 *Journal*, 18 December 1825, pp. 40–1.

20 See *Life*, pp. 7.16–20.

21 See Claire Lamont 'Essay on the Text', *Chronicles of the Canongate*, p. 294.

22 Seamus Cooney points out that 'Scott's allusions here imply that he felt anonymity was deeply connected with his creative power'. See 'Scott's Anonymity – Its Motives and Consequences', *Studies in Scottish Literature* 10 (1973), pp. 207–19 (p. 211).

23 W. J. Overton, 'Scott, the Short Story and History: "The Two Drovers"' in *Studies in Scottish Literature*, 21 (1986), pp. 210–25 (p. 222).

24 *Journal,* 28 May 1826, p. 151.

25 Claire Lamont, 'Essay on the Text', p. 296.

26 Scott to Ballantyne, 9 June 1826, quoted in Claire Lamont, 'Essay on the Text', p. 296.

27 Claire Lamont, 'Essay on the Text', p. 297.

28 Ibid. p. 298.

29 See Claire Lamont, 'Introduction' in Walter Scott, *Chronicles of the Canongate* (London: Penguin, 2003), pp. xix–xix (p. xix) for a discussion of this dynamic.

30 A. O. J. Cockshut, *The Achievement of Walter Scott* (London: Collins, 1969), p. 57.

31 Kenneth McNeil describes Doune market as 'a kind of polyglot border zone in which English and Highlander come together': Kenneth McNeil, 'The Limits of Diversity: Using Scott's "The Two Drovers" to Teach Multiculturalism in a Survey or Nonmajors Course' in *Approaches to Teaching Scott's Waverley Novels*, pp. 123–9 (p. 125).

32 Seamus Cooney argues that the 'quarrel, thus, is more than a mere clash of two individuals. It is essentially a clash of two ways of life, two cultures':

See 'Scott and Cultural Relativism: "The Two Drovers"' *Studies in Short Fiction* 15:1 (Winter, 1978), pp. 1–9 (p. 3).

33  Ibid. p. 6. Kenneth McNeil observes that the judge's perspective 'signals the final message of the story: when cultural differences *cannot* be accommodated, when competing notions of justice cannot occupy the same national space, the dominant culture must and will prevail, by force if necessary'. See Kenneth McNeil, 'The Limits of Diversity', pp. 126–7.

34  Reading the novel from a post-colonial perspective Molly Youngkin argues that because of his status as a 'colonial subject' Middlemas is 'one of those individuals living "in the inbetween", as both Bhabha and Spivak characterise the condition of the colonised'. See '"Into the woof, a little Thibet wool': Orientalism and Representing "Reality" in Walter Scott's *The Surgeon's Daughter'*, *Scottish Studies Review* 3:1 (Spring, 2002), pp. 33–57 (p. 39).

35  J. M. Rignall, 'Walter Scott, J. G. Farrell, and Fictions of Empire' in *Essays in Critcism*, Volume XLI, Number 1 (1991), pp. 11–27 (p. 21).

36  Caroline McCracken-Flesher, '*Pro Matria Mori*: Gendered Nationalism and Cultural Death in Scott's "The Highland Widow"', *Scottish Literary Journal* 21:2 (1994), pp. 69–78 (p. 77).

37  Frank Jordan, 'Chrystal Croftangry, Scott's Last and Best Mask', *Scottish Literary Journal* 71 (1980), pp. 185–92 (p. 185).

38  Marilyn Orr '"Almost Under the Immediate Eye": Framing Displacement' in *Scott in Carnival*, pp. 60–71 (p. 68).

39  Caroline McCracken-Flesher, *Possible Scotlands*, p. 158.

40  Frank Jordan comments that 'In settling in the Canongate for the duration of his life Chrystal has shed his last illusion, dropped his last pretension, except perhaps that of authorship. This last illusion is one, however, in which his creator Walter Scott indulges him: to redeem the past via imagination was not, in Scott's eyes, destructive of the personality, not if imagination were used to expose and enrich reality rather than to conceal and impoverish it'. Frank Jordan, 'Chrystal Croftangry, Scott's Last and Best Mask', p. 187.

# Chapter 6

# Last Words: *Count Robert of Paris, Reliquiae Trotcosienses* and *Castle Dangerous*

Of all Scott's fiction his last works, *Count Robert of Paris*, *Reliquiae Trotcosienses* and *Castle Dangerous* have been perceived as the most problematic. Frequently dismissed by critics they have been seen as flawed productions, the consequence of Scott's late illnesses and intellectual decline. A. O. J. Cockshut, for example, states that Scott's last texts are simply an act of '[labouring] steadily on with the task of covering blank paper with ink'[1] while Christopher Harvie describes them as 'eminently forgettable projects'.[2] Catherine Jones sees these novels as a 'retreat into the formulaic'.[3] While recognising that *Count Robert* is Scott's 'most powerful exercise in grotesquerie' John Sutherland nevertheless calls the novel an 'abortion'.[4] James Anderson sums up the common response to Scott's last novels by stating that of them 'it is best to say nothing; they were written after paralysis had begun to destroy Scott's genius . . . The writing of 1830 and 1831 is dull and wordy'.[5]

These late texts by Scott were also perceived as problematic at their inception. Scott's advisers, Cadell and Lockhart, saw them as inherently flawed, limited by the condition of Scott's health at the point when they were being written. In his *Life* J. G. Lockhart describes how James Ballantyne informed Scott 'that he considered the opening chapters of Count Robert as decidedly inferior to any thing that had ever before come from that pen'. Focussing on the subject matter of the tale he 'dwelt chiefly on the hopelessness of any Byzantine fable'.[6] Lockhart reports that by December, Ballantyne and Robert Cadell travelled to Abbotsford to try to dissuade Scott from writing *Count Robert of Paris*.[7] What Lockhart does not say is that in his opinion, and that of Cadell, the problem with *Count Robert* lay not with the subject matter but with the fact that Scott, who had suffered a stroke earlier in the year, was incapable of writing new fiction and that he should 'content himself with working at notes and prefaces'.[8] Similar problems were perceived with *Castle Dangerous*, which was begun after *Count Robert* but completed simultaneously. Scott's printer, James Ballantyne, complains that the proofs have given him 'great difficulty'[9] and both Cadell and Lockhart refer to Scott's general confusion surrounding the whole enterprise. Cadell comments that Scott's amanuensis, William Laidlaw, reports that Sir Walter 'could not get on with Castle Dangerous [as] his ideas get confused'.[10] As a consequence as soon as Scott had left for the Mediterranean in 1831 Cadell and Lockhart set about revising these texts, tidying up what they saw as their errors, clarifying what they considered to be confusions, and perhaps most significantly of all, radically rewriting the conclusion to *Count Robert*.[11] As J. H. Alexander points out, 'It is clear that Lockhart and Cadell had it in mind to effect radical revisions once the author was out of the country', noting that 'Lockhart observes that Cadell "so managed that the Novels just finished should remain in types, but not thrown off, until the author should have departed; so as to give opportunity for revising and abridging them"'.[12]

In order to distract him from writing these novels Cadell and Lockhart also suggested an alternative project. Following Scott's stroke in 1830 Robert Cadell visited him at Abbotsford to suggest that, rather than writing new novels, he should concentrate on the notes and introductions for the Magnum Opus. However Lockhart reports that Scott was not disposed to adopt this plan. As a means of persuading him Cadell 'suggested very kindly . . . that before entering upon any new novel, he should draw up a sort of *catalogue raisonnée* of the most curious articles in his library and museum. Sir Walter', he continues, 'grasped at this, and began next morning to dictate to Laidlaw what he designed to publish in his usual novel shape, under the title of "Reliquiae Trottcosienses, or the Gabions of Jonathan Oldbuck."'[13] In the fly leaf of his diary for 1831 Cadell notes that he has 'a contract with Sir Walter for a work in 2 Vols to be named Reliquae Trotcosienses'[14] and the contract itself suggests that Scott was paid £750 for the work and that five thousand copies were to be printed.[15] However, *Reliquiae* was never published in Scott's lifetime and was suppressed until edited by myself and Gerard Carruthers in 2004. As David Hewitt points out, in their savage editing of both *Count Robert of Paris* and *Castle Dangerous* and in their suppression of *Reliquiae Trotcosienses*, Cadell and Lockhart 'seem to have thought that oblivion was preferable to the exhibition of what they thought was the obvious diminution of Scott's powers.'[16]

Admittedly the justification for seeing these later productions by the Author of Waverley as flawed lies, to some extent, with Scott himself who in his *Journal* describes the pains which producing these texts caused him. For example, while the idea for *Count Robert of Paris* is first mentioned as early as 16 April 1829[17] Scott was to suffer a stroke in

February 1830, followed by another two in just over a year, and as a result there was much delay in the production of the novel. In his *Journal* for the period Scott describes the effects of his stroke on the writing process commenting 'I myself am sensible that my fingers begin to stammer, that is to write one word instead of another very often.'[18] While the difficulty was partly remedied by employing William Laidlaw as an amanuensis Scott reports being at a loss when he is absent. In April, for example, Laidlaw having been given a day's holiday, Scott again notes a problem: 'I have a hideous paralytick custom of *stuttering* with my pen and cannot write without strange blunders'.[19] As he concludes the novel he is clearly weary, recording on 30 April that he is 'not much pleased with [his] handy work'.[20] By September, when he is completing *Castle Dangerous*, he states 'I have been very ill and if not quite unable to write I have been unfit to do. I have wrought however at two Waverly things but not well and what is worse past mending.'[21] This sense of failure, or at least of the flawed nature of the texts, was also reflected in their first edition publication. At Lockhart's suggestion *Count Robert of Paris* and *Castle Dangerous* were eventually published as *Tales of My Landlord, Fourth and Last Series* with an Introductory Address by Jedidiah Cleishbotham where he makes apology for the deficiencies of the novels. Adopting the conceit that these are again the productions of the (now deceased) Peter Pattieson, Cleishbotham comments that he is 'disappointed at finding them by no means in that state of correctness, when as we say of a writing, it is prepared for press. There were not only parts of the manuscript omitted, and others, intended doubtless to be detailed, and united with the principal story, left completed, but there were evident mistakes which a careful revision would have cleared away.'[22]

However, in spite of these frequent comments on the difficulties he experiences in writing these texts, elsewhere Scott notes that he 'cannot find any failure in his intellect' and his conclusion is supported by the fact that work goes on at a much better pace when Laidlaw is acting as an amanuensis.[23] Moreover, Scott's choice of vocabulary is interesting; his use of terms such as 'stammer' and 'stutter' seems to imply a kind of time lag between what he thinks and what he is capable of writing so that the problem is not so much one of Scott being incapable of creating coherently, but rather, one of his being unable to transmit these thoughts to the page. Indeed, he seems reasonably happy with *Count Robert* at certain points in its production recording that 'The plot is . . . a good plot and full of expectation',[24] and that in March he is 'driving on the *Count*

*Robert of Paris* right mer[r]ily'.[25] This casts a particular light on Scott's difficulties with these late texts. Commenting on the manuscript of *Count Robert*, J. H. Alexander notes that 'the passages in Scott's hand are largely coherent, but they show abundant evidence of his failing health', such as 'crabbed and irregular writing'.[26] 'Words are often malformed, most frequently with a superfluous minim inserted'.[27] As a consequence it becomes clear that Scott's difficulties seem to be related to motor skills rather than intellect. In support of this Alexander notes that errors are far less frequent in that portion of the manuscript in Laidlaw's hand, so that 'it is highly probable that Scott dictating was less liable to confusion than Scott writing'.[28] Similar conclusions can be drawn from the experience of editing the manuscript of *Reliquiae Trotcosieneses*, which is partly in Scott's own hand and partly in that of William Laidlaw to whom it was dictated. As Gerard Carruthers and myself note, 'That part of the manuscript in Scott's own hand shows clear signs of failure in motor skills resulting from Scott's strokes of 1830, that "stammer" in his handwriting which he describes so poignantly in his *Journal* for the period. The result is a marked deterioration in the formation of individual letters when compared to Scott's writing in, for example, all but the final Waverley Novels. There is also evidence that Scott frequently loses the thread of a sentence in the course of writing it, leading one sentence to collapse in on another.' However what was also equally clear to us as editors was that although 'what Scott intended to write is not always fully articulated on the page' nevertheless the text 'displays all the brightness and wit of Scott's intellect'.[29]

While Scott may have had difficulties physically writing these texts, and while the manuscripts may exhibit some of the failures that Jedidiah complains of, they are not 'past mending' as Scott fears in his *Journal*. David Hewitt notes in his Introduction to *Reliquiae* that the reconstruction of this text has been possible because 'the underlying literary structure is manifest, even though in local areas it may be obscured'[30] and, similarly, Alexander concludes that the vast majority of the alterations to Scott's text for the purpose of clarification and correction of error made by Cadell and Lockhart are unnecessary since Scott's work is far more coherent than they believed.[31] As he points out regarding Cadell's interventions in *Count Robert*: 'Sometimes what he did is essential; sometimes it is no more than possibly desirable; and often it seems quite unnecessary. It is as though he expected the text in front of him to be more faulty than it actually is.'[32] Lockhart's position is similar. Described by Alexander as 'hypercritical'[33] he too makes many changes, often in ways that a careful reassessment shows to be unnecessary. For example, to give a flavour of this intervention and the ways it has been rejected in the Edinburgh Edition text of *Count Robert*, Alexander reports that he has made over 400 emendations to just one portion of the novel (around 170 first edition pages) thus rejecting around half of the changes made by Cadell and Lockhart in this section alone: 'Some 165 emendations involve rejecting clarifications that seem unnecessary and pedestrian rather than helpful' he states, while 'some 110 general stylistic changes are rejected, mostly as being pointless'.[34] The result of such editing of the novel as a whole is a text much closer to that which Scott originally intended:

> The novel as now presented is much closer to that envisaged by its author than the first-edition or Magnum texts. It is freed from the major censorships applied to it by Cadell and Lockhart, as well as from many minor tonings-down and conventionalisations. Stylistically it is more adventurous. Relieved of much unnecessary spelling-out, it is a good deal sharper. More demanding for readers in its strangeness of plot and expression . . . it offers an experience both challenging and rewarding.[35]

Alexander reports a similar situation with regard to *Castle Dangerous*, with many of the interventions to this text also being rendered unnecessary by the careful reconstruction wrought for the Edinburgh Edition. 'The corrections known to be by Cadell and by Lockhart' he writes, 'are often appropriate, but just as frequently they seem to be quite unnecessary (though they must have appeared desirable to Cadell and Lockhart), and sometimes they are positively deleterious'. As a consequence, 'of Cadell's 1900-odd changes . . . some 1000 have been rejected. Of Lockhart's 650, some 347 have been rejected'.[36]

There can be no doubt that Alexander's reconstruction of Scott's intentions for both *Count Robert* and *Castle Dangerous* is a triumph of textual editing. However, if, as this reconstruction would seem to imply, these 'apoplectic' novels are the product not of an author in decline producing texts of which it is 'best to say nothing', but of one who is still largely in command of his intellectual faculties and hungry to continue in his project of writing fiction, what can these texts, along with *Reliquiae Trotcosienses*, offer to our understanding of Scott's late fiction, and his fiction as a whole?

Recent critical attention has suggested that these works are worth revisiting. Caroline McCracken-Flesher offers an interesting commentary on *Castle Dangerous* in *Possible Scotlands* and Ian Duncan has also written about the significance of *Count Robert* in *Scott's Shadow*.[37]

Moreover if we revisit these late works in the context of the present study it becomes clear that these texts are not unfortunate embarrassments but are in many ways the logical culmination of Scott's fictional career. It has been argued here that a concern with narrative form runs throughout Scott's writing and that in his work (both poetry and fiction) he moves from an initial concern with the relationships between meaning and forms of narrative discourse to an ever more anxious investigation of the fact that indeterminacy is inherent in the very linguistic materials from which discourse is constituted. *The Heart of Mid-Lothian* is recognised as a turning point, offering a site where its author offers a critique of both Enlightenment and Romantic models of the relationship between meaning and language. Within this paradigm the novels of the early 1820s can be seen to demonstrate Scott exploring the potential redundancy of the novel form implied by such a realisation. In the last chapter it was proposed that in his later works Scott moves beyond this exhaustion to offer experimental works that suggest how creativity might proceed in the face of epistemological indeterminacy. By following this trajectory Scott's writing career arguably reflects and develops the eighteenth-century origins of the novel and prefigures the self-reflexive postmodern anxieties and liberations of contemporary fiction. Seen within this framework what Alexander calls the 'stylistic adventurousness' of the last texts, and their 'strangeness of plot and expression' are not the result of an author losing his ability to create but, rather, symptomatic of one exploring the very limits of the novel form. The tensions within *Count Robert*, *Reliquiae* and *Castle Dangerous* are, it will be argued here, generated by Scott's anxiety with the very substance of fiction writing and the ways in which the problems he has recognised as inherent in it might be resolved.

This becomes clearer if we look more closely at *Count Robert of Paris*, a text that includes within it an account of the potentially 'exhausted' nature of art and its redundant and parodic relationship to society. *Count Robert of Paris* is set in the eleventh century during the early years of the crusades. To reach Jerusalem the European crusaders must pass through Constantinople, described here as the decayed remnant of the Greek Empire. This is manifested in the works of art which decorate the city:

> But the men who did great actions, and those, almost equally esteemed, by whom such deeds were celebrated, in poetry, in painting, and in music, had ceased to exist. The nation, though still the most civilized in the world, had passed beyond that period of society, when the desire of fair fame is of itself the sole or chief motive for the labour of the historian or the poet, the painter

or the statuary, while in their turn they confer upon those whom they consider as meriting it, a species of immortality . . . leaving nothing but feeble recollections, which produced no emulation. (p. 4)

Art in these circumstances is redundant, 'used up' to borrow Barth's phrase, and the public life of this civilisation is also presented as an empty show devoid of any real meaning or content, 'encumbered with unmeaning ceremonies' inspired by a 'wish to add seriousness and an importance to objects, which, in their trivial nature, can admit no such distinction' (p. 7).[38] As Graham McMaster notes Constantinople as it is depicted here by Scott is 'a city of art, yet an art in which something has gone wrong'.[39] As readers of Scott are aware, often his opening chapters provide us with a key as to how we are to read the novel that follows and here such despondency about art in a decaying civilisation (and at the hands of a decaying artist) seems to suggest that the novel should be read as exploring a more general anxiety about the relationship of art to society. Moreover, as the novel proceeds it becomes increasingly apparent that this anxiety also extends more specifically to an immediate and fundamental concern with Scott's own artistic medium of language and its capacity to operate effectively.

This is evident in that the civilisation presented here is one that functions, like that in *The Fortunes of Nigel*, via a *lingua Franca* (p. 22) or web of languages. As a consequence it is clear that people living side by side in Constantinople are incapable of communicating with each other. The first appearance of the Varangian Hereward, the real hero of the text, for example, is characterised by a conversation that draws attention to a lack of linguistic commonality. Spotting him by the city gate one citizen of Constantinople enquires of another whether it is likely that he is lurking there to eavesdrop. The second citizen responds:

> "That is not likely . . . these Varangians do not speak our language, and are not extremely well fitted for spies, since few of them pretend to any intelligible notion of the Grecian tongue." (p. 14)

*Count Robert of Paris*, consequently, revisits the concerns relating to language found throughout Scott's writing and a discussion of the limitations of it is built into its very plot. All of the characters in this text attempt to deceive, control, and gain power over each other, and language is depicted as a crucial component in achieving these ends. Indeed the central aspect of the plot – the request by the crusaders to pass through

Constantinople – is described by Alexius as nothing more than a war of words, a competition between different kinds of rhetoric to determine who can best control it. "'Here are loud words'" he says of the crusaders' demands, "'but the wind which whistles loudest is not always most dangerous to the vessel . . . we will flatter their vanity till we get time and opportunity for more effectual defence . . . if words can pay debt, there is no fear of our exchequer becoming insolvent'" (p. 67). Later, he again reiterates that it is via the power of words that the battle will be won: "'We will deal with them in all Christian practice'", he tells his counsellors, "'and by using fair words to one, threats to another, gold to the avaricious, power to the ambitious, and reasons to those that are capable of listening, we doubt not to prevail upon those Franks . . . to acknowledge us as their common superior'" (p. 83).

However, in spite of Alexius's confidence in the power of rhetoric his faith is repeatedly undercut in this text, which draws attention, rather, to the emptiness of words and their lack of agency. This is nowhere more evident than in the character of the cynic Agelestes. Philosophers such as he, Hereward comments, may appear to assume power via language but in the end this is impotent, since the spaces between words and meaning, what we might call slippage, render words redundant. Language, thus cut adrift from referentiality, is no more than a 'battery of sophisms'. "'I have understood'", he states, "'that the masters of this idle science make it their business to substitute, in their argumentations, mere words instead of ideas; and as they never agree upon the precise meaning of the former, their disputes can never arrive at a fair or settled conclusion, since they do not agree in the language in which they express them. Their theories, as they call them, are built on the sand, and the wind and the tide shall prevail against them.'" (p. 91). It is, therefore, hardly surprising that it is the fate of the greatest word-smith, Agelestes, to be killed in one of the most bizarre incidents in the novel when he is strangled by the orang-utang Sylvan. As Ian Duncan has acknowledged the appearance of this near-human ape in *Count Robert* may not be as strange as it first seems. 'Edinburgh in the late Enlightenment (until the 1830s)' he writes, 'was the British institutional center for pre-Darwinian theorizing about human origins, and Scott would have been familiar with the polygenetic thesis of Lord Kames, as well as the notorious claims of Lord Monboddo . . . that the orangutan was a human subspecies that only lacked speech'. And he points out that 'The Romantic vogue for the orangutan', was predicated on the fact that it was 'a figure on the threshold of humanity, language, and culture'.[40]

In this text Sylvan *does* inhabit the liminal space identified by Duncan. However, while he may be on the 'threshold of language', communicating through gesture and expression and seemingly understanding all that is said to him, what is actually more significant is the fact that he cannot speak. As Clare A. Simmons notes, in the eighteenth-century, and in particular for Rousseau, the 'orang-outang was the encouraging symbol of un-socialized humanity', its 'communication . . . through action, not words' making it 'truest of all' in *Count Robert*.[41] Indeed, it is this that makes him, for Hereward at least, the most honourable character since Sylvan alone is freed from the problematic medium of language. As the Man of the Wood utters a 'chattering noise' in response to Hereward's questioning, Hereward states, '"I understand thee . . . thou wilt tell no tales . . . and faith I will trust thee rather than the better part of my own two-legged race, who are eternally circumventing or murdering each other"' (p. 206). The problematics surrounding language are reiterated with particular clarity in *Count Robert of Paris*, and it is Scott's acute awareness of the anxieties surrounding his own artistic medium which contributes to the demanding strangeness of its plot and expression.

Hereward's suggestion that an over-reliance on words can lead to the substitution of 'mere words instead of ideas' and the inability to 'arrive at a fair or settled conclusion' may, indeed, be taken as an apt description of the whole novel. It is acknowledged that the bare bones of plot are seldom the real point in Scott's fiction, but rather, as Franco Moretti suggests, that he is the master of the 'filler', a narrative device that inhabits the spaces between the details of plot.[42] This was a feature of the novel noted by James Ballantyne, who cited it as one of his reasons for objecting to the manuscript. 'I confess I think 24 pages an enormous length for a single conversation, of no great interest perhaps, between Achilles & Hereward' he writes to Scott having read the opening of the novel, 'but it would be grievous to stop before the experiment is fairly made. *You* are of the opinion the subject is an excellent one: whereas *I* do not even know what the subject is'.[43] As Ballantyne implies here 'filler', to borrow Moretti's terminology, becomes a substitute for plot as if such distractions or digressions have actually become the primary subject matter of the text, thus evading the impulse to close the novel down into any form of determinacy, or 'subject' as he puts it. Moreover, one might argue that Ballantyne would have been none the wiser having come to the end of the novel for if its plot and characterisation are problematic so too is its controversial conclusion; inevitably, the impulse to evade is also reflected here. Scott frequently shows his intellectual resistance to closure, but again this is particularly marked in *Count Robert*. While there are a great many words in this text very little actually happens, and most of the details of the plot – such as an attempted coup against Alexius – are in fact narrative dead ends. In spite of all the fuss about the novel's ending in terms of plot it is, by the time we reach it, redundant since the events upon which it rests have already largely been resolved by the death of the key players or the machinations of Alexius.

It is worth reiterating the details of the novel's controversial conclusion here. These are anticipated when the Emperor's son-in-law, Nicephorus Briennius, challenges Count Robert's wife Brenhilda to meet in the lists, the prize being her hand should he be victorious. However, it transpires that Brenhilda cannot fight as she is pregnant and much of the last section of the novel is taken up with how to resolve this dilemma. In fact, by the time the appointed hour arrives Nicephorus has made his peace with his wife Anna Comnena and the outcome of the fight, except as a matter of honour, is largely irrelevant to the working out of the plot. At the appointed day Nicephorus is subject to house arrest by the Emperor and Anna Comnena, the literary princess of Constantinople, resolves to meet with Brenhilda in his place.

It was this detail that so embarrassed Lockhart and Cadell and they warned the author that to insist on such an ending would cost him thousands of pounds in sales. Scott lacked the will, or the desire, to provide an alternative, however, abandoning the novel by 12 May stating that he 'resolved to lay by *Robert of Paris*' as to think about it 'makes [his] head swim'.[44] As soon as he left for the Mediterranean in October, therefore, Lockhart set about revising the conclusion, his 'principal endeavour', according to Alexander, being 'to eliminate all reference to the duel between Brenhilda and Anna'.[45] The result is that in the first edition Brenhilda is too indisposed to leave her apartment and Count Robert appears to fight with Hereward in the lists.

John Sutherland argues that Scott never finished the novel because 'he was so incapacitated that solving the narrative problems of the final volume (more particularly, the women's gladiatorial combat) was beyond him. The final trip to the Mediterranean intervened'.[46] However, Scott *did* provide an ending to his text and it is restored in the Edinburgh Edition. Moreover, if we read the novel as being one that is dealing with the fundamental problems surrounding the effectiveness of language then it is a fitting one and one that suggests that Scott is far more in control of his material and his thematic purposes than previously recognised.

Confronted by the possibility that his daughter and Brenhilda will fight, the Emperor Alexius proposes that, rather than bear arms, his "'beloved daughter shall put to this illustrious Countess a question, or riddle, like that of the sphynx, to which the said Countess shall return an answer according to best judgement'" (p. 338). The Grecian audience, we are told, 'received with shouts a proposal congenial enough to the garrulous and wordy character of their nation' (pp. 338–9). However, in this novel, which has dealt with the inadequacies of exchanging mere words for ideas, and which has foregrounded the fact that battles of rhetoric are pointless since the combatants can seldom agree on the meaning of their terms, things are not to be resolved so easily. "'Am I a child'" asks the indignant Brenhilda, looking at the riddle she has been presented with "'that you meet my open challenge with scrawled spells, containing such charms, for any thing I know, as were used by the false wizzard whom I beheld Satan strangle in my very presence'" (p. 339). Words, the exchange implies, offer no stable access to any kind of ontological certainty and as such cannot be substituted for action.

In this strange novel, however, itself constituted out of words of course, no other form of determinacy can take the place of the riddle and the impasse that this creates mirrors the position that the author, himself a 'false wizzard' is in; caught within language there is nothing he can substitute for its contingencies. In Scott's version a duel does take place between the two women but the pregnant Brenhilda stumbles and falls before a blow is ever struck. Hereward and Count Robert also fight but again in what is essentially a parody of a duel since by this point nothing is at stake. The ending of the novel, consequently, like the long conversation with which it opens, is not an attempt to reach narrative closure but, rather, is designed to foreground the fact that nothing can actually be revealed by words other than the endless and on-going circuit of signification. While Scott concludes by quoting the authorities of Edward Gibbon and Anna Comnena on the events he has described he consequently offers no assurance that their accounts have offered any access to any 'real' version of the past or captured the truth of it. Nor does he offer any such assurance for his own narrative: rather, in his farewell statement that closes the text, he suggests that plot can only ever be indeterminate, part of an on-going exchange of words between author and reader:

It cannot be a matter of doubt that the object of an author of a work of fiction is, to fix the public attention, and for that purpose obtain novelty at whatever rate; if he has not the fortune to unite this necessary qualification with a probable tale of a domestic nature, the public good-naturedly permits him to lay his scene in distant countries, among stranger nations, whose manners are imagined for the purpose of the story—nay, whose powers are extended beyond those of human nature, so that there are no limits within the power of a reasonable enchanter, to which the fictitious author may not extend his own capacity, in despite of the limits of natural, and even moral impossibility. (pp. 362–3)

Here, the Author of Waverley, who seemingly began his fictional career with an attempt to find the best form of words in which to capture the past seems to acknowledge the futility of this endeavour. In *Count Robert of Paris* Scott's long consideration of the limits of language reaches its natural conclusion; it is not to be trusted; it is an act of sophistry, it is a vehicle of deceit; it is a poor substitution for action. As a consequence the novelist cannot capture the past through language; he can only ever be a 'reasonable enchanter', what Brenhilda – with a gesture towards one of Scott's many sobriquets – calls a 'false wizzard' incapable of offering epistemological certainty of any kind but telling parodic stories that move beyond 'the limits of the natural' and defy 'even moral impossibility'.

## Reliquiae Trotcosienses

Scott explores similar ideas in *Reliquiae Trotcosienses or the Gabions of the Late Jonathan Oldbuck Esq. of Monkbarns*. This late text also takes as its subject matter the problematic nature of communicating the past via words and like much of Scott's later fiction responds to this situation by acts of self-reflexivity and self-parody. As described above Cadell's initial proposal was that Scott should be distracted from writing fiction by compiling a *catalogue raisonnée* of the most curious articles in his library and museum at Abbotsford. However, while *Reliquiae* is in one sense a 'catalogue' of Scott's library it is, as the following discussion will show, also far more than this.

For many commentators Scott's collecting activities and his home at Abbotsford seems to offer a continuation of what they see as an essentially empirical impulse in his work and a desire to collect, record, and describe the past both in his antiquarian pursuits and in his fiction. As Hugh Cheape, Trevor Cowie and Colin Wallace put it 'Scott was as much alive to the significance of material culture to the historian as he was to that of conventional sources. This is well seen in the building and finishing of Abbotsford, in the enthusiastic and detailed description of costume and artefacts in his novels, and in his appetite for collecting objects as well as facts'.[47] Iain Brown offers a more direct comparison, suggesting that 'Abbotsford, one might say, is the *Waverley* novels in stone'.[48]

This impulse to see direct links between the fiction and Scott's home was well established by the mid-nineteenth-century and was supported by the publication of the Abbotsford Edition of the Waverley Novels between 1842 and 1847, an edition elaborately illustrated, often with engravings of the collections at Abbotsford themselves. A notice for it reads:

> It was a favourite pursuit of Sir WALTER SCOTT throughout life, but especially in his most active period, to collect and arrange objects of Art connected with the historical events and personages recorded and illustrated by his pen; and it cannot be doubted that a Series of Engravings, representing the Pictorial and Antiquarian Museum of Abbotsford, would furnish the most instructive graphic commentary that the body of his Writings could receive from any one source whatever. This collection, therefore, valuable in itself, and doubly interesting as having been made by such a hand, has now been studied with care, and its various curiosities faithfully copied for the exclusive purposes of an Edition of the Waverley Novels, which is to bear the title of The Abbotsford Edition.[49]

*Waverley*, consequently, is illustrated with, among other things, cut and thrust and toledo swords, a target and swords, and a hunting horn from Hermitage Castle, all taken from the Abbotsford collections. Rather more controversially, an engraving of the window in the hall at Abbotsford is taken as an illustration for Waverley-Honour while one of the Abbotsford gateway serves to illustrate the entrance to Tully-Veolan. Other novels follow the same pattern; the illustrators have a field day with *The Antiquary*, drawing on the whole range of the Abbotsford collections to illustrate the novel. Pleasant though it may be to read Scott's novels in the Abbotsford Edition it is nonetheless troubling in several ways. Certainly, as the above illustrations to *Waverley* suggest, the editors were not afraid to be cavalier with historical detail; spurs from Bannockburn and Otterburn illustrate a novel about the Jacobite Rising for example. Such an approach may have contributed to a general sense that Scott himself was frequently slap-dash with details of historical accuracy, simply plundering the past arbitrarily for his fiction. While Scott was, of course, not afraid to play with historical detail (one thinks of the appearance of the Countess of Derby in *Peveril of the Peak* for example) he was seldom *unknowingly* inaccurate when it came to history. Indeed, the experience of the editors of The Edinburgh Edition of the Waverley Novels has been to discover that even when Scott appears to be wrong about some detail of history, he is frequently referring to information and circumstances unknown to the modern editor. More perniciously, however, the Abbotsford Edition is also troubling because it apparently draws a direct correlation between Scott's home and antiquarian collections and his fiction, as if, unproblematically, historical artefact can be taken to illustrate the complexities of the Waverley novels themselves.

This is not to say that there is no connection between the Waverley Novels and Scott's antiquarian collections but the relationship is clearly more complex than the Abbotsford Edition implies. Scott himself recognised that his house was in some ways a continuation of his fiction writing activities and wrote to Lord Montagu in 1822 that '[i]t is worth while to come were it but to see what a romance of a house I am making'.[50] Elsewhere he refers to Abbotsford as a 'Conundrum Castle'[51] acknowledging the whimsical nature of it. However, as these references imply it is clear that for Scott the connection between his home and his novels is that both are 'romances' of sorts, not that his antiquarian activities at Abbotsford reinforce an empirical impulse at work in his fiction. This becomes even more apparent when we consider the dynamics at work within *Reliquiae*.

Certainly it is clear that in spite of the fact that Cadell had suggested to him that he write a 'catalogue' Scott himself was suspicious of any such enterprise and wary of the very idea of a straightforward record of his own collections. In January 1828 a Mr Stewart visited Scott wishing to include a description of Abbotsford in a (rather unfortunately titled) series on *Views of Gentlemen's Seats*. Afterwards Scott comments in his *Journal*:

> I must take care he does not in civility over-puff my little assemblage of curiosities. Scarce any thing can be meaner than the vanity which details the contents of china closets—basins, ewers and Chamberpots. Horace Walpole with all his talents makes a silly figure when he gives an upholsterer's catalogue of his goods and chattles at Strawberry hill.[52]

It is therefore hardly surprising that Scott wrote an altogether different kind of text. Cadell refers to the *Reliquiae* in his diary as 'a *novel* in two volumes' and although it is incomplete it is clear that this is what Scott had in mind since in its structure it reflects the familiar architecture of a Waverley text, being divided into an 'Introduction', 'Proem' and 'Preface' (or series of self-reflexive framing narratives), and three sections, mapping onto the volumes of its larger counterparts. Moreover, the 'Proem' makes explicit that what is being presented here is not a straightforward catalogue of Scott's library but a far more parodic account of the collections and collecting activities of the titular hero of his novel *The Antiquary*, Jonathan Oldbuck. Thus the preface, as so often in Scott's work, self-reflexively contextualises the work which is to follow and provides a key as to how it is to be read. Most significantly it revisits questions that vex Scott from the outset of his career offering a satirical commentary on the possibility of capturing the past either by antiquarian pursuits or by narrative.

This is evident if we consider the opening sentences of this Proem, which refers to the curious title of the piece which is taken from a truly dreadful poem called *The Muses Threnodie* by Henry Adamson – a poem about Perth's antiquities and the Ruthven Conspiracy:

> We are told by an author of the present day whose friends as well as enemies, if he has either, will confess that he is a voluminous writer, that there is a certain advantage in giving a book to the public under a title which conveys an intelligible meaning, yet which does not lead the reader to injury by inducing him to form an exaggerated idea of the amusement which he is destined to receive from the contents. Our late excellent friend Jonathan Oldbuck Esq. of Monkbarns, to whose library the public is now indebted for the amusement which these sheets may impart, seems to have followed his contemporary's receipt to the utmost by using a word in the title which not only conveys no distinct meaning of the contents but which never did so, and is not more intelligible now than it would have been a century ago in the year 1700, except perhaps by a few antiquaries about the town of Perth, who would have understood what was meant by "Gall's gabions." These words, or the single word "gabions" taken by itself has, in the neighbourhood of that ancient burgh, a distinguished and precise signification of its own, which has we believe been adopted by a few at least of the celebrated book club which sends forth its reprints on a scale only second to the Roxburghe itself. (p. 5)

The unintelligible word 'Gabions', the narrator goes on to tell us, was one coined by an antiquarian collector in Perth who taught his fanatical followers to 'distinguish the objects of his whimsical curiosity by the name of "gabions," which became so far a correct phrase as with those at least among Dr Ruthven's friends who sympathized with him in his love of their curiosities, and agreed in the cant name by which they were distinguished' (p. 5). Much of the rest of the Proem is then taken up with quoting Adamson's poem and giving an account of this poet and his antiquarian friends. The Proem, consequently, sets up a context for the 'catalogue' that follows within which the whole business of antiquarian collection and its relationship to the past is satirised. Scott, instructed by Lockhart and Cadell to write a history of Abbotsford in order to distract him from writing novels, in fact produces here a strange hybrid kind of text; no simple 'catalogue of upholstery' but a fictionalised account of his own collections which is part biography, part factual account but also a strangely self-parodying text that calls into question apparent epistemological certainty in the forms of both the relationship between word and meaning, as well as that between the physical object of antiquarian collection and its relationship to any kind of knowable past.

The imperative of antiquarianism, as it flourished in the eighteenth century, was essentially an Enlightenment one borne out of a faith that empirical truth about the past could be located by piecing together the artefacts which represent its material culture. Many have seen the Waverley Novels project and the notes and introductions that accompany Scott's texts as embodying a similar relationship to the historical record.[53] However, *Reliquiae* suggests that an altogether more complex relationship between the past and narrative is being formulated by the Author of Waverley for not only does it satirise antiquarian collecting and the epistemological certainty upon which it is built, it in fact simultaneously reflects an important creative impulse that resonates throughout Scott's last fictions for *Reliquiae* reminds the reader that, in spite of the fact that the past cannot be captured within discourse, the imperative to tell stories remains.

This can be seen in the very structure of the text. The narrator of *Reliquiae* sets out for himself a careful plan as to how he is to proceed; he will first describe the house and then the objects that it contains and, somewhat unusually, Scott reports that he indeed wrote a plan for this text.[54] However, as the Author of Waverley has observed elsewhere, he is incapable of writing up to such schemes[55] and inevitably he cannot stick to one here. Describing the hall at Abbotsford, for example, he comments upon a peculiar suit of armour that includes a sword marked out with the days of the Catholic saints. He goes on:

> In a word, it is a calendar to direct the good knight's devotions. The other suit of armour, which is also complete in all its parts, was said when it came into my possession to have belonged to a knight who took arms upon Richmond's side at the Field of Bosworth and died I think of his wounds there. If one was disposed to give him a name, in all certainty the size of his armour might claim that he was John Cheney, the biggest man of both armies on that memorable day. I venture to think—for I feel myself gliding into the true musing style of an antiquarian disposed in sailors' phrase 'to

spin a tough yarn'—I incline, I say, to think that the calendar placed in the hand of the little French knight in the right-hand niche, originally belonged to the gigantic warrior of Bosworth Field. (pp. 33–4)

What he has done here, he notes, is to '[infringe] on his order' (p. 34) by describing his gabions ahead of the house. But this is, in fact, how narrative is generated in this text as Scott uses his antiquarian collections as springboards for story, 'tough yarns' as he calls them. *Reliquiae*, and its overt departure from its author's self proclaimed scheme, thus reminds the reader that while antiquarian collections may not offer a coherent narrative of the past they do provide the imaginative spaces within which stories about it may exist. As David Hewitt puts it, what emerges here is an oblique relationship between artefact and fact, and one which suggests that 'For the Author of Waverley the past can never be finally located, but only approached via complex, multiplex and elusive acts of narration; via fictions which, just as they seem to offer us some fixed referent for the personal and national histories which they recount, repeatedly subvert their own conclusions, offering up a myriad of possibilities and opening spaces for further narrative.'[56] While *Reliquiae* serves to question what some have seen as the foundations of the Waverley Novels project, the ability to collect, record and describe the past with any kind of epistemological certainty, however, its position is not one of despair. It is, in fact, a funny text, and one of the pleasures of transcribing the manuscript lay in a growing realisation that in it one could still find Scott's sense of humour. For example, at the time when it was being written Scott was still amusing himself by going on excursions with a group of friends known as the Blair-Adam Club; the in-jokes, games and disguises found in the novels then continue in this late satiric, self-parodying and self-reflexive text. As such, *Reliquiae* functions to remind us that while there may be no form of words in which the past can finally be located, nevertheless the fragments of it that are left to us may yet offer a key to artistic generation.

## Castle Dangerous

As with *Count Robert* Cadell and Lockhart made significant changes to *Castle Dangerous* after Scott had left for Malta and, as we have seen above, many of these have been rejected in the Edinburgh Edition. The flaws they and Ballantyne perceived in this text were similar to those they saw in *Count Robert*; Ballantyne, for example, objected to the length of one conversation asking, rather plaintively, 'Could not the long conversation between Aymer and Bertram be shortened, or divided? It already occupies more than 30 pages, and is going on'.[57] The ending of the text again also came under revision although it is less clear why this was the case. J. H. Alexander suggests that as with *Count Robert* this may have been on grounds of taste, but that, whatever the reason, the cuts have the effect of destroying Scott's intended rhetorical effect:

> It is very likely that the unflinching presentation of Fleming's attitude to Lady Margaret seemed unacceptable to Cadell (and possibly also Lockhart): that would be this novel's equivalent to the pregnant combat excised from *Count Robert of Paris*. It would have been possible to cover this objection by cutting only the second half of the section. It may be that the protracted to-ing and fro-ing of the negotiations seemed excessive, though they were certainly part of Scott's conception of the dynamics of the scene and of the characters' roles in it.[58]

By cutting these lengthy conversations and negotiations within Scott's novel Cadell and Lockhart fail to recognise that, just as in *Count Robert*, these ongoing discursive elements are part of the fabric of the text; not a symptom of Scott's decay but, rather, a response to his realisation that all the past can offer is the stories we choose to tell of it ourselves.

This dynamic is evident, however, if we look more closely at *Castle Dangerous*, Scott's last and most neglected novel. Like *Count Robert*, *Castle Dangerous* is haunted by a sense of exhaustion and redundancy. Images of death and decay pervade this late fiction. This is apparent, for example, in the passage where Aymer de Valence is confronted by what appears to be the supernatural appearance of a Douglas knight and, in order to unravel the apparent mystery, is directed to 'old Goodman Powheid, who has the charge of the muniments' (p. 89). On arriving at Powheid's home Aymer observes that it seems like a '"charnel-house of the dead"' and his guide agrees, commenting that '"when an auld bedral dwells near the dead, he is living . . . among his customers"' (p. 90). The home of the suitably named Lazarus is comprised of stones reclaimed from graves, and the fuel for the fire is similarly comprised of 'the relics of mortality', which is employed to expel 'the damps of the grave' (p. 92). When Aymer enquires of this old man about the House of Douglas, Powheid points out, in words that are in many ways reminiscent of Rebecca's well-known denunciation of chivalry in *Ivanhoe*,[59] that in spite of all their glorious deeds, the family are now consigned to death:

Look around, Sir Knight, you have above and around you the men of whom we speak. Beneath us, in a little aisle . . . there lies the first man whom I can name as memorable among those of this mighty line . . . Others, his descendants, called Orodh or Hugh the first and Orodh or Hugh the second, William the first of that honourable name, and Gilmour, the theme of many a minstrel song, commemorating achievements done under the oriflamme of Charles the Great, Emperor of France, have all consigned themselves to their last sleep, nor has their memory been sufficiently preserved from the waste of time. (pp. 93–4)

Other episodes in the novel also cast the constant shadow of death. This is particularly true of one strangely dream-like sequence in the novel when Lady Augusta, abandoned by Margaret de Hautlieu, enters a thicket to be confronted by the 'Knight of the Sepulchre' whose 'armour was ingeniously painted, so as to represent a skeleton; the ribs being constituted by the corslet and its back-piece' (p. 134). This knight hands her over to his attendants who then lead Lady Augusta, blind-folded, through ruins and tunnels in 'an atmosphere which was close to a smothering degree, and felt at the same time damp, and disagreeable to the smell, as if from the vapours of a new made grave' (p. 144) and which 'oppressed her like that of a charnel-house' (p. 145). It is unclear what this lengthy episode actually adds to the plot of the novel beyond signifying that Lady Augusta has fallen into the hands of the Scots. This, however, is perhaps to miss the point for allusions such as these seem less motivated by the need to move the narrative forward than by serving some kind of metaphorical key to the underlying concerns of the text. As Alexander puts it, 'The reader soon accepts that this is a dreamlike fiction, in which transitions are sometimes abrupt and characters like the sacristan appear and disappear in response to imaginative requirements rather than as part of more conventional plotting'.[60] In Scott's earlier work, such as *The Tale of Old Mortality*, memorials of death are frequently introduced with the implication that the historical novel itself seems to operate, like them, as an act of commemoration by which the past is recorded, preserved, and kept alive in the mind of the reader.[61] In this text, however, these monuments do not enact such commemoration but function, rather, as a *memento mori*, a reminder of the shadow of death which has hung over so much of Scott's writing. And the question that haunts this novel is the extent to which it, as a work of art, may serve as a vehicle by which to redeem the 'waste of time' signified by human endeavour.

Certainly, these strange episodes contribute to the 'dreamlike' aspect of the text and to what Alexander also describes as the 'disturbing and haunting reading experience' that it evokes.[62] This 'haunting' element is, however, also generated by the fact that this novel is *literally* haunted by traces of Scott's earlier work and echoes of both his poetry and fiction. As Alexander point out, *Castle Dangerous* is not a venture into new material for Scott. Just as *Reliquiae* revisits *The Antiquary* here Scott is drawing on material he has known from childhood and which he had told himself 'on three occasions before making it central to a work of fiction: in the 'Essay on Chivalry' (1817), the first series of *Tales of a Grandfather* (1828), and the first volume of his *History of Scotland* (1829)'.[63] *Castle Dangerous*, then, is not new material, but familiar material re-worked and re-visited.

This sense of a text haunted by earlier texts is also evident in the opening sections of the novel and the introduction there of Bertram the Minstrel. *Castle Dangerous* begins with a scene that overtly directs Scott's readers back to the very beginnings of his career and his first long narrative poem *The Lay of the Last Minstrel*. *Castle Dangerous*, like the *Lay*, is set in the Scottish Borders and, as in the tale that the minstrel tells in Scott's poem, it is a Borders at war with the English. After setting the scene Scott introduces two travellers, one of whom is 'a person well, and even showily dressed . . . who bore at his back, as wandering minstrels wont, a case, containing a small harp, rote, or viol, or some such species of musical instrument' (p. 6). This introduction to the novel, consequently, invites readers to recall Scott's earlier poem and the ways in which the figure of the minstrel resonates through his early writing. Other echoes with Scott's poetry are also to be found. For example, Bertram is visiting Castle Dangerous for the purpose of 'get[ting] among romances and chronicles, and the contents of a fine old library' (p. 24) and with the specific intention of discovering the lost book of Thomas the Rhymer. 'Thomas the True Speaker' features in *Minstrelsy of the Scottish Border* and the completion of his poem for *Minstrelsy* was one of Scott's first poetic endeavours. By refiguring him here Scott is both referencing his early career and, crucially, foregrounding the fact that he is imaginatively re-engaging with those issues concerning poetic utterance, the status of the minstrel, and the relationship of poetry to our understanding of the self and the past that informed his early work.

*Castle Dangerous*, then, is not simply a formulaic reworking of Scott's earlier writing but a creative revisiting of it. As such it serves as a marker of how far Scott has travelled in his understanding of the role of the poet and his relationship to society in the course of his long writing career. As noted above, *Castle Dangerous* opens with a description of the minstrel Bertram and the Lady Augusta making their way into Scotland

and much space in the opening chapters is devoted to a description of the role of the minstrel. Indeed, part of the lengthy conversation between Sir Aymer and Bertram to which Ballantyne so objected concerns itself with this very subject. Questioned by Aymer as to why he has endangered his life by coming to Scotland, Bertram responds by comparing the role of the minstrel to that of the knight: "'You long to see adventures worthy of notice,'" he tells him, "'and I . . . seek a scanty and precarious, but not a dishonourable living, by preparing for eternal memory, as well as I can, the particulars of such exploits, especially the names of those who were the heroes of these actions'" (p. 26). "'I have known,'" he continues "'not poets only, but even chroniclers . . . who spared neither toil nor danger when the question was how to acquire a true knowledge of the facts which they intended to transmit to posterity'" (p. 27). The role of the minstrel Bertram outlines here seems initially to be very similar to that presented in Scott's earlier work: confident that 'words' and 'action' are indeed the same he sees it as the function of the poet to record and transmit events of historical significance, thereby preserving them for future generations. However, in spite of this seeming affirmation of the role of the minstrel his function in *Castle Dangerous* emerges in this late text as far more complex and ambiguous than Bertram's initial statements imply. While in his 1802 introduction to the *Minstrelsy* Scott wrote that 'there has hardly been found to exist a nation so brutishly rude, as not to listen with enthusiasm to the songs of their bards',[64] by the time that he wrote 'Introductory Remarks on Popular Poetry' in 1830 he notes that 'poets were a fabling race from the very beginning of time, and so much addicted to exaggeration, that their accounts are seldom to be relied on without corroborative evidence.'[65] He elaborates upon this less favourable view of the minstrel in the companion essay 'Imitations of the Ancient Ballad':

> The invention of printing necessarily occasioned the downfall of the Order of Minstrels, already reduced to contempt by their own bad habits, by the disrepute attached to their profession, and by the laws calculated to repress their license. When the Metrical Romances were very many of them in the hands of every one, the occupation of those who made their living by reciting them was in some degree abolished, and the minstrels either disappeared altogether, or sunk into mere musicians, whose utmost acquaintance with poetry was being able to sing a ballad.[66]

This degenerate construction of the minstrel's role is also one proposed in *Castle Dangerous*. Sir John Walton, for example, suggests that while it may have stood higher in former days the profession is now one of "'a detractor of God and a deceiver of man'" (p. 47) and De Valence expresses a similar view proposing that minstrels have fallen from the "'higher pretensions of that noble order'" so that they are motivated only by "'love of gain'" (p. 70).

Indeed, while Bertram continues his conversation with Aymer this more ambivalent construction of minstrelsy becomes increasingly apparent. Telling a tale of the Douglas family, and thus seemingly carrying out the role he has outlined for himself, Bertram immediately undermines his own position. Confronted by an alternative version of the details, for example, he is forced to concur "'I know not that'" (p. 30). Challenged by Aymer that the tale he tells disrespects Edward the First he states that he will "'avoid disputable topics'" and when called into question on matters of opinion he admits that it is up to the individual to "'determine which has most falsehood'". In spite of the fact that he reiterates that he "'must tell the truth'" (p. 31) it is apparent that this is far more complex than is initially implied since "'the same tale can be told another way'" (p. 32). The epistemological uncertainty that has been interrogated in Scott's fiction, consequently, undermines the role of the minstrel and what he can achieve.

These conclusions are the logical culmination of Scott's ever increased awareness of the limited nature of language and its potential (or lack of potential) to articulate the past and it is hardly surprising to find these ideas reiterated here in his last work. This is apparent even in the tale of the apparition of 'Thomas the True Speaker' who, in spite of his name, seems to communicate on very dubious authority. The tale, as Aymer points out, seems "'quite apocryphal in the sober hours of the morning'" (p. 39) and is certainly at least second hand. Moreover, Thomas communicates in "'an antique language . . . which few could have comprehended'" and which must consequently be 'translated'; a term now loaded with significance in Scott's fictional world (p. 39). If the language of even the 'truest' of speakers occupies this ambiguous category it is hardly surprising that the language of others serves to confuse rather than elucidate.

As we might now have come to expect in Scott's work the 'plot' elements which make up the narrative of *Castle Dangerous* – although as we shall see this is perhaps not the most appropriate word for them – hinge upon the failures of language to communicate effectively. The first of these, the love involvement between Lady Augusta and Sir John Walton has, indeed, been inspired by a minstrel's tale, for in spite of her later reservations and her journey to Scotland to resolve the situation, it is this which has inspired Augusta to launch the challenge by which Walton may win her hand. She recounts the story to Margaret de Hautlieu in her guise of Sister Ursula:

> "Here stopt the harp; and I shame to say, that I myself, as if moved to enthusiasm by the song of the minstrel, arose, and taking from my neck the chain of gold which supported a crucifix of special sanctity, I made my vow, always under the King's permission, that I would give my hand, and the inheritance of my fathers, to the good knight, being of noble birth and lineage, who should keep the Castle of Douglas in the King of England's name, for a year and a day". (p. 108)

Elsewhere, further details which may be said to constitute plot in this strangely plotless novel are also generated by linguistic confusion or ambiguity. The quarrel between Aymer de Valence and Sir John Walton, for example, is caused by an overheard, and misunderstood, conversation by the squire Fabian and his decision to further misrepresent what he has heard by 'carry[ing] the tale to [his] master' (p. 49). As the narrator tells us 'The mother of mischief . . . is no bigger than a midge's wing' (p. 49), yet such linguistic misconstruction can have dire effects so that, as the motto to Chapter 6, taken from Coleridge, tells us, 'words of high disdain, / And insult to his heart's dear brother' can lead to a situation where 'whispering tongues can poison truth' (p. 51). In this instance, both miscommunication and failure to communicate contribute to a situation where the men are nearly fatally at odds so that while 'explanation might have produced a complete agreement in the sentiments of both' (p.68), instead fragments of conversation are 'overheard by some of the squires and pages, and bandied about among them from one to another, until it entirely lost the accent and tone of good humour in which it had been originally spoken' and reconciliation seems impossible (p. 65). Similar confusion also arises from the written word in this novel for while the letter that Lady Augusta writes as she escapes from the convent is meant to clarify her situation it only obscures the reality of it and leads the abbot to conclude that it is '"Midsummer madness"' (p. 119) and Sir John to read the note with an eye that 'wandered over the characters without apparently conveying any distinct impression to his understanding' (p. 124). Even the words of the minstrel are ineffectual in this novel. While his search for Thomas the Rhymer's Book of Prophecies at Castle Dangerous seems to form yet another of the many plot lines, the recitation of them, which in some ways could be seen as a kind of culmination of Scott's writing career, is presented in the most deflated way. 'The minstrel', we are told, 'began to recite verses, which, in our time, the ablest interpreter could not make sense out of', while '[t]he archer listened to these mystic prognostications, which were not the less wearisome than they were, in a considerable degree, unintelligible' (p. 156). Language here has no agency and as a result minstrelsy is no longer privileged as prophecy or 'truth' but is only a kind of mischief-making, words being used as a vehicle to '"create rumours of plots, conspiracies, and bloody wars"', thus causing '"the very mischances which they would be thought only to predict"' (p. 158).

As so often in Scott's later fiction, then, linguistic communication cut adrift from any fixed meaning is either misleading or ineffectual. Yet in spite of this, just as in *Count Robert*, there is a great deal said in this text, and although it is much shorter than some of Scott's others, it demonstrates the impulse articulated in *Reliquiae* to 'spin a tough yarn', to keep telling stories. Haunted though it may be by a sense of redundancy and death *Castle Dangerous* does not signify the 'exhaustion' of the novel form but, rather, the imperative encapsulated within it to continue to generate narrative. While death may haunt this 'dreamlike fiction' Scott is not sleep-walking towards it but, rather, exploring the ways in which the 'death' wrought by the closed nature of language may yet be evaded. Nowhere is this more evident than in the section that Ballantyne so objected to, the conversation between Aymer and Bertram. This lengthy conversation takes place as Bertram and Sir Aymer de Valence are travelling to Douglas Castle. At the outset, the reader is informed that the purpose of this conversation is seemingly to pass the time, and to keep lines of communication open:

> The view was monotonous and depressing, and apparently the good knight Aymer sought some amusement in occasional talk with Bertram, who, as was usual with his craft, possessed a fund of knowledge, and a power of conversation, well suited to pass away a dull morning. Anxious as the minstrel was in picking up some information as he might be able to procure concerning the present state of the castle, he of course embraced every opportunity of sustaining the dialogue. (p. 25)

After those exchanges already discussed about why the minstrel has come to Scotland, Aymer requests that Bertram gives him his '"own minstrel account"' of the legends that have encouraged his visit and on this basis Bertram begins a 'long story' in which he gives an account of the history of the Douglasses. In turn, Sir Aymer then gives his 'edition of the story' of the 'Douglas Larder' episode. Story in turn inspires story and Bertram again takes up the thread. Moreover, as in *Redgauntlet*, story is figured here overtly as story; as Bertram introduces the appearance of True Thomas during the siege of the castle, he comments that "'the rote or the viol easily changes its time and varies its note'" (p. 37) thus foregrounding the narratorial strategies at work within his tale: "'I have heard this story told at a great distance from the land in which it happened, by a sworn minstrel of the house of Douglas'", he continues, providing the narrative frame for his own account (p. 37). This lengthy conversation, then, is less of a dialogue than a vehicle for story-telling and as such in many ways prefigures the novel that follows, which is not driven by plot, but by a deeper and more urgent imperative.

This is suggested by the 'plot' lines described above, which are, in fact, driven less by normal conventions than, as Alexander indicates, by a series of abrupt 'transitions' by 'characters like the sacristan [who] appear and disappear in response to imaginative requirements rather than as part of more conventional plotting'.[67] Indeed, rather than following the pattern of narrative 'crux' followed by resolution and denouement the novel offers a series of narrative false starts and dead ends, and finally shatters into a series of tangentially related stories none of which can be easily identified as the main plot line.[68] This is illustrated by its opening where readerly expectations are confounded by an inability to identify the key elements of the plot. While Bertram and his page seem to be the main characters at the beginning, another element is soon introduced by the quarrel between Thomas Dickson and his son Charles. Yet while this seems to imply some element that will gain significance as the plot develops this is in fact more or less a narrative dead end. The introduction of True Thomas and his Book of Prophecies also portends some kind of narrative significance: "'The fated hour of removing this book is not yet come'", Thomas announces, seemingly setting up a line of narrative development, "'the time of its removal shall come'" (p. 40). Yet, as we have seen, the book (like the one that features so prominently in the *Lay*) turns out to be of little significance and has no real implications for narrative development. Another plot line is implied by the quarrel between Sir Aymer and Walton, but, in spite of all that is made of it, again this has no real implications for the novel's denouement and is in the end easily resolved. When Valence visits the town of Douglas the reader feels that they may at last be given some clue to what is driving this story since Powheid is introduced as one who may 'possess the knowledge which may assist' the knight (p. 89). Again, however, any expectation of clarification is frustrated when Powheid offers no real enlightenment but, yet again, only a series of stories, 'the recitation of the pedigree of the House of Douglas' (p. 94) which Aymer dismisses (perhaps ironically) as 'a fiction too gross to charm to sleep a schoolboy tormented with the toothach' (p. 96). Finally, with the (not altogether surprising) revelation about half way through the novel that the youth Augustine is in fact Lady Augusta the reader finally feels that they have discovered the true plot line of this text. Yet even this is to some extent frustrated for the emphasis seems almost immediately to shift from her own love entanglement to that of Margaret de Hautlieu – revealed yet again via embedded story. At the end of the novel those plot lines which the reader has struggled to identify seem simply to dissipate; while a battle between the English and Scottish knights is anticipated upon the arrival of Pembroke he in fact simply fails to show, which causes Walton's brow to become 'overclouded' but simultaneously 'placed him at liberty to take measures for the safety of the Lady of Berkely' (p. 185). The siege of the castle is ended by an act of 'chivalry' which sidesteps the fact that Augusta's and Walton's safety was 'resting on the precarious issue of a desperate combat' (p. 185) and the novel's conclusion seems less concerned with those who have seemingly been its main players but with Margaret and Malcolm Fleming, characters introduced late in the day. The novel ends not with denouement but with what Alexander describes as a 'protracted to-ing and fro-ing of the negotiations', which seems to have irked those who were involved in the cutting of its conclusion. Rather than following the trajectory we have come to expect of the novel, or the teleological movement so often identified as part of Scott's creativity, this text fractures into a series of broken narratives where the telling of the tale seems more significant than the conclusions reached by it. It is an imperative driven by something more urgent than the need to pass the time, or by a desire to 'labour steadily on with the task of covering blank paper with ink'. It is, rather, one driven by the realisation that the only way to defeat the epistemological certainties of language that have death at their centre is to work not towards closure, but towards digression.

It is this dynamic, I would suggest, that drives all of the late fiction. Having recognised that the 'poverty' of words he identifies as intrinsic to the novel form is incapable of offering access to anything other than a web of linguistic evasion and confusion, and that at the heart of a desire to pin language down into a fixed conclusion there can only be silence or 'death', the Author of Waverley side-steps into a new kind of narrative; one driven not by the minstrel's desire to communicate 'true knowledge' but one driven by the imperative of digression or evasion. John Barth identifies this impulse as lying at the heart of his own writing and that of the whole art of fiction. Figuring *The Arabian Nights* as a trope for the novelistic imperative he comments:

> [T]he story of deflowered Scheherazade, yarning tirelessly through the dark hours to save her neck, corresponds to a number of things at once, and flashes meaning from all its facets. For me its rich dark circumstances, mixing the subtle and the coarse, the comic and the grim, the realistic and the fantastic, the apocalyptic and the hopeful, figure, among other things, both the estate of the fictioner in general and the particular endeavours and aspirations of this one, at least, who can wish nothing better than to spin like that vizier's excellent daughter, through what nights remain to him, tales within tales within tales . . . until he and his scribblings are fetched low by the Destroyer of Delights.[69]

The trope of Scheherazade was resonant with meaning for many postmodern writers for they recognised with Barth that it 'flashes meaning from all its facets' encapsulating within it far more than simply the desire to keep telling stories but, rather, a recognition that it is by such acts that we resist closing language down into the fixed teleological system which has at its centre death. It is this impulse that also provides the key to understanding the strangely dislocating but compelling narrative spaces constituted by *Count Robert of Paris*, *Reliquiae Trotcoienses* and *Castle Dangerous*. These texts offer a coherence that arises not from plot or structure (or at times even from the clarity of individual sentences) but from the questions that vex Scott throughout his writing career; questions that are at the heart of the novel form and what it can achieve. Can the past be captured in words? If so what form should they take? And if not, how can the writer proceed in the face of the limited nature of his own medium? Caught within the poverty of words is fiction just an empty sham like the statues described in Constantinople or is there some worth (or even compulsion) in the enduring desire that Scott exhibits in his last novels to keep telling stories, Scheherazade-like, in the face of his own imminent death. As John Barth argues, it is by such acts that the novel moves beyond its own 'exhaustion', and redeems the 'waste of time' that falls like a shadow across *Castle Dangerous* and all of Scott's last work. While the referential, teleological impulse within language may have death at its centre, the act of narrative is an act of resistance: 'We tell stories and listen to them because we live stories and live in them', Barth comments. 'Narrative equals language equals life: To cease to narrate, as the capital example of Scheherazade reminds us, is to die'.[70]

*Notes*

1  A. O. J. Cockshut, *The Achievement of Walter Scott,* p. 101.
2  Christopher Harvie, 'Scott and the Image of Scotland' in *Sir Walter Scott; The Long-Forgotten Melody*, ed. by Alan Bold (London: Vision and Barnes & Noble, 1983), pp. 17–42 (p. 39).
3  Catherine Jones, *Literary Memory*, p. 152.
4  John Sutherland, *The Life of Sir Walter Scott: A Critical Biography*, p. 344 and p. 343.
5  James Anderson, *Sir Walter Scott and History and other papers* (Edinburgh: The Edina Press, 1981), p. 171.
6  *Life*, p. 7.236.
7  *Life*, p. 7.246.
8  *Life*, p. 7.218.
9  See J. H. Alexander, 'Essay on the Text', *Castle Dangerous,* p. 212.
10  J. H. Alexander. 'Essay on the Text', *Castle Dangerous*, p. 212.
11  For a comprehensive description of the changes that they made to these late novels see J. H. Alexander's 'Essay on the Text' for both *Count Robert of Paris* and *Castle Dangerous.*
12  J. H. Alexander, 'Essay on the Text', *Castle Dangerous*, p. 216.
13  *Life*, p. 7.218.
14  NLS MS 21021, f.1r.
15  See NLS, MS 745, f.211.
16  David Hewitt, 'Introduction', *Reliquiae Trotcosienses*, p. xix.
17   J. H. Alexander, 'Essay on the Text', *Count Robert of Paris*, p. 382.
18  *Journal*, 21 Jan 1831, p. 628.
19  *Journal*, 5 April 1831, p. 645.
20  *Journal*, 30 April 1831, p. 650.
21  *Journal*, September 1831, p. 659.
22  'Introductory Address, by Jedidiah Cleishbotham, M.A in 'Appendix to the Text', *Castle Dangerous*, p. 198.
23  *Journal*, 5 April 1831, p. 645.
24  *Journal*, 28 Jan 1831, p. 630.
25  *Journal*, 14 March 1831, p. 639.
26  J. H. Alexander, 'Essay on the Text', *Count Robert of Paris*, p. 407.
27  Ibid. p. 407.
28  Ibid. p. 408.
29  Gerard Carruthers and Alison Lumsden, 'Note on the Text', *Reliquiae Trotcosienses*, pp. 73–81 (p. 73).
30  David Hewitt, 'Introduction', *Reliquiae Trotcosienses*, p. xix.
31  J. H. Alexander, 'Essay on the Text', *Count Robert of Paris*, p. 426. This

was also recognised before the appearance of The Edinburgh Edition by Philip Hobsbaum and Kurt Gamerschlag. See Philip Hobsbaum, 'Scott's "Apoplectic" Novels' in *Scott and his Influence: The Papers of the Aberdeen Scott Conference, 1982*, pp. 149–56 and Kurt Gamerschlag, 'The Making and Un-Making of Sir Walter Scott's *Count Robert of Paris*', *Studies in Scottish Literature* 15 (1980), pp. 95–123.

32  See J. H. Alexander, 'Essay on the Text', *Count Robert of Paris*, p. 426.

33  Ibid. p. 415.

34  Ibid. p. 413.

35  Ibid. p. 431.

36  J. H. Alexander, 'Essay on the Text', *Castle Dangerous*, p. 265.

37  See Caroline McCracken-Flesher, *Possible Scotlands*, pp. 164–87 and Ian Duncan, *Scott's Shadow*, p. 112.

38  Jerome McGann comments on the ways in which the opening of the novel offers a 'pastiche of Comnena's notoriously decadent prose' that 'turns reflexively on Scott's own tale, suggesting that we might register certain equations between Comnena and Scott' and the ways in which he has become 'increasingly elaborate and formulaic'. See Jerome McGann, 'Walter Scott's Romantic Postmodernity', pp. 124–5.

39  Graham McMaster, *Scott and Society*, p. 208. McMaster argues that the novel is held together by a symbolic exploration of the dialectics between art / the city and nature / simplicity. See p. 214.

40  Ian Duncan, *Scott's Shadow,* p. 112.

41  Clare A. Simmons, 'A Man of Few Words: The Romantic Orang-Outang and Scott's *Count Robert of Paris*', *Scottish Literary Journal* 17.1 (1990), pp. 21–34 (pp. 25 and 31).

42  Franco Moretti, 'Serious Century' in Moretti, pp. 2.364–400 (p. 388).

43  See J. H. Alexander, 'Essay on the Text', *Count Robert of Paris*, p. 388.

44  *Journal*, 12 May 1831, p. 654.

45  J. H. Alexander, 'Essay on the Text', *Count Robert of Paris*, p. 429.

46  John Sutherland, *The Life of Walter Scott: A Critical Biography*, p. 343.

47  Hugh Cheape, Trevor Cowie and Colin Wallace 'Sir Walter Scott, The Abbotsford Collection and the National Museums of Scotland' in *Abbotsford and Sir Walter Scott: The Image and the Influence*, ed. by Iain Gordon Brown (Edinburgh: Society of Antiquaries of Scotland, 2003), pp. 49–89 (p. 49).

48  Iain Gordon Brown, 'Scott, Literature and Abbotsford' in *Abbotsford and Sir Walter Scott: The Image and the Influence*, pp. 4–36 (p. 5).

49  Walter Scott, Abbotsford Edition of the Waverley Novels (Edinburgh and London: Robert Cadell and Houlston & Stoneman, 1842–7), p. 3.

50  Letter to Lord Montagu, March 1822, *Letters*, p. 7.111.

51  *Journal*, 7 January 1828, p. 411.

52  Ibid. 4 January 1828, p. 410.

53  In fact it could be argued that this paratextual material is not designed to reinforce authority in Scott's work but to undermine it by illustrating that which is 'in excess' of any one discourse.

54  Letter to Robert Cadell, 12 July 1831, NLS MS 1752, f.387.

55  The best iteration of this is to be found in the famous introductory epistle to *The Fortunes of Nigel* where Scott writes about the 'demon on the feather of [his] pen' which prevents him following a laid down scheme.

56  David Hewitt, 'Introduction', *Reliquiae Trotcosienses*, p. xvi.

57  See J. H. Alexander, 'Essay on the Text', *Castle Dangerous*, p. 212.

58  Ibid. pp. 277–8.

59  See Graham Tulloch's introduction to the Penguin edition of *Ivanhoe* for an excellent commentary on this passage: Walter Scott, *Ivanhoe*, ed. by Graham Tulloch (London: Penguin, 1998), pp. xi–xxix.

60  J. H. Alexander, 'Essay on the Text', *Castle Dangerous*, p. 279.

61  For a discussion of *The Tale of Old Mortality* as an act of commemoration see Alison Lumsden, 'Scott, Stevenson and Scottish History' in *The Edinburgh Companion to Robert Louis Stevenson*, ed. by Penny Fielding (Edinburgh: Edinburgh University Press, 2010), pp. 70–85.

62  J. H. Alexander, 'Essay on the Text', *Castle Dangerous*, p. 280. Philip Hobsbaum similarly notes that the novel operates by a 'substratum of significant imagery': 'Scott's "Apoplectic" Novels', p. 154.

63  J. H. Alexander, 'Essay on the Text', *Castle Dangerous*, p. 209.

64  Walter Scott, 'Introduction', *Minstrelsy of the Scottish Border*, p. 1.xci.

65  Walter Scott, 'Introductory Remarks on Popular Poetry', p. 14.

66  Walter Scott, 'Imitations of the Ancient Ballad', pp. 3–4.

67  J. H. Alexander, 'Essay on the Text', *Castle Dangerous*, p. 279.

68  Philip Hobsbaum dismisses the novel on the grounds that it 'lacks a defining plot': 'Scott's "Apoplectic" Novels', p. 154.

69  John Barth, 'Muse Spare Me' in *The Friday Book*, pp. 55–9 (p. 59).

70  John Barth, 'Tales Within Tales Within Tales', p. 236.

# Afterword

Wittgenstein's statement '*The limits of my language* mean the limits of my world' is made in his early *Tractatus Logico-Philosophicus* and it was one that he was to modify in the notebooks that became the posthumous *Philosophical Investigations*. Recognising that the position he had reached in *Tractatus* trapped him within a prison-house of language he negotiated a way beyond this impasse by suggesting that meaning within the closed circuit of signification proceeds by *grammar*: 'For a *large* class of cases', he continues, 'though not for all—in which we employ the word "meaning" it can be defined thus: the meaning of a word is its use in the language'.[1] Meaning, he concludes (thus curiously echoing Hume), is an evolving of contexts, so that communication proceeds not by any absolute relationship between signifier and signified, word and object, but by the contextual relations within a series of utterances. Such a solution is essentially pragmatic, suggesting that each manoeuvre in human interchange must be renegotiated within its own parameters: 'What *we* do', he states, 'is to bring words back from their metaphysical to their everyday use'[2] so that the result of his new philosophy is the 'uncovering of one or another piece of plain nonsense and of bumps that the understanding has got by running its head up against the limits of language'.[3]

For some commentators Wittgenstein's conclusions thus both pre-empt and offer a solution to the apparent crisis articulated by post-structuralist criticism, which figured the recognition of language as a self-reflexive system as a moment of trauma. As a consequence, his solution is crucial to postmodern writers who, perhaps against all odds, sought a means of 'replenishment' in the face of the 'the novel in crisis' wrought by post-structuralism's conclusions. As Charles Altieri puts it: 'Wittgenstein's basic discovery has been crucial to the spirit of post-modern literary thought, even if his particular solution has been largely ignored'.[4] Derrida suggests a similar strategy for proceeding in the face of the problems his philosophical critique has raised by reminding us of the richness of the 'irreducible excess of the syntactic over the semantic'.[5] Both commentators suggest, then, a way out of the philosophical linguistic impasse they recognise by a liberation from the teleological impulse intrinsic in the semantic; in referential naming of names, in categorisation, in the Enlightenment impulse towards a search for ultimate knowledge. Instead we are reminded of the syntactic, a method of procedure which relies on the infinite fluidity of the spaces between words, the subtle connections and relationships within discourse, which may provide a site to posit some kind of meaning. At the moment when, to use Derrida's phrase, 'language invades the universal problematic', the site of interest moves elsewhere. The question is no longer, how do we find epistemological certainty – the perfect fixed system – but how do we proceed in the knowledge of its absence.[6]

As Altieri suggests, Wittgenstein's later philosophical project is one mirrored by the development of the novel in the late twentieth century. Approaching a moment of apparent 'exhaustion' and redundancy the novel, as John Barth recognises, does not disappear as a genre, but in fact reinvents itself. And it does so not by simply rejecting earlier forms, but by re-examining, via what we now know as postmodernity or metafiction, its own first principles. This, Barth suggests, is what is involved in the project that he identifies as a 'literature of replenishment':

> If the modernists, carrying the torch of romanticism, taught us that linearity, rationality, consciousness, cause and effect, naïve illusionism, transparent language, innocent anecdote, and middle-class moral conventions are not the whole story, then from the perspective of these closing decades of our century we may appreciate that the contraries of those things are not the whole story either. Disjunction, simultaneity, irrationalism, anti-illusionism, self-reflexiveness, medium-as-message, political olympianism, and a moral pluralism approaching moral entropy—these are not the whole story either.
>
> A worthy program for postmodernist fiction, I believe, is the synthesis or transcension of these antitheses, which may be summed up as premodernist and modernist modes of writing. My ideal postmodernist author neither merely repudiates nor merely imitates either his twentieth-century modernist parents or his nineteenth-century premodernist grandparents.[7]

Barth's observations are helpful for they remind us that in spite of its name 'postmodernity' does not necessarily exist in a linear relationship to what has gone before but, rather, revisits the very foundations upon which the novel rests, prompting us to reflect that its impulses were never essentially imitative but interpretative and that the turn towards realism or verisimilitude (which as Roland Barthes recognised implies a kind of epistemological if not ontological stability) that the novel in English took in the nineteenth century should be seen as an anomaly rather than a norm. 'A novel', Barth writes, 'works like the *camera obscura*. The arbitrary facts that make the world – devoid of ultimate meaning and so familiar to us that we can't really see them any longer, like the furniture of our living room – these facts are passed through the dark chamber of the novelist's imagination, and we *see* them, perhaps for the first time'.[8] As a consequence the story-teller's art is one of 'making up stories attractive enough to induce people to spend their time reading what he writes precisely despite the presumption that it's all made up in his head'.[9]

Barth's description of 'the literature of replenishment' also alerts us, therefore, to the fact that we should not be surprised to find the problems that so vexed novelists of the late twentieth century (and indeed their solutions) manifested in earlier innovators of the novel form. While Barth recognises that '*one* characteristic preoccupation, among others, of the modernists and protomodernists was the problematics, not only of language, but of the medium and processes of literature: a manifestation of their heightened authorial self-consciousness' he also acknowledges that 'these protomodernists, to be sure, are anticipated by the late eighteenth- and nineteenth-century romantics'.[10]

*Walter Scott and the Limits of Language* has set out to explore whether the 'reflexive, self-conscious, and more-or-less experimental' tendencies that have been recognised in Scott's fiction in recent years are similarly generated by a preoccupation with 'the problematics of language' and the attempt to find a way to proceed in the face of them. Taking its cue from trends in recent criticism of Scott and of the novel more generally, from the Enlightenment debates on language (and particularly Hume's scepticism) which suggestively prefigure Wittgenstein's conclusions, and from Scott's own commentaries (both within his fiction and beyond it) on the function and problematics surrounding literature, it has, it is hoped, foregrounded the fact that throughout Scott's work a scepticism concerning language has been a key, even fundamental source of both tension and creativity.

By considering Scott in this way, however, it was also hoped that a re-examination of his fiction could contribute to our understanding of the novel more generally, demonstrating how this most significant of practitioners contributes to a disruption of the 'tidy little story' of the novel discredited by John Brenkman. I hope this study has achieved this, and that, in some small way, it will contribute to our understanding of Scott's place in the development of the novel form. However, in the course of writing this study I also became increasingly aware that the concern with the limitations of language which I recognised in Scott may, indeed, be a concern which stimulates and invigorates all creative writing. In his discussion of the 'literature of replenishment' John Barth moves increasingly towards an understanding that what he recognises as typical of the postmodern novel is, in fact, true of all fiction. Retracting his original assessment of the novel as 'exhausted' he states 'I agree with Borges that literature can never be exhausted, if only because no single literary text can ever be exhausted—its "meaning" residing as it does in its transactions with individual readers over time, space, and language.'[11] While I stated at the outset of this study that I wanted to avoid eliding difference or giving the impression that all fiction is, ultimately, the same, it does nevertheless seem that approaching Scott through the paradigm of his concern with the limits of language serves as a reminder that such a concern, is, perhaps, intrinsic to the art of fictional narrative, whether in prose or verse.

Catherine Gallagher suggests that novel reading may suspend 'the constant maintenance of active scepticism' required by other 'mandatory suppositional acts'.[12] However, novel *writing*, it might be argued, always contains within it an act of sceptical interrogation of its own communicative capacities. It is that, perhaps, after all, that makes it a privileged form of discourse. Creative writers, one suspects, have known all along what it has taken criticism until the twentieth century to conclude; that language as Robert Louis Stevenson puts it, 'is but a poor bull's-eye lantern wherewith to show of the vast cathedral of the world'.[13] John Barth, writing as a practitioner rather than as critic, recognises that this is the logical conclusion of his reflections on the novel:

> One might add that if this is true, then not only is all fiction fiction about fiction, but all fiction about fiction is in fact fiction about life. Some of us understood that all along.[14]

But if writers have always known that 'all fiction [is] fiction about fiction' it is, perhaps, post-structuralism which has provided the critical vocabulary for our own time best fitted to articulate this. If, approaching Scott in the aftermath of all that theory has taught us, we revisit his work with an expectation that we will find moments of interrogation of the communicative capacities of language within it, it transpires that we find, in fact, an epistemologically sceptical yet generative creative anxiety inscribed *throughout* it. From *The Lay of the Last Minstrel* to *Castle Dangerous* we find within Scott's works a consummate concern with the limits of language and, above all, a restless search for the ways in which the writer can liberate both text and reader from the 'poverty', 'wild waste' and 'magic maze' of words.

*Notes*

1  Ludwig Wittgenstein, *Philosophical Investigations*, p. 20.

2  Ibid. p. 48.

3  Ibid. p. 48.

4  Charles Altieri, 'Wittgenstein on Consciousness and Language: A Challenge to Derridean Literary Theory', *Modern Language Notes*, 91 (1976), pp. 1397–423 (p. 1411).

5  Jacques Derrida, *Dissemination*, translated by Barbara Johnson (London: Athlone, 1981), p. 221.

6  Jacques Derrida, *Writing and Difference*, translated by Alan Bass (London: Routledge and Kegan Paul, 1978), p. 280.

7  John Barth, 'The Literature of Replenishment', p. 203.

8  John Barth, 'How to Make a Universe' in *The Friday Book*, pp. 13–25 (p. 21).

9  John Barth, 'The Future of Literature and the Literature of the Future' in *The Friday Book*, pp. 161–5 (p. 162).

10  John Barth, 'The Self in Fiction, or, "That Ain't No Matter. That is Nothing"', p. 209.

11  John Barth, 'The Literature of Replenishment', p. 205.

12  Catherine Gallagher, 'The Rise of Fictionality', p. 347.

13  Robert Louis Stevenson, 'Walt Whitman', *Familiar Studies of Men and Books*, The Works of Robert Louis Stevenson, Tusitala Edition, vol. 27 (London: William Heinemann, 1923), p. 59.

14  John Barth, 'Tales Within Tales Within Tales', p. 236.

# Bibliography

## Works by Scott

Scott, Walter, 'Introduction to *Minstrelsy of the Scottish Border'*, *Minstrelsy of the Scottish Border* 2 vols (Kelso: James Ballantyne for T. Cadell and W. Davis, Strand, London, 1802), pp. 1.i–cx.

——, *The Lay of the Last Minstrel: A Poem* (London and Edinburgh: Longman, Hurst, Rees, and Orme and A. Constable and Co., 1805).

——, *The Lay of the Last Minstrel* (1805), *Poetical Works of Sir Walter Scott, Bart.* (Edinburgh and London: Robert Cadell, 1833–4), vol. 6.

——, *Marmion; A Tale of Flodden Field* (Edinburgh and London: Archibald Constable and Company and William Miller and John Murray, 1808).

——, *The Lady of the Lake*: *A Poem in Six Cantos* (Edinburgh and London: John Ballantyne and Co. and Longman Hurst, Rees, and Orme, and William Miller, 1810).

——, *Waverley* (1814), ed. by P. D. Garside, Edinburgh Edition of the Waverley Novels 1 (Edinburgh: Edinburgh University Press, 2007).

——, *Guy Mannering* (1815), ed. by P. D. Garside, Edinburgh Edition of the Waverley Novels 2 (Edinburgh: Edinburgh University Press, 1999).

——, *The Antiquary* (1816), ed. by David Hewitt, Edinburgh Edition of the Waverley Novels 3 (Edinburgh: Edinburgh University Press, 1995).

——, *The Tale of Old Mortality* (1816), ed. by Douglas Mack, Edinburgh Edition of the Waverley Novels, 4b (Edinburgh: Edinburgh University Press, 1993).

——, *The Heart of Mid-Lothian* (1818), ed. by David Hewitt and Alison Lumsden, Edinburgh Edition of the Waverley Novels 6 (Edinburgh: Edinburgh University Press, 2004).

——, *The Bride of Lammermoor* (1819), ed. by J. H. Alexander, Edinburgh Edition of the Waverley Novels 7a (Edinburgh: Edinburgh University Press, 1995).

——, *Ivanhoe* (1820), ed. by Graham Tulloch, Edinburgh Edition of the Waverley Novels 8 (Edinburgh: Edinburgh University Press, 1998).

——, *The Pirate*, ed. by Mark Weinstein with Alison Lumsden, Edinburgh Edition of the Waverley Novels 12 (Edinburgh: Edinburgh University Press, 2001).

——, *The Fortunes of Nigel* (1822), ed. by Frank Jordan, Edinburgh Edition of the Waverley Novels 13 (Edinburgh: Edinburgh University Press, 2004).

——, *Peveril of the Peak* (1822), ed. by Alison Lumsden, Edinburgh Edition of the Waverley Novels 14 (Edinburgh: Edinburgh University Press, 2007).

——, *Redgauntlet* (1824), ed. by G. A. M. Wood with David Hewitt, Edinburgh Edition of the Waverley Novels 17 (Edinburgh: Edinburgh University Press, 1997).

——, *Chronicles of the Canongate* (1827), ed. by Claire Lamont, Edinburgh Edition of the Waverley Novels 20 (Edinburgh: Edinburgh University Press, 2000).

——, *Count Robert of Paris* (1831), ed. by J. H. Alexander, Edinburgh Edition of the Waverley Novels 23a (Edinburgh: Edinburgh University Press, 2006).

——, *Castle Dangerous* (1831), ed. by J. H. Alexander, Edinburgh Edition of the Waverley Novels 23b (Edinburgh: Edinburgh University Press, 2000).

——, *Reliquiae Trotcosienses Or The Gabions of the Late Jonathan Oldbuck Esq. of Monkbarns*, ed. by Gerard Carruthers and Alison Lumsden (Edinburgh: Edinburgh University Press in association with The Abbotsford Library Project Trust, 2004).

——, Abbotsford Edition of the Waverley Novels (Edinburgh and London: Robert Cadell and Houlston & Stoneman, 1842–7).

——, General Preface', *Waverley Novels*, 48 vols (Edinburgh: Constable and Co. 1829–33).

——, 'Henry Fielding', *The Prose Works of Sir Walter Scott*, 28 vols (Edinburgh: Robert Cadell, 1834–6), pp. 3.77–116.

——, 'Samuel Richardson', *The Prose Works of Sir Walter Scott*, 28 vols (Edinburgh: Robert Cadell, 1834–6), pp. 3.3–76.

——, 'Robert Bage', *The Prose Works of Sir Walter Scott*, 28 vols (Edinburgh: Robert Cadell, 1834–6), pp. 3.441–464.

——, 'Tobias Smollett', *The Prose Works of Sir Walter Scott*, 28 vols (Edinburgh: Robert Cadell, 1834–6), pp. 3.117–190.

——, Daniel De Foe', *The Prose Works of Sir Walter Scott*, 28 vols (Edinburgh: Robert Cadell, 1834–6), pp. 4. 228–281.

——, 'Tales of My Landlord', *The Prose Works of Sir Walter Scott*, 28 vols (Edinburgh: Robert Cadell, 1834–6), pp. 19.1–86.

——, 'Kirkton's Church History', *The Prose Works of Sir Walter Scott*, 28 vols (Edinburgh, 1834–6), pp. 19.213–282.

——, 'Essay on Romance', *The Prose Works of Sir Walter Scott*, 28 vols (Edinburgh, 1834–6), 6.1–216.

——, '*Emma*: a Novel', *Quarterly Review*, xiv (1815–16); reprinted in *Sir Walter Scott on Novelists and Fiction*, ed. by Ioan Williams (London: Routledge and Kegan Paul, 1968), pp. 225–36.

——, 'Introductory Remarks on Popular Poetry', *The Poetical Works of Sir Walter Scott, Bart.*, ed. by J. G. Lockhart, 12 vols (Edinburgh and London: Robert Cadell, 1833–4), pp. 1.5–91.

——, 'Essay on Imitations of the Ancient Ballad', *Poetical Works of Sir Walter Scott, Bart.*, ed. by J. G. Lockhart, 12 vols (Edinburgh and London: Robert Cadell, 1833–4), pp. 4.3–78.

——, 'Introduction to *The Lay of the Last Minstrel*', *Poetical Works of Sir Walter Scott, Bart.*, ed. by J. G. Lockhart, 12 vols (Edinburgh and London: Robert Cadell, 1833–4), pp. 6.5–31.

——, *The Journal of Sir Walter Scott*, ed. by W. E. K. Anderson (Oxford: Clarendon Press, 1972).

——, *The Letters of Sir Walter Scott*, ed. by H. J. C. Grierson, 12 vols (London: Constable, 1932–7).

## Manuscript Sources

NLS MS. 1548: *The Heart of Mid-Lothian*.

NLS MS 323 f. 204r; f. 222r–v: Note by Robert Cadell stating works contracted for with the Author of Waverley.

NLS MS 791, f. 311v: Constable to James Ballantyne, 22 July 1822.

NLS MS 21059, f. 133r: Scott to James Ballantyne, October 1822.

NLS MS 21059, f. 141r: Scott to James Ballantyne, 5 November 1822.

NLS MS 21021, f. 1r.: Robert Cadell's diary for 1831.

NLS, MS 745, f. 211 Contract for *Reliquiae Trotcosienses* [6 September 1830].

NLS MS 1752, f. 387: Letter to Robert Cadell, 12 July 1831.

## Secondary Materials

Alexander, J. H. and David Hewitt 'Preface' in J. H. Alexander and David Hewitt, eds, *Scott in Carnival: Selected Papers from the Fourth International Scott Conference, 1991* (Aberdeen: Association for Scottish Literary Studies, 1993), pp. vii–viii.

Alexander, J. H., '*The Lay of the Last Minstrel': Three Essays* (Salzburg: Institut für Englische Sprache und Literatur Universität Salzburg, 1978).

——, *The Reception of Scott's Poetry by His Correspondents: 1796–1817*, 2 vols (Salzburg: Institut für Anglistik und Amerikanistik Universität Salzburg, 1979).

——, '*Marmion': Studies in Interpretation and Composition* (Salzburg: Institut für Anglistik und Amerikanistik Universität Salzburg, 1981).

——, *Two Studies in Romantic Reviewing: Edinburgh Reviewers and the English Tradition: The Reviewing of Walter Scott's Poetry 1805–1817* (Salzburg: Institut für Englische Sprache und Literatur Universität Salzburg, 1976).

Altieri, Charles, 'Wittgenstein on Consciousness and Language: A Challenge to Derridean Literary Theory', *Modern Language Notes* 91 (1976), pp. 1397–423.

Anderson, Carol, 'The Power of Naming: Language, Identity and Betrayal in *The Heart of Midlothian'* in J. H. Alexander and David Hewitt, eds, *Scott in Carnival: Selected Papers from the Fourth International Scott Conference, 1991* (Aberdeen: Association for Scottish Literary Studies, 1993), pp. 189–201.

Anderson, James, *Sir Walter Scott and History with other papers* (Edinburgh: The Edina Press, 1981).

Bal, Mieke, 'Over-writing as Un-writing: Descriptions, World-Making and Novelistic Time' in Franco Moretti, ed., *The Novel*, 2 vols (Princeton and Oxford: Princeton University Press, 2006), pp. 2.571–610.

Barth, John, *The Friday Book: Essays and Other Nonfiction* (New York: G. P. Putnam's Sons, 1984).

Barthes, Roland, *Writing Degree Zero*, translated from the French by Annette Lavers and Colin Smith (London: Jonathan Cape, 1967).

Beiderwell, Bruce, ed., *Romantic Enlightenment: Sir Walter Scott and the Politics of History*. Spec. issue of *European Romantic Review* 13.3 (2002), pp. 223–324.

Blair, Hugh, *Lectures on Rhetoric and Belles Lettres*, new edition, 3 vols (Edinburgh: Bell and Bradfute, 1811).

Bloom, Harold, *The Ringers in the Tower: Studies in Romantic Tradition* (Chicago and London: University of Chicago Press, 1971).

Brenkman, John, 'Innovation: Notes on Nihilism and the Aesthetics of the Novel' in Franco Moretti, ed., *The Novel*, 2 vols (Princeton and Oxford: Princeton University Press, 2006), pp. 2. 808–38.

Brink, André, *The Novel: Language and Narrative from Cervantes to Calvino* (Basingstoke: Macmillan Press, 1998).

Broadie, Alexander, 'Introduction: What was the Scottish Enlightenment?' in *The Scottish Enlightenment: An Anthology*, ed. by Alexander Broadie (Edinburgh: Canongate Classics, 1997), pp. 3–31.

Brown, Iain Gordon, 'Scott, Literature and Abbotsford' in Iain Gordon Brown, ed., *Abbotsford and Sir Walter Scott: The Image and the Influence* (Edinburgh: Society of Antiquaries for Scotland, 2003), pp. 4–36.

Brown, Marshall, 'Poetry and the novel' in Richard Maxwell and Katie Trumpener eds, *The Cambridge Companion to Fiction in the Romantic Period* (Cambridge: Cambridge University Press, 2008), pp. 107–28.

Buckingham, George, Duke of, *The Rehearsal* in *The Rehearsal and The Critic*, with a preface by Cedric Gale (New York: Barron's Educational Series, 1960).

Burke, John J., 'The Romantic Window and the Postmodern Mirror: The Medieval Worlds of Sir Walter Scott and Umberto Eco' in J. H. Alexander and David Hewitt, eds, *Scott in Carnival: Selected Papers from the Fourth International Scott Conference, 1991* (Aberdeen: Association for Scottish Literary Studies, 1993), pp. 556–68.

Burnet, James, Lord Monboddo, *Of the Origin and Progress of Language*, 2nd edition, 6 vols (Edinburgh: J. Balfour and T. Cadell, 1774–1809).

Buzard, James, 'Translation and Tourism: Scott's *Waverley* and the Rendering of Culture', *Yale Journal of Criticism* 8 (1995), pp. 31–59.

Campbell, George, 'The Philosophy of Rhetoric' in *The Scottish Enlightenment: An Anthology*, ed. by Alexander Broadie (Edinburgh: Canongate Classics, 1997), pp. 685–96.

Chandler, James, *England in 1819: The Politics of Literary Culture and the Case of Romantic Historicism* (Chicago: University of Chicago Press, 1998).

Cheape, Hugh, Tevor Cowie and Colin Wallace, 'Sir Walter Scott, the Abbotsford Collection and The National Museums of Scotland' in Iain Gordon Brown, ed., *Abbotsford and Sir Walter Scott: The Image and the Influence* (Edinburgh: Society of Antiquaries for Scotland, 2003), pp. 49–89.

Clark, Arthur Melville, *Sir Walter Scott: The Formative Years* (Edinburgh and London: William Blackwood, 1969).

Cochrane, J. G. *Catalogue of the Library at Abbotsford* (Edinburgh: Bannatyne Club, 1838).

Cockshut, A. O. J., *The Achievement of Walter Scott* (London: Collins, 1969).

Cole, Lucinda and Richard G. Swartz, '"Why Should I Wish for Words?": Literacy, Articulation and the Borders of Literary Culture' in Mary A. Favret and Nicola J. Watson, eds, *At the Limits of Romanticism: Essays in Cultural, Feminist, and Materialist Criticism* (Bloomington and Indianapolis: Indiana University Press, 1994), pp. 143–69.

Colley, Linda, *Britons: Forging the Nation, 1707–1837* (New Haven: Yale University Press, 1992).

Cooney, Seamus, 'Scott's Anonymity – Its Motives and Consequences', *Studies in Scottish Literature* 10 (1973), pp. 207–19.

——, 'Scott and Progress: The Tragedy of "The Highland Widow"', *Studies in Short Fiction* 11:1 (Winter, 1974), pp. 11–16.

——, 'Scott and Cultural Relativism: "The Two Drovers"', *Studies in Short Fiction* 15:1 (Winter, 1978), pp. 1–9.

Craig, Cairns, 'Coleridge, Hume, and the chains of the Romantic imagination' in Leith Davis, Ian Duncan and Janet Sorensen, eds, *Scotland and the Borders of Romanticism* (Cambridge: Cambridge University Press, 2004), pp. 20–37.

——, *Out of History: Narrative Paradigms in Scottish and English Culture* (Edinburgh: Polygon, 1996).

——, *Associationism and the Literary Imagination: From the Phantasmal Chaos* (Edinburgh: Edinburgh University Press, 2007).

Currie, Mark, ed., *Metafiction* (London and New York: Longman, 1995).

Dale, Gillian M., 'Jeanie Deans, *The "Heart" of Midlothian*, and Feminist Ethical Theory' in J. H. Alexander and David Hewitt, eds, *Scott in Carnival: Selected Papers from the Fourth International Scott Conference, 1991* (Aberdeen: Association for Scottish Literary Studies, 1993), pp. 202–15.

D'Arcy, Julian Meldon, *Subversive Scott: The Waverley Novels and Scottish Nationalism* (Reykjavik: University of Iceland Press, 2005).

Derrida, Jacques, *Writing and Difference*, translated by Alan Bass (London, 1978).

——, *Dissemination*, translated by Barbara Johnson (London: Athlone, 1981).

Duncan, Ian, *Modern Romance and Transformations of the Novel: The Gothic, Scott, Dickens* (Cambridge: Cambridge University Press, 1992).

——, Ann Rowland and Charles Snodgrass, eds, *Scott, Scotland and Romantic Nationalism*, Special ed. *Studies in Romanticism* 40:1 (Spring, 2001).

——, *Scott's Shadow: The Novel in Romantic Edinburgh* (Princeton and Oxford: Princeton University Press, 2007).

——, 'Hume and the Scottish Enlightenment' in Ian Brown, Thomas Owen Clancy, Susan Manning and Murray Pittock, eds, *The Edinburgh History of Scottish Literature*, 3 vols (Edinburgh: Edinburgh University Press, 2007), 2.71–79.

——, 'Scotland and the novel' in Richard Maxwell and Katie Trumpener, eds, *The Cambridge Companion to Fiction in the Romantic Period* (Cambridge: Cambridge University Press, 2008), pp. 251–64.

——, 'Scott, the History of the Novel, and the History of Fiction' in Evan Gottlieb and Ian Duncan, eds, *Approaches to Teaching Scott's Waverley Novels* (New York: The Modern Language Association of America, 2009), pp. 88–96.

Favret, Mary A. and Nicola J. Watson, eds, *At the Limits of Romanticism: Essays in Cultural, Feminist, and Materialist Criticism* (Bloomington and Indianapolis: Indiana University Press, 1994).

Ferris, Ina, 'The Reader in the Rhetoric of Realism: Scott, Thackeray and Eliot' in J. H. Alexander and David Hewitt, eds, *Scott and his Influence: The Papers of the Aberdeen Scott Conference, 1982* (Aberdeen: Association for Scottish Literary Studies, 1983), pp. 382–92.

——, *The Achievement of Literary Authority: Gender, History, and the Waverley Novels* (Ithaca and London: Cornell University Press, 1991).

——, 'The Indefatigable Word: Scott and the Comedy of Surplusage' in J. H. Alexander and David Hewitt, eds, *Scott in Carnival: Selected Papers from the Fourth International Scott Conference, 1991* (Aberdeen: Association for Scottish Literary Studies, 1993), pp. 19–26.

——, 'Translation from the Borders: Encounter and Recalcitrance in *Waverley* and *Clan-Albin*', *Eighteenth-Century Fiction* 9.2 (1997), pp. 203–22.

Fielding, Henry, *The History of Tom Jones*, ed. by R. P. C. Mutter (London: Penguin, 1985).

Fielding, Penny, *Writing and Orality: Nationality, Culture, and Nineteenth-Century Scottish Fiction* (Oxford: Clarendon Press, 1996).

Findlay, L. M., '"Perilous Linguists": Scots, wha hae their Foucault Read' in J. H. Alexander and David Hewitt, eds, *Scott in Carnival: Selected Papers from the Fourth International Scott Conference, 1991* (Aberdeen: Association for Scottish Literary Studies, 1993), pp. 27–39.

Forbes, Duncan, 'The Rationalism of Sir Walter Scott', *Cambridge Journal* 7 (1953), pp. 20–35.

Freeman, Michael and Andrew D. E. Lewis, eds, *Law and Literature* (Oxford: Oxford University Press, 1999).

Gallagher, Catherine, 'The Rise of Fictionality' in Franco Moretti, ed., *The Novel* 2 vols (Princeton and Oxford: Princeton University Press, 2006), pp. 1.336–63.

Gamerschlag, Kurt, 'The Making and Un-Making of Sir Walter Scott's *Count Robert of Paris*', *Studies in Scottish Literature* 15 (1980), pp. 95–123.

Garside, Peter, 'Scott and the "Philosophical" Historians', *Journal of the History of Ideas* 36 (1975), pp. 497–512.

Gaston, Patricia S., *Prefacing the Waverley Novels: A Reading of Sir Walter Scott's Prefaces to the Waverley Novels* (New York: Peter Lang, 1991).

Gifford, Douglas, 'Scott's Fiction and the Search for Mythic Regeneration' in J. H. Alexander and David Hewitt, eds, *Scott and his Influence: The Papers of the Aberdeen Scott Conference, 1982* (Aberdeen: Association for Scottish Literary Studies, 1983), pp. 180–8.

——, Sarah Dunnigan and Alan MacGillivray (eds), *Scottish Literature in English and Scots* (Edinburgh: Edinburgh University Press, 2002).

Goody, Jack, 'From Oral to Written: An Anthropological Breakthrough in Storytelling' in Franco Moretti, ed., *The Novel*, 2 vols (Princeton and Oxford: Princeton University Press, 2006), pp. 1.3–36.

Gordon, Jan B., '"Liquidating the Sublime": Gossip in Scott's Novels' in Mary A. Favret and Nicola J. Watson, eds, *At the Limits of Romanticism: Essays in Cultural, Feminist, and Materialist Criticism* (Bloomington: Indiana University Press, 1994), pp. 246–68.

Goslee, Nancy Moore, *Scott the Rhymer* (Lexington: University Press of Kentucky, 1988).

——, '"Some Hidden Movement": Signs of Embarrassment in Scott's Poetic Language' in J. H. Alexander and David Hewitt, eds, *Scott in Carnival: Selected Papers from the Fourth International Scott Conference, 1991* (Aberdeen: Association for Scottish Literary Studies, 1993), pp. 72–88.

Gottlieb, Evan, *Feeling British: Sympathy and National Identity in Scottish and English Writing, 1707–1832* (Lewisburg: Bucknell University Press, 2007).

Gottlieb, Evan and Ian Duncan, eds, *Approaches to Teaching Scott's Waverley Novels* (New York: The Modern Language Association of America, 2009).

Groom, Nick, 'Romantic poetry and antiquity' in James Chandler and Maureen N. McLane, eds, *The Cambridge Companion to British Romantic Poetry* (Cambridge: Cambridge University Press, 2008), pp. 35–52.

Hale, Dorothy J., ed., *The Novel: an Anthology of Criticism and Theory 1900–2000* (Oxford: Blackwell Publishing, 2006).

——, 'Introduction' to 'Part III: Structuralism, Narratology, Deconstruction' in Dorothy J. Hale, ed., *The Novel: An Anthology of Criticism and Theory* (Oxford: Blackwell Publishing, 2006), pp. 186–204.

Hamilton, Paul, *Metaromanticism: Aesthetics, Literature, Theory* (Chicago: University of Chicago Press, 1993).

Harvie, Christopher, 'Scott and the Image of Scotland' in Alan Bold, ed., *Sir Walter Scott: The Long-Forgotten Melody* (London: Vision and Barnes & Noble, 1983), pp. 17–42.

Hayden, John O., ed., *Scott: The Critical Heritage* (London: Routledge and Kegan Paul, 1970).

Hewitt, David, 'Walter Scott' in *The History of Scottish Literature*, 4 vols (Aberdeen: Aberdeen University Press, 1988), pp. 3.65–85.

——, 'The Phonocentric Scott' in J. H. Alexander and David Hewitt, eds, *Scott in Carnival: Selected Papers from the Fourth International Scott Conference, 1991* (Aberdeen: Association for Scottish Literary Studies, 1993), pp. 581–92.

——, 'Introduction' in Walter Scott, *Redgauntlet*, ed. by G. A. M. Wood with David Hewitt (London: Penguin, 1997), pp. xiii–xxxi.

——, 'Introduction' in *Reliquiae Trotcosienses Or The Gabions of the Late Jonathan Oldbuck Esq. of Monkbarns*, ed. by Gerard Carruthers and Alison Lumsden (Edinburgh: Edinburgh University Press in association with The Abbotsford Library Project Trust, 2004), pp. xi–xxii.

——, 'Teaching *The Heart of Mid-Lothian*' in Evan Gottlieb and Ian Duncan, eds, *Approaches to Teaching Scott's Waverley Novels* (New York: The Modern Language Association of America, 2009), pp. 150–6.

Hobsbaum, Philip, 'Scott's "Apoplectic" Novels' in J. H. Alexander and David Hewitt, eds, *Scott and his Influence: The Papers of the Aberdeen Scott Conference, 1982* (Aberdeen: Association for Scottish Literary Studies, 1983), pp. 149–56.

Home, Henry, Lord Kames, *Elements of Criticism*, 4th edition, 2 vols (Edinburgh: A. Kincaid and J. Bell, 1769).

——, *Sketches of the History of Man*, 3rd edition, 2 vols (Dublin: James Williams, 1779).

Hume, David, *Selected Essays*, ed. by Stephen Copley and Andrew Edgar (Oxford: Oxford University Press, 1993).

Inglis, Tony, 'Introduction' in Walter Scott, *The Heart of Mid-Lothian*, ed. by Tony Inglis (London: Penguin, 1994), pp. ix–l.

Irvine, Robert P., *Enlightenment and Romance: Gender and Agency in Smollett and Scott* (Oxford and New York: Peter Lang, 2000).

Jameson, Frederic, *The Prison-house of Language: A Critical Account of Structuralism and Russian Formalism* (Princeton: Princeton University Press, 1972).

Jefferson, D. W., *Walter Scott: An Introductory Essay* (Edinburgh: Dunedin Academic Press, 2002).

Jones, Catherine, *Literary Memory: Scott's Waverley Novels and the Psychology of Narrative* (Lewisburg: Bucknell University Press, 2003).

Jordan, Frank, 'Chrystal Croftangry, Scott's Last and Best Mask', *Scottish Literary Journal* 7:1 (1980), pp. 185–92.

——, 'Scott, Chatterton, Byron and the Wearing of Masks' in J. H. Alexander and David Hewitt, eds, *Scott and his Influence: The Papers of the Aberdeen Scott Conference, 1982* (Aberdeen: Association for Scottish Literary Studies, 1983), pp. 279–89.

Kerr, James, *Fiction against History: Scott as Storyteller* (Cambridge: Cambridge University Press, 1989).

Kirkton, James *The Secret and True History of the Church of Scotland, from the Restoration to 1678*, ed. by C. K. Sharpe (London and Edinburgh: Longman, Hurst, Rees, Orme, and Brown, London; and John Ballantyne, Edinburgh, 1817).

Lamont, Claire, 'Introduction' in Walter Scott, *Waverley*, ed. by Claire Lamont (Oxford: Oxford University Press, 1986), pp. vii–xx.

——, 'Walter Scott: Anonymity and the Unmasking of Harlequin' in E. J. Clery, Caroline Franklin and Peter Garside, eds, *Authorship, Commerce and the Public: Scenes of Writing, 1750–1850* (Basingstoke: Palgrave Macmillan, 2002), pp. 54–66.

——, 'Introduction' in Walter Scott, *Chronicles of the Canongate* (London: Penguin, 2003), pp. xi–xxix.

Land, Stephen K., *From Signs to Propositions: The Concept of Form in Eighteenth-Century Semantic Theory* (London: Longman, 1974).

Langan, Celeste, 'Understanding Media in 1805: Audiovisual Hallucination in *The Lay of the Last Minstrel*' in Ian Duncan, Ann Rowland and Charles Snodgrass, eds, *Scott, Scotland and Romantic Nationalism*, Special ed. *Studies in Romanticism* 40:1 (Spring, 2001), pp. 49–70.

——, and Maureen N. McLane, 'The medium of Romantic poetry' in James Chandler and Maureen N. McLane, eds, *The Cambridge Companion to British Romantic Poetry* (Cambridge: Cambridge University Press, 2008), pp. 239–62.

——, '"The Poetry of Pure Memory": Teaching Scott's Novels in the Context of Romanticism' in Evan Gottlieb and Ian Duncan, eds, *Approaches to Teaching Scott's Waverley Novels* (New York: The Modern Language Association of America, 2009), pp. 67–76.

Leavis, F. R., *The Great Tradition: George Eliot, Henry James, Joseph Conrad* (London: Chatto and Windus, 1962; 1948).

Leith, Davis, *Acts of Union: Scotland and the Literary Negotiation of the British Nation, 1707–1830* (Stanford, CA: Stanford University Press, 1998).

Levine, George, *The Realist Imagination: English Fiction from Frankenstein to Lady Chatterley* (Chicago and London: University of Chicago Press, 1981).

Lima, Luiz Costa, 'The Control of the Imagination and the Novel' in Franco Moretti, ed., *The Novel*, 2 vols (Princeton and Oxford: Princeton University Press, 2006), pp. 1.37–68.

Lincoln, Andrew, *Walter Scott and Modernity* (Edinburgh: Edinburgh University Press, 2007).

Lockhart, J. G., *Memoirs of the Life of Sir Walter Scott, Bart.*, 7 vols (Edinburgh: Robert Cadell, 1837–8).

Lodge, David, *The Art of Fiction Illustrated from Classic and Modern Texts* (London: Penguin, 1992).

Lukács, Georg, *The Historical Novel*, translated by Hannah and Stanley Mitchell (Lincoln, NE and London: University of Nebraska Press, 1983).

Lumsden, Alison, 'Burns, Scott and Intertextuality' in Gerard Carruthers, ed., *The Edinburgh Companion to Robert Burns* (Edinburgh: Edinburgh University Press, 2009), pp. 125–36.

——, 'Scott, Stevenson and Scottish History' in Penny Fielding, ed., *The Edinburgh Companion to Robert Louis Stevenson* (Edinburgh: Edinburgh University Press, 2010), pp. 70–85.

Lyotard, Jean-François, *The Postmodern Condition: A Report on Knowledge*, translated from the French by Geoff Bennington and Brian Massumi (Manchester: Manchester University Press, 1984).

McCracken-Flesher, Caroline, 'A Wo/man for a' that? Subverted Sex and Perverted Politics in *The Heart of Midlothian*' in J. H. Alexander and David Hewitt, eds, *Scott in Carnival: Selected Papers from the Fourth International Scott Conference, 1991* (Aberdeen: Association for Scottish Literary Studies, 1993), pp. 232–44.

——, '*Pro Matria Mori*: Gendered Nationalism and Cultural Death in Scott's "The Highland Widow"', *Scottish Literary Journal* 21.2 (1994), pp. 69–78.

——, 'Narrating the (gendered) Nation in Walter Scott's *The Heart of Midlothian*', *Nineteenth-Century Contexts* 24.3 (2002), pp. 291–316.

——, *Possible Scotlands: Walter Scott and the Story of Tomorrow* (Oxford: Oxford University Press, 2005).

McGann, Jerome, 'Walter Scott's Romantic Postmodernity' in Leith Davis, Ian Duncan and Janet Sorensen, eds, *Scotland and the Borders of Romanticism* (Cambridge: Cambridge University Press, 2004), pp. 113–29.

McIntosh, Ainsley, '*Marmion; A Tale of Flodden Field.* A Critical Edition' (Unpublished PhD thesis, University of Aberdeen, 2009).

McKeon, Michael, ed., *Theory of the Novel: A Historical Approach* (Baltimore and London: Johns Hopkins University Press, 2000).

McLane, Maureen N., *Balladeering, Minstrelsy, and the Making of British Romantic Poetry* (Cambridge: Cambridge University Press, 2008).

McMaster, Graham, *Scott and Society* (Cambridge: Cambridge University Press, 1981).

McNeil, Kenneth, 'The Limits of Diversity: Using Scott's "The Two Drovers" to Teach Multiculturalism in a Survey or Nonmajors Course' in Evan Gottlieb and Ian Duncan, eds, *Approaches to Teaching Scott's Waverley Novels* (New York: The Modern Language Association of America, 2009), pp. 123–9.

Manning, Susan, *Fragments of Union: Making Connections in Scottish and American Writing* (Basingstoke: Palgrave, 2002).

Maxwell, Richard, 'The historiography of fiction in the Romantic period' in Richard Maxwell and Katie Trumpener, eds, *The Cambridge Companion to Fiction in the Romantic Period* (Cambridge: Cambridge University Press, 2008), pp. 7–21.

——, 'The historical novel' in Richard Maxwell and Katie Trumpener, eds, *The Cambridge Companion to Fiction in the Romantic Period* (Cambridge: Cambridge University Press, 2008), pp. 65–87.

Merikoski, Ingrid A., ed., *Well Temper'd Eloquence* (Edinburgh: David Hume Institute, 1996).

Miller, J. Hillis, 'Reading Narrative' in Dorothy J. Hale, ed., *The Novel: An Anthology of Criticism and Theory* (Oxford: Blackwell Publishing, 2006), pp. 242–56.

Millgate, Jane, *Walter Scott: The Making of the Novelist* (Toronto: University of Toronto Press, 1984).

——, *Scott's Last Edition: A Study in Publishing History* (Edinburgh: Edinburgh University Press, 1987).

——, '"Naught of the Bridal": Narrative Resistance in *The Lay of the Last Minstrel*', *Scottish Literary Journal*, 17.2 (November, 1990), pp. 16–26.

Moretti, Franco, *Atlas of the European Novel*, 1800–1900 (New York: Verso, 1998).

——, ed., *The Novel*, 2 vols (Princeton and Oxford: Princeton University Press, 2006.

——, 'Serious Century' in Franco Moretti, ed., *The Novel*, 2 vols (Princeton and Oxford: Princeton University Press, 2006) pp. 2.364–400.

North, Roger, *Examen: Or, An Enquiry into the Credit and Veracity of a Pretended Complete History* (London, 1740).

Ong, Walter J., *Orality and Literacy: The Technologizing of the World* (London: Methuen, 1982).

Orr, Marilyn, "'Almost Under the Immediate Eye': Framing Displacement' in J. H. Alexander and David Hewitt, eds, *Scott in Carnival: Selected Papers from the Fourth International Scott Conference, 1991* (Aberdeen: Association for Scottish Literary Studies, 1993), pp. 60–71.

Overton, W. J. 'Scott, the Short Story and History: "The Two Drovers"', *Studies in Scottish Literature*, 21 (1986), pp. 210–25.

Penelhum, Terence, *David Hume: An Introduction to his Philosophical System* (West Lafayette, IN: Purdue University Press, 1992).

Pittock, Murray, ed., *The Reception of Sir Walter Scott in Europe* (London and New York: Continuum, 2006).

——, *Scottish and Irish Romanticism* (Oxford: Oxford University Press, 2008).

Politi, Jina, 'The Ideological Uses of Intertextuality: The Case of *Redgauntlet*' in Alexander, J. H. and David Hewitt, eds, *Scott in Carnival: Selected Papers from the Fourth International Scott Conference, 1991* (Aberdeen: Association for Scottish Literary Studies, 1993), pp. 345–57.

——, 'Discourses of History and Discourse on History at the Time of the Historical Novel', *Scottish Literary Journal* 21.2 (1994), pp. 55–68.

Rignall, J. M., 'Walter Scott, J. G. Farrell, and Fictions of Empire', *Essays in Critcism*, Volume XLI, Number 1 (1991), pp. 11–27.

Robertson, Fiona, *Legitimate Histories: Scott, Gothic, and the Authorities of Fiction* (Oxford: Clarendon Press, 1994).

——, 'Walter Scott' in Ian Brown, Thomas Owen Clancy, Susan Manning and Murray Pittock, eds, *The Edinburgh History of Scottish Literature*, 3 vols (Edinburgh: Edinburgh University Press, 2007), pp. 2. 183–90.

Rothery, C. I., 'Scott's Narrative Poetry and the Classical Form of the Historical Novel' in J. H. Alexander and David Hewitt, eds, *Scott and his Influence: The Papers of the Aberdeen Scott Conference, 1982* (Aberdeen: Association for Scottish Literary Studies, 1983), pp. 63–74.

Rowland, Ann Wierda, 'Romantic poetry and the romantic novel' in James Chandler and Maureen N. McLane, eds, *The Cambridge Companion to British Romantic Poetry* (Cambridge: Cambridge University Press, 2008), pp. 117–35.

Rubenstein, Jill, 'Scott Scholarship and Criticism: Where Are We Now? Where Are We Going?' in J. H. Alexander and David Hewitt, eds, *Scott in Carnival: Selected Papers from the Fourth International Scott Conference, 1991* (Aberdeen: Association for Scottish Literary Studies, 1993), pp. 594–600.

Schlossman-Robb, Ann, *'The Honour of Men, and the Truth of Women': Disguise and Its Cultural Implications in the Waverley Novels* (Unpublished PhD thesis, University of Aberdeen, 1997).

Schoene, Berthold, 'A Passage to Scotland: Scottish Literature and the Postcolonial British Tradition', *Scotlands* 2:1 (1995), pp. 107–22.

Shaw, Harry E., ed., *Critical Essays on Sir Walter Scott* (New York: Hall, 1996).

——, *The Forms of Historical Fiction: Sir Walter Scott and his Successors* (Ithaca: Cornell University Press, 1983).

——, *Narrating Reality: Austen, Scott, Eliot* (Ithaca: Cornell University Press, 1999).

Shklovsky, Viktor, 'Sterne's *Tristram Shandy*: Stylistic Commentary' in Dorothy J. Hale, ed., *The Novel: An Anthology of Criticism and Theory* (Oxford: Blackwell Publishing, 2006), pp. 31–53.

Simmons, Clare A., 'A Man of Few Words: The Romantic Orang-Outang and Scott's *Count Robert of Paris*', *Scottish Literary Journal* 17.1 (1990), pp. 21–34.

Smith, Adam, 'Considerations Concerning the First Formation of Language' in *The Scottish Enlightenment: An Anthology*, ed. by Alexander Broadie (Edinburgh: Canongate Classics, 1997), pp. 695–714.

Sorensen, Janet, *The Grammar of Empire in Eighteenth-Century British Writing* (Cambridge: Cambridge University Press, 2000).

——, '"Something Glee'd": The Uses of Language in Scott's Waverley Novels' in Evan Gottlieb and Ian Duncan, eds, *Approaches to Teaching Scott's Waverley Novels* (New York: The Modern Language Association of America, 2009), pp. 38–49.

Stein, Richard L., 'Historical Fiction and the Implied Reader: Scott and Iser', *Novel* 14:3 (Spring, 1981), pp. 213–31.

Stevenson, Robert Louis, 'Books Which Have influenced Me' in *Essays Literary and Critical*, The Works of Robert Louis Stevenson, Tusitala Edition, vol. 28 (London: William Heinemann, 1923).

——, 'Walt Whitman', *Familiar Studies of Men and Books*, The Works of Robert Louis Stevenson, Tusitala Edition, vol. 27 (London: William Heinemann, 1923).

Sutherland, John, *The Life of Walter Scott: A Critical Biography* (Oxford and Cambridge, MA: Blackwell, 1995).

Sutherland, Sheena, *Scott's Voices: An Analysis of Discourse Competition in the Waverley Novels* (Unpublished PhD thesis, University of Aberdeen, 1997).

Todd, William and Ann Bowden, eds, *Sir Walter Scott: A Bibliographical History, 1796–1832* (New Castle, DE: Oak Knoll, 1998).

Trumpener, Katie, *Bardic Nationalism: The Romantic Novel and the British Empire* (Princeton: Princeton University Press, 1997).

——, 'National Character, Nationalist Plots: National Tale and Historical Novel in the Age of *Waverley*, 1806–1830', *ELH* 60.3 (1993), pp. 685–731.

Tulloch, Graham, *The Language of Walter Scott: A Study of his Scottish and Period Language* (London: André Deutsch, 1980).

——, 'The Use of Scots in Scott and Other Nineteenth Century Scottish Novelists' in J. H. Alexander and David Hewitt, eds, *Scott and his Influence: The Papers of the Aberdeen Scott Conference, 1982* (Aberdeen: Association for Scottish Literary Studies, 1983), pp. 341–50.

——, 'Imagery in *The Highland Widow*', *Studies in Scottish Literature* 21 (1986), pp. 147–57.

——, 'Introduction' in Walter Scott, *Ivanhoe*, ed. by Graham Tulloch (London: Penguin, 1998), pp. xi–xxix.

Wallace, Tara Ghoshal, 'Thinking Globally: *The Talisman* and *The Surgeon's Daughter*' in Evan Gottlieb and Ian Duncan, eds, *Approaches to Teaching Scott's Waverley Novels* (New York: The Modern Language Association of America, 2009), pp. 170–6.

——, *Imperial Characters: Home and Periphery in Eighteenth-century Literature* (Cranbury, NJ: Associated University Presses, 2010).

Watson, J. R., *English Poetry of the Romantic Period 1789–1830* (London: Longman, 1985).

Watt, James, 'Orientalism and empire' in Richard Maxwell and Katie Trumpener, eds, *The Cambridge Companion to Fiction in the Romantic Period* (Cambridge: Cambridge University Press, 2008), pp. 129–42.

White, Hayden, *Metahistory: The Historical Imagination in Nineteenth-Century Fiction* (Baltimore: Johns Hopkins University Press, 1973).

Wickman, Matthew, *The Ruins of Experience: Scotland's 'Romantick' Highlands and the Birth of the Modern Witness* (Philadephia: University of Pennsylvania Press, 2007).

Williams, Ioan, ed., *Sir Walter Scott On Novelists and Fiction* (London: Routledge and Kegan Paul, 1968).

Wilt, Judith, *Secret Leaves: The Novels of Walter Scott* (Chicago and London: University of Chicago Press, 1985).

Wittgenstein, Ludwig, *Tractatus Logico-Philosophicus*, translated by D. F. Pears and B. F. McGuinness (1921; London and New York: Routledge, 1997).

——, *Philosophical Investigations*, translated by G. E. M. Anscombe (1953; Oxford; Blackwell, 1989).

Wu, Duncan, *Romanticism: An Anthology* 3rd edition (Oxford: Blackwell, 2006).

Youngkin, Molly, '"Into the woof, a little Thibet wool": Orientalism and Representing "Reality" in Walter Scott's *The Surgeon's Daughter*', *Scottish Studies Review* 3:1 (Spring, 2002), pp. 33–57.

Zimbardo, Rose A., *A Mirror to Nature: Transformations in Drama and Aesthetics 1660–1732* (Lexington: University Press of Kentucky, 1986).

# Index